The machinic city

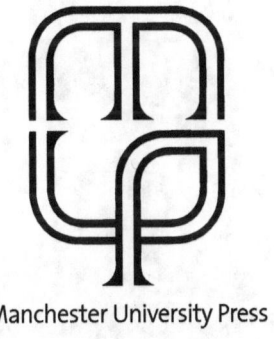

Manchester University Press

MATERIALISING THE DIGITAL

Series editors
Adam Fish and Hannah Knox

Materialising the Digital seeks to interrogate the infrastructures, relationships and imaginaries of digital technologies through situated, empirical analyses of the production, circulation and use of digital devices and systems.

Positioned at the intersection of media studies, STS, anthropology and sociology, the series provides original, critical and theoretically innovative understandings of the implications of digital technologies for contemporary social life. The series will provide a solid ground from which to engage and critique the persistence of utopian, functionalist and dystopic visions of technological futures.

Previously published
Ethnography for a data-saturated world   Hannah Knox and Dawn
  Nafus (eds)

The machinic city

Media, performance and participation

Marcos P. Dias

MANCHESTER UNIVERSITY PRESS

Published by Manchester University Press
Oxford Road, Manchester M13 9PL

www.manchesteruniversitypress.co.uk

British Library Cataloguing-in-Publication Data
A catalogue record for this book is available from the British Library

ISBN 978 1 5261 3578 0 hardback
ISBN 978 1 5261 7906 7 paperback

First published 2021

The publisher has no responsibility for the persistence or accuracy of URLs for any external or third-party internet websites referred to in this book, and does not guarantee that any content on such websites is, or will remain, accurate or appropriate.

Typeset by
Servis Filmsetting Ltd, Stockport, Cheshire

For my wife and daughters.

Contents

List of figures

Acknowledgements

This book is the result of a long process of discovery, serendipity and enjoyment. It slowly took shape over a period of ten years during my studies, teaching and research in Ireland and Australia, and was informed by performance art projects across several countries. However, most importantly, it was influenced by many people along the way, to whom I am very grateful.

I would like to thank all the artists who supported my research and gave me permission to use their images in this book, including Blast Theory, Rimini Protokoll, Rafael Lozano-Hemmer, Dante or Die and Liam Young. I am particularly indebted to Blast Theory artists Matt Adams, Nick Tandavanitj and Ju Row Farr for facilitating my ethnographic research on *A Machine To See With* in Brighton by giving me access to their archives, production meetings, project testing and for arranging interviews with participants and collaborators.

I am very grateful to Scott McQuire and Nikos Papastergiadis, my supervisors during my PhD studies in the University of Melbourne, who provided me with expert advice, support and encouragement to publish my work. Thanks to all my colleagues from the School of Culture and Communication in the University of Melbourne and the Technology and Culture Reading Group (TCRG) for the conversations, ideas and guidance, including: Tom Apperley, Sean Cubitt, Michael Dieter, Robbie Fordyce, Anna Jackson, Rachael Kendrick, Dale Leorke, Camilla Møhring Reestorff, Bjørn Nansen, Romana Rosalie, Nate Tkacz and Luke van Ryn. The fun and informal weekly readings under the tree beside Tsubu bar informed this book in many ways.

Thanks to all my colleagues from Trinity College Dublin, Dundalk Institute of Technology and Maynooth University for their support, guidance and inspiration. My sincere gratitude to Marie Redmond, Glenn Strong and Feargal Fitzpatrick for giving me advice and assistance during the early phase of my academic career and to Linda Doyle for providing me with access to the facilities in the CTVR/the Telecommunications Research Centre in Dublin during my PhD studies. Thanks to Michiel de Lange, Jussi Parikka, Maria Pramaggiore and Stephanie Rains for their generous advice on book publishing at various stages of the process.

I would also like to thank my colleagues from Dublin City University, where I currently teach and research. I am very fortunate to be part of a thriving and collaborative academic community.

My sincere thanks to my editor Tom Dark, for seeing the potential in my proposal and for the expert guidance provided in the last three years.

I also thank my extended families in Brazil and Ireland for their encouragement and I celebrate the memory of my father Francisco Martins Dias, who was also a lecturer and would have loved to see this book materialise. Finally, I want to thank my wife and my daughters for their ongoing support. This book is dedicated to you.

This book received financial support from the Faculty of Humanities and Social Sciences Book Publication Scheme at Dublin City University.

Introduction

The machine-city

What is the social and spatial experience of urban living in the twenty-first century? It inevitably – and increasingly – involves interactions with machines. Many of these consist of media machines that process vast amounts of data from both the surrounding environment and remote databases. Take a walk through your city. Leaving your home behind, you are likely to be carrying a very powerful information and communication machine in your pocket (your mobile phone). As you cross the street, an automated software system located in a citywide traffic control centre controls how long you need to wait for the pedestrian light to go green, as the system tries to minimise traffic congestion around your area (perhaps by prioritising car traffic instead of you). As you wait, CCTV cameras are keeping an eye on you; if you happen to live in a country that exerts tight control on citizen's social interactions, facial recognition systems will identify you in a matter of seconds, letting the authorities know your social track record, who you hang out with, and where you have been for the last week. It will also compare your identity to a vast database of criminal records, and if there is a match it will only be a matter of minutes before you are caught; there is also the possibility that you might be mistakenly identified as a criminal, as these systems are not perfectly accurate.

As you walk towards the bus stop, an autonomous vehicle crosses your path. Controlled by a combination of artificial intelligence and several sensors, it scans the surrounding environment, assembling a 3D representation of you by emitting pulsed laser light (LIDAR) in your direction, and reduces its speed as you attempt to jaywalk (because your public transport app is telling you that you will be late for your meeting). As you arrive at the nearest bus stop, a digital information display indicates that the bus is slightly delayed. You stress out as the app increases the time by which you will be late. As you board the bus, you remind yourself that the bus driver might soon be replaced by an autonomous driving system. You walk straight past the driver and scan your radio-frequency iden- tification (RFID) bus card at a terminal before taking a seat. As you arrive at work, you scan a different RFID card at the turnstile, and it lets you through. Your wallet contains several more RFID cards, some of which you haven't used for a while. A few weeks ago you decided to buy a fancy aluminium-clad wallet to safeguard your information after reading about a card hacking scandal. An assistant sits at the reception desk beside the turnstile, looking idle, with his head down checking his social media apps. The last time you spoke to him was about a month ago, when your access card failed, and he let you through manually. You wonder how he is still holding onto his job and hasn't yet been replaced by a helpline number to address these minor inconveniences.

While media machines are essential for navigating the con- temporary city, several other types of machines and machine- infrastructures are essential for the sustainability of the city: electricity, water, sewage, mobile and Internet infrastructure net- works, transport machines of all types, buildings, urban furniture, traffic lights and so on. All of these machines have to work together so that the city does not descend into chaos. We might include ourselves in this list, if we accept that we are also machines – posthumans, cyborgs, information junkies – just another node in an overarching machine-system that must keep moving forward, faster, in a predictable and repetitive cycle. This implies a synchro- nisation of the rhythm of humans and machines. At the beginning of the twentieth century, Simmel ([1903] 1950: 413) described the new-found efficiency of the city through 'the punctual integration of all activities and mutual relations into a stable and impersonal time schedule' in his account of metropolitan life. According to him, this was dealt by the urban citizen through a reprogramming of the mind to adapt to the rhythms of the machine-city: 'Modern mind has become more and more calculating. The calculative exactness of practical life ... corresponds to the ideal of natural science: to transform the world into an arithmetic problem, to fix every part of the world by mathematical formulas' (Simmel, [1903] 1950: 412).

In contemporary urban living, the rationalisation of urban life and the synchronisation of human and machine rhythms is symbolised by the impact of digitally mediated communication machines on our embodied practices. Mitchell (2003: 19) describes the blurring of boundaries between human beings and the networked systems of the city as the new condition of urban living: 'My biological body meshes with the city; the city itself has become not only the domain of my networked cognitive system, but also – and crucially – the spatial and material embodiment of that system.' As we are assembled with the machine apparatus of the city, we are subject to its limitations and inefficiencies as we deal with traffic jams, power outages, surveillance system misidentification and incorrect updates provided by digital information displays. Despite its potential failures, the vision of the machine as a technical apparatus that is crucial to the improvement of urban life has been a key factor in the planning of contemporary cities.

The model of the city as a machine was epitomised by the 1933 Athens Charter, a key manifesto of modernist urban planning issued by the Congrès Internationaux d'Architecture Moderne (CIAM), which envisioned a functionalist city plan that could theoretically be implemented anywhere in the world, regardless of environmental, social and cultural constraints (Sadler, 1999: 22). This included a hierarchical and modular urban network with clear separation of functions (leisure, work, residential, industrial). Le Corbusier – a key figure in the conceptualisation of the Athens Charter – proposed the concept of a 'machine for living' as 'the basic element of his utopian vision of the modern city' (Graham and Marvin, 2001: 72). Le Corbusier identified the machine as an essential element for human progress: 'Science has given us the machine. The machine gives us unlimited power. And we in our turn can perform miracles by its means. We have in our hands a technical equipment which is the sum of man's acquired knowledge' (Le Corbusier, 1987: 150).

The machine-city vision of the Athens Charter is structured through a top-down model of city planning and governance driven by the expectation of efficient, predictable and rational urban exchanges. This expectation, however, does not take into account the agency of the most complex machines in the city – individual citizens – and their needs and desires, which interfere with the expected functionality of the urban machine apparatus. In contrast to Le Corbusier's vision, Mitchell's definition of the hybrid human-machine provides us with a grounded perspective on contemporary urban life, where our social and spatial exchanges are mediated – rather than dictated – by complex assemblages of machines that come in many shapes and forms.

The importance of this assemblage is the basis of what I define as the machinic city, where the key to understanding contemporary urban life is to analyse the relation between machine actants (including the human-machine), rather than to pit humans against machines, or to praise machines as a universal technological solution for improving life in the city. But how – as citizens – can we reflect on the implications of this assemblage, where our lives are mediated by complex information and media machines that are embedded in the urban fabric? Towards this aim, I argue that we must pay closer attention to aesthetic machines and their ability to enable us to reflect upon our interaction with and within the contemporary mediated city. I focus in particular on digitally mediated performance art as a form of aesthetic machine that can generate spaces of deliberation on our role as an actant within the assemblage that constitutes the machinic city. Mediated performance art overlays artistic narratives onto urban space, which are mediated through innovative technological assemblages and that demand participation and reflection. This unusual assemblage generates performative events in urban space where stage and audience are combined.

Other aesthetic machines also have the ability to generate spaces for deliberation on contemporary life issues, co-opting media forms and design strategies for this particular purpose. For example, video games have been adapted to generate persuasive narratives that deal with social and cultural issues. Bogost (2007: ix) defines this as procedural rhetoric, or 'the art of persuasion through rule-based representations and interactions [that are] tied to the core affordances of the computer'. He also states that video games can 'disrupt and change fundamental attitudes and beliefs about the world, leading to potentially significant long-term social change' (2007: ix). Bogost co-founded a game development practice called Persuasive Games that produced several video games that fit under his definition of procedural rhetoric. For example in *Fatworld*, a video game that explores the politics of nutrition, the player has 'to construct menus and recipes, decide what to eat and what to avoid, exercise (or not), and run a restaurant business to serve the rest of [their] town' (Persuasive Games, 2020). The aim to generate deliberation is clearly stated in the description of the goals of the game: 'The game's goal is not to tell people what to eat or how to exercise, but to demonstrate the complex, interwoven relationships between nutrition and factors like budgets, the physical world, subsidies, and regulations'(Persuasive Games, 2020).

Another example of an aesthetic machine that generates spaces for deliberation can be found in the area of adversarial design, a practice that confronts the expectations of functionalist design by using 'design as provocation ... to create awareness for political issues and as part of social processes' (Hansson et al., 2018: 3). In doing so, adversarial design enables reflection on taken-for-granted everyday interactions that depend on the efficient design and integration of products and infrastructures. For example, as part of STATIC!, a design research project by the Interactive Institute, a series of erratic home appliances were created 'as a means of increasing our awareness of how energy is used and for stimulating changes in energy behavior' (Interactive Institute, 2020). Yet the project also reveals the hidden connections between the appliances, the electricity grid and between multiple households. Some of their suggested design approaches include: a TV set that displays 'black areas at the top and bottom of the screen' when 'another household start[s] using more and more energy', indicating that personal 'consumption is reduced when others expand theirs'; an iron that 'might behave like one individual in a herd of appliances' and increases its energy use as other surrounding appliances increase their energy use; and a radio that 'tunes in to stations depend[ing] on the energy consumption in its vicinity' (Ernevi, Palm and Redström, 2007: 74, 75).

Digitally mediated performance art projects combine strategies and outcomes from the procedural rhetoric of persuasive video games and the provocative strategies of adversarial design. When these projects are performed in urban space, they interfere with and temporarily reconfigure the functional spaces of the city. They also combine rule-based interactions mediated by repurposed functional technologies (such as automated call centre systems and digital information displays) with ambiguous artistic narratives. However, the ability of performance art projects to enable spaces of deliberation is complicated by the ever-changing nature of the contemporary mediated city.

As the technical machine apparatus embedded in urban space becomes more autonomous, making decisions and performing in urban space independently of human intervention, we must reflect on how this affects us as urban citizens. The machine apparatus is not immediately obvious to us: it is either concealed, too complex to be easily grasped or its outcomes are too subtle (yet highly effective). The individual components of this machine apparatus can either operate through predefined and predictable states or inefficient, unpredictable and uncontainable states; and they can move dynamically between these two states.

In this book I foreground the importance of not-so-efficient machines – persuasive, erratic, dysfunctional, ambiguous – to safeguard our human condition against the backdrop of ubiquitous and pervasive machines that mediate urban life. In particular, I focus on the role of not-so-efficient machines that materialise through the narratives of performance art projects. Such projects incorporate and reflect upon the machines – efficient and not-so-efficient – that mediate urban life. My general argument is that performance art can act as a probe to help us reflect on contemporary urban living, as human and machine agency become increasingly intermingled and digital media is overlaid onto the urban fabric. The machinic assemblages enabled by performance art projects in urban space that are facilitated by digital media technologies demonstrate the importance of a relational understanding of how agency is distributed across the city, defocusing – but not disabling – the agency of technical machines.

Such projects generate hybrid spaces where embodiment intersects with digitally mediated communication machines and artistic narratives within spatial boundaries that are emergent and changeable. These projects draw from a rich history of avant-garde art movements, reflecting on contemporary urban living and also speculating on the future of the city. Therefore the focus of this book is to define the role of performance art – and particularly digitally mediated performance art – towards creating a space for deliberation and reflection on the machinic nature of the contemporary city, where the experience of the assemblage of media, performance and participation defines contemporary urban living. I adopt an open-ended definition of performance art, generally described as live performances that combine 'diverse disciplines and media', with the use of provocation as a strategy to respond to change – 'whether ... political ... or cultural, or dealing with issues of current concern' – and that are capable of triggering reflection in the participant (Goldberg, 1998: 12, 13). Such projects define participants as performers, whose 'responses to an art work are essential to the completion of the work', regardless of the mode of interaction (Goldberg, 1998: 9).

Machines that make art

The original concept for this book came from observing an unusual performance taking place on a cold night in the Trinity College campus in Dublin's city centre in 2008. This performance was unusual in many ways: it was part of Lightwave, the inaugural event of the Science Gallery, a non-profit gallery situated on the campus, described as a 'living experiment [...] where science and art collide' (Science Gallery, 2019a). The performance was called *Laser Bombing* by Graffiti Research Lab (see Figure I.1).

The promotional blurb in the event's brochure stated that *Laser Bombing* would 'allow any graffiti writer or ordinary citizen to communicate on the same scale as advertisers, corporations and governments using a 60-milliwatt laser, 1800 watts of audio and a very big projector' (Science Gallery, 2019b). This sense of empowerment was certainly present when I came across the performance.

Through an innovative and mobile assemblage of digital technologies – a projector, a laptop, a webcam and a laser pen – Graffiti Research Lab's installation empowered Dublin citizens to

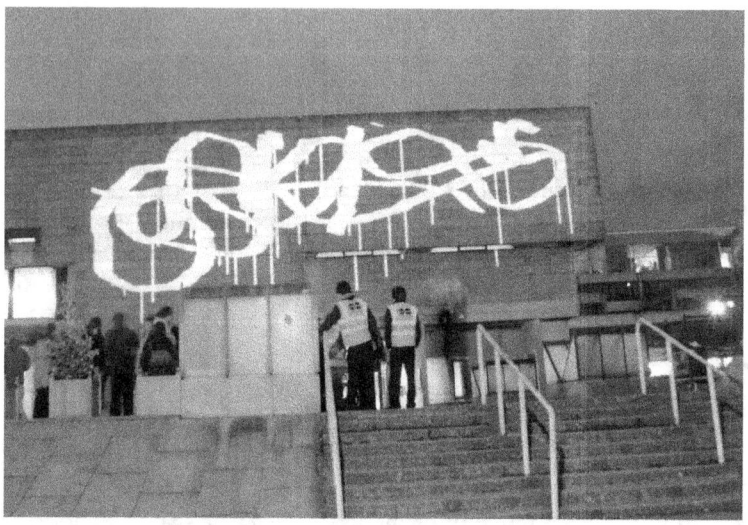

Figure I.1 Graffiti Research Lab – *Laser Bombing*

draw gigantic, non-permanent inscriptions on the monumental bare concrete walls of Trinity College's Berkeley Library, a symbolic icon of Brutalist architecture. Participants used a battery-operated laser pointer pen – considerably more powerful than the ones commonly used to deliver slide presentations – to draw and write onto the wall of the library. A web camera connected to a laptop tracked the movement of the laser's light beam on the wall. A software program developed by the artists captured the path drawn by the participants and projected it onto the wall with the help of a powerful (yet portable) projector situated approximately twenty metres away from the library's wall. As an ad hoc crowd gathered in front of the library, participants informally shared the laser pen to participate. Their inscriptions on the wall overlapped and formed emerging patterns composed of multi-layered drawings and writings, including political statements and personal messages. After a few minutes the software program deleted all the inscriptions, leaving a blank canvas ready to be drawn onto over and over again. A portable electric generator powered the web camera, laptop and projector, and the whole equipment was assembled on top of a trailer attached to a bicycle, enabling the installation to be easily redeployed.

The experience amplified the gesture of writing to a colossal scale. Standing ten metres away from the wall, I was able to write in letters that were taller than me. The experience was empowering, and symbolised a form of transgressive communication that, despite its monumental scale and impact, disappeared once the event was over. *Laser Bombing*'s powerful form of communication enabled an open and unpredictable performance where participation was an essential component. Artist Evan Roth from Graffiti Research Lab stood next to the projector, behind the crowd at the bottom of the staircase leading to the library, controlling the laptop, while a group of participants unknown to each other took turns with the laser pen. There were no specific rules guiding the sharing of the laser pen. The event temporarily hijacked the surrounding public space through a form of non-destructive graffiti. Yet it could have also been easily hijacked: anyone could have brought their own laser pen and started a new inscription, which would subsequently be captured by the web camera, processed by the computer software and projected onto the library's wall.

This reinforces the unpredictability of the event and its potential as an emergent performative intervention in an otherwise carefully monitored yet publicly accessible space (Trinity's main campus) used mainly for education and touristic purposes. While engaging as a participant I was able to observe the social interaction patterns emerging through the performance. Participants informally shared the laser pen during the performance without direct interference or guidelines from the artists, while passers-by were perplexed by the unusual light display. The performative intervention in one of the most symbolic urban spaces in Dublin generated a focal point of attention that contrasted – and competed with – the sombre, and equally powerful statement of the Brutalist facade of the Berkeley Library.

Media, performance and participation

Laser Bombing symbolises the potential of performance art to reflect on how contemporary urban space is assembled through a combination of built environment and digital technologies, where both inform how we interact with the city. *Laser Bombing* involves three main elements – media, performance and participation – which are also key factors in how we interact with urban space. I will briefly describe the importance of these three elements towards my aim of investigating the potential of performance art to enable us to reflect on contemporary urban living.

First, media is a key constitutive element of contemporary urban life. Media forms such as cinema, photography and postcards have translated the city from a space of built forms into a mediated space. For example, as McQuire (2008: 45) points out: 'the postcard played a critical role in disseminating the modern city as a visual spectacle [feeding] the emerging apprehension of the city as a collection of fragments, a terrain comprising multiple perspectives, a space which can no longer be contained by the single authoritative shot'. McQuire (2008: 131) states that 'media consumption is increasingly occurring in public space', as the built environment becomes an assemblage of mediated forms in the shape of signature buildings, the branding of ambitious urban redevelopments, and electronic displays covering the entire visible surface of buildings.

Digital media accelerates the process of mediatising the city, by enabling convergence of media forms, intensifying relations between the different actants in the city (including citizens, built environment, media displays and transport and communication infrastructure networks) and the reconfiguration of social relations. McQuire argues that the new social experience of the media city is defined by relational space, where social relations are emergent and unpredictable: 'As media become increasingly mobile, scalable and interactive, the new mode of social experience in the media city is characterized by what I term *relational space* [...] I am referring to the contemporary condition in which the horizon of social relationships has become radically open' (2008: 21, 22; original emphasis).

Easterling (2016: 13) argues that the infrastructure space of the city is a medium of information that shares the modular potential and universal reach of computer operating systems. This implies that the city itself is a programmable interface, where a 'set of instructions' replaces the master plan as a new urban development process defined by an 'interplay between variables' (Easterling, 2016: 80). Easterling's argument underpins the extent to which the city and digital media forms are interchangeable, a key factor in performance art projects that reflect on the future of urban living, as I will discuss later in Chapter 6.

Second, performance is an integral aspect of our everyday lives as we interact with digitally mediated space. The city can be interpreted as a stage, or a collective of stages, where citizens – bridging the role between audience and actors – enact emergent performances. However, concurrently, the city is also a performer, as it has its own collective of actants. The assemblage of the performances of citizens and city actants – mediated by digital communication technologies – presents a complex site of investigation that can be probed by performance art projects. The artistic narratives behind such projects interrogate the relational nature of urban actants while introducing serendipity, failure, ambiguity and uncertainty into the performance of the technological apparatus of the city. However, performance art is not an autonomous probe; it is also reconfigured and influenced by the performance of the city and its assemblage of actants, as I will illustrate through my case studies.

Finally, participation refers to our individual and collective interaction with the mediated city and performance art projects. Urban planners must make particular assumptions about how we interact with urban space that inform the design of urban space. Yet citizens interact with such spaces according to their individual needs and desires. In a similar way, artists define particular narratives and outcomes for performance art projects, however, it is up to each individual participant to interpret these narratives and engage with the performance through their own means. Therefore, we cannot speak of a consensual interaction with the mediated city. Nor can we speak of a consensual interpretation of the artistic narrative of any given performance art project.

Our ability to interpret the narrative of both urban life and performance art projects to meet our own needs, desires and beliefs is representative of the importance of dissensus as a desirable factor of urban or cosmopolitan life. As Latour (2004: 453) points out, the ideal of 'one cosmos' as representative of cosmopolitanism is not attainable in contemporary society. Yet for national and local government authorities seeking to control urban areas through totalitarian systems of control – through a discreet but highly effective

assemblage of digital surveillance, data-mining and rating systems –
consensus is the default mode of operation towards defining a
predictable and controllable form of cosmopolitanism. According
to Latour (2004: 457; original emphasis), while cosmopolitanism
intends to enable citizens to 'recognize that they all inhabit the same
world', it is the task of cosmopolitics to enable us to 'see how this
"same world" can be slowly *composed*' rather than pre-empted.
Latour (2004: 454) refers to Stengers' definition of cosmopolitics,
where cosmos is not a 'finite list of entities' and the role of politics
is to curtail the tendency to foreclose cosmos. Instead, he states,
cosmos 'must embrace, literally, everything – including all the
vast numbers of non-human entities making humans act' (Latour,
2004: 454).

These non-human entities and their agential capabilities are
essential components of performance art projects, as I will argue
through my case studies. As Stengers (2005: 995) points out, the
task of politics is 'to create a space for hesitation regarding what it
means to be "good" [while] cosmos refers to the unknown constituted by … multiple, divergent worlds and to the articulations of
which they could eventually be capable'. Performance art is a form
of micro-cosmopolitics that enables reflection on how we collectively inhabit urban space, generating temporary and multiple cosmoses through the agency of both human and non-human actants.
These temporary cosmoses illustrate the importance of the concept
of the machinic city as representative of contemporary urban living,
in contrast to the model of the machine-city.

The machinic city

The concept of the machinic city does not oppose or provide an
alternative to the machine-city. Instead, it probes the relations
between the several actants in contemporary mediated cities, including those that have been modelled on the fundamental principles of
the machine-city. For example, Brasilia (see Figure I.2), a city built
between 1956 and 1960 in a remote area to become the new capital
of Brazil, was modelled on the principles of the Athens Charter. Its
rational grid-like structure is overlaid with logical circulation for

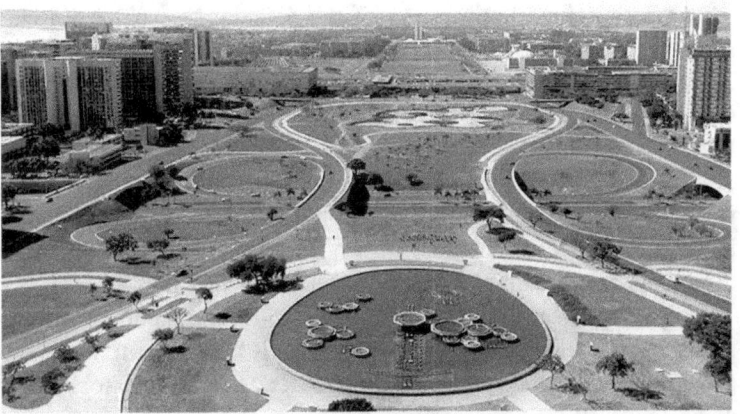

Figure I.2 Brasilia – aerial view

transportation and divided into clear functional sectors (residential, commercial, industrial and leisure). The planning of Brasilia ignored an urban feature – the *esquina* (street corner) – that is considered the main hub of social life in historically grounded cities across Brazil. While *esquinas* were absent from Brasilia's original plans, they emerged informally, as bars situated in the commercial sectors ignored the strict planning rules and placed chairs and tables in the green areas and footpaths located outside the official boundaries of the bars. These became focal points of attraction for socialising, and eventually became the de facto *esquinas* in Brasilia, driven by an emerging assemblage of actants who took little notice of the strict planning rules of the city. This example illustrates the performative potential of the concept of the machinic city, where unscripted (and emerging) narratives provide a counterpoint to the consensual model of the machine-city.

Therefore, I argue that the conceptual model of the machinic city enables us to grasp our current state of urban affairs while probing the relational nature of urban actants (including the agency of non-human actants). This model is informed by both empirical studies and philosophical frameworks of the machine that are not limited to the definition of the machine as a technical apparatus. The term 'machinic city' has been employed previously in Adrian Franklin's (2010) *City Life*, but in a different context. Franklin uses the term to define the influence of the machine as technical apparatus in the transformation of cities at the end of the eighteenth century and beginning of the nineteenth century across England through industrialisation. Referring to *Coketown* – the term used by Charles Dickens to describe these cities, Franklin (2010: 30) describes how the logic of the machine displaces human agency: 'It was as if the new machinery itself played a part in, was an agent in, and extended a machinic logic and ethic to life in Coketown displacing the humanity of previous city life.'

Despite the negative effects on the physical and mental health of industrial workers at the time, there was also excitement about the potential of the machine as both an aesthetic and a regulatory form, or as Law (2003: 6, 7) argues, a form of machinic pleasure that involves a degree of renunciation of agency and is associated with the pleasure of 'being cared for' by the machine and the 'luxury of non-responsibility'. In his account of the early industrialisation of England, Franklin (2010: 32) outlines the influence of the machine as a form of 'aesthetics of the steam age', where any negative effects of the machine apparatus were normalised: 'The city machinescape of grime, discharge and noise was inscribed on the bodies of the workers, their skin, their clothes and their homes – but also on their thinking. For the working classes, coal smoke signified the epicentre of successful domesticity.'

The machinic aesthetic represents the influential power of machines on social relations – from the steam machines of early industrial towns to smart phones in contemporary society. However, in contemporary urban space, the side effects of the machinic aesthetic are less prominent and more ubiquitous. The process of blackboxing of digital technologies (Latour, 2000: 304), where the machine's internal complexity is hidden (and we only deal with its inputs and outputs) is coupled with the ubiquity of digital media, as such technologies 'weave themselves into the fabric of everyday life until they are indistinguishable from them' (Weiser, 1991: 94). This coupling enables the machine to permeate most social encounters in our everyday lives, while making it harder for us to acknowledge its side effects on our wellbeing. As machines move towards the background of the urban fabric, they become more pervasive and influential than ever.

The aesthetic machine

The concept of the machinic city as an assemblage of human and non-human actants draws from Lewis Mumford's (2014) conceptualisation of the megamachine as a collective machine. Mentioning the Great Pyramid of Giza as an example of a megamachine, Mumford (2014: 385) states: 'By operating as a single mechanical unit of specialized, subdivided, interlocking parts, the one hundred thousand men who worked on that pyramid could generate ten thousand horsepower.' This collective machine's efficiency was enabled 'by a combination of divine command and ruthless military coercion [where] a large population was made to endure grinding poverty and forced labour at dull repetitive tasks' (Mumford, 2014: 385). According to Mumford (2014: 387) the contemporary version of the megamachine is equally oppressive, where a 'system of total control exercised by a military-scientific-industrial elite' under the imperative of universal automation attempts to curtail the 'spontaneous manifestations of life that cannot be fed in to the machine'. Mumford's argument is not directed against the machine itself, but against the structures of power underpinning the machinic assemblages of contemporary society.

Mirroring Franklin's (2010) account of the normalisation of the machinic aesthetic during the early industrialisation of England, Mumford (1934: 323) states: 'the most durable conquests of the machine lay not in the instruments themselves ... but in the modes of life made possible via the machine and in the machine'. These emerging modes of life involve, as Mumford points out, the ways in which artists responded to – and incorporated – the new aesthetic forms of the machine. Félix Guattari (1995: 107) emphasises the importance of a non-mechanist definition of the role of the machine in our society, where the creativity of the aesthetic machine is assembled with the creativity of the techno-science machine (rather than being opposed to it): 'We have to shed our mechanist visions of the machine and promote a conception which encompasses all of its aspects: technological, biological, informatic, social, theoretical and aesthetic.'

The conceptualisation of the aesthetic machine by Guattari is of key importance to my argument that performance art can help us to reflect on everyday life in the contemporary mediated city. Guattari (1995: 105) states that the aesthetic paradigm occupies a 'key position of transversality with respect to other Universes of value', enabling emerging modes of subjectivity. Guattari situates the aesthetic machine as neither an autonomous machine, nor a machine that is hierarchically more important than other machines. Instead, the aesthetic machine traverses social, technical and urban machines, assembling them into machinic assemblages where meaningful exchanges and reflections between participants take place (both human and non-human) without necessarily restructuring these machines.

The task of assembling the aesthetic and techno-science machines was undertaken through traditional art forms such as painting and sculpture, but also through media forms emerging in the nineteenth century and their unique machinic features: photography and motion pictures. In relation to motion pictures, Mumford (1934: 343) argues that they are capable of recreating 'in symbolic form a world that is otherwise beyond our direct perception or grasp'. While foregrounding the potential of the motion picture as a form of deliberation on the increasing complexity of life, Mumford also emphasises that the 'observer … partly determines the picture' (Mumford, 1934: 342). Or in other words, the observer participates in the construction of meaning. Mediated performance art also invites the participant to reflect on urban life and to construct meaning through their personal interpretation of the artistic narrative, but most importantly it achieves this through embedding itself in urban space and becoming part of the urban fabric.

Some of the performance art projects that I discuss as case studies in this book consist of temporary interventions that have a discreet visual and physical impact on the infrastructure of the city, yet are capable of generating affect, reflection and a variety of emotional responses in participants, as they interact with artistic narratives, city actants, unusual technological assemblages, bystanders and other participants. These temporary interventions might be invisible to busy citizens engaging in their everyday routines, but from the participant's point of view they consist of significant interventions where at times it is difficult to draw the line between reality and fiction.

By acknowledging the performative potential of the aesthetic machine, I argue that it is important to investigate it *in situ*. To this effect, I have become yet another performative machine-component in some of the performances that I have researched in the process of writing this book as I observed participants, became a participant, took part as a tester in one of the projects (on behalf of the artists) and interviewed participants, artists and technical support members. During this process, I was continually interpellated by the disruptive agency of the city and its collective of actants and had to adapt my research methods on the move. While these mishaps foregrounded my inefficiencies as a research machine, they also unveiled unexpected lines of enquiry and unscripted performances, as I will discuss later. Mediated performance art projects – in particular those that take place in urban space – provide unique probes into contemporary urban life that differ from more structured approaches, such as through the procedural rhetoric of video games and the interventions of adversarial design in domestic environments. The aesthetic machine of performance art questions the perceived role of the machine as a technologically deterministic agent through narratives that engage participants in challenging, uncanny, ambiguous, unexpected, enlightening and open-ended experiences. Such experiences depend on both the interpretation of the artistic narrative by the participant, but also on the unexpected agency of city actants, and therefore are machinic – and unpredictable – in nature.

Structure

My strategy towards outlining the importance of performance art as an approach to reflecting on urban life is to present case studies upfront, and subsequently analyse them through a theoretical framework that combines philosophy, performance, media and urban studies. Some of the case studies that I present have been the subject of my ethnographic research described above, but I also include other relevant projects that I was unable to experience in person. In Chapter 1, I describe my experience as a participant in Blast Theory's *A Machine To See With*, to reflect on the participatory potential of performance art. My experience illustrates the importance of tracing the relations between an emergent assemblage of actants, in order to understand their role in mediating agency. Blast Theory is an internationally renowned artist group that has been producing award-winning digitally mediated performance art projects for over two decades. I describe some of their projects to illustrate different approaches, strategies and outcomes of performance art.

In Chapter 2, I provide a breakdown of the actants in *A Machine To See With*, dividing them into three main categories – design, technology and city actants. This analysis provides a detailed account of a performance art project – from design to development to performance – while also introducing some of the machine-components that I argue are constitutive of both performance art and the machinic city. This account highlights the performative potential of not-so-efficient machines, illustrating how they may lead to positive social outcomes when they fail to fulfil their intended aims.

In Chapter 3, I reconceptualise the machine as a performative device with abstract potential. By presenting an example of a performative encounter described to me by a participant, I provide an account of a technically deficient but socially efficient assemblage of machines. This is followed by a description of the core machines that mediate contemporary urban life and that are also key components of performance art. Finally, I describe the importance of machinic subjectivity and of a broader definition of the machine towards enabling us to reflect on the mediated contemporary city.

Chapter 4 focuses on the aesthetic machine, addressing both the criticism of its association with techno-science machines and the innovative aesthetic machines that emerged in twentieth-century avant-garde art movements, such as Futurism and the Russian Agit-Theatre of Attractions. This is followed by an analysis of the influence of the cinematic machine as a device to explore the potential of urban space. Towards the end of this chapter, I describe the importance of the post-1960s performative turn as a foundation for contemporary performance art, including the Neo-Concretists' experiments with embodied encounters, the Situationists' interventions in functional urban living, and Fluxus and Happenings' experiments with open-ended and ambiguous narratives. This chapter concludes with a reflection on the assemblage of the aesthetic machine with the digital paradigm and an analysis of autonomous aesthetic machines made possible by recent technological achievements.

In Chapter 5 I provide a critical reflection on how participation unfolds in the digitally mediated environment of the machinic city by referring to a series of large-scale projects by artist Rafael Lozano-Hemmer – including *Solar Equation*, performed in Melbourne in 2010 – and also to my participation in *Ciudades Paralelas*, a series of performance interventions in functional urban spaces curated by Lola Arias and Rimini Protokoll artist Stefan Kaegi in the city of Cork (in Ireland) in 2012. My account of participation is based on Jacques Rancière's (2009a) critique of the emancipated spectator and on Eco's (1989) conceptualisation of the 'open work', and highlights the importance of dissensus as a key factor in the participatory outcome of both performance art and the machinic city.

Finally, in Chapter 6 I turn my focus towards future machines to argue that any speculation of the future of social and spatial relations in the city must not be carried out through technocentric dystopian narratives but instead by acknowledging – and investigating – assemblages of human, technology and urban actants. I argue that performance art's potential to speculate on the future of the machinic city emerges through two main affordances: first, its capacity to trigger reflection on current uses of digitally mediated technologies, such as in Dante or Die's performance *User Not Found* (2018), which reflects on the issue of the digital data that we produce outliving us; and second, through its ability to speculate on future urban scenarios that artist Liam Young (in Griffiths, 2015) describes as an 'exaggerated present'. To illustrate these affordances, I talk about my participation in *User Not Found* and also describe a series of projects by Liam Young, who describes himself as a speculative architect. I also analyse the importance of the concept of collaboration towards generating future machines by describing *2097: We Made Ourselves Over* (2017a), a project by Blast Theory that was informed by their collaboration with experts in several areas of knowledge and that unfolded through several outputs, including live performances in the cities of Hull (in the UK) and Aarhus (in Denmark), through a series of fictional films and a custom-made app.

I argue that performance art and its assemblage of both efficient and not-so-efficient machines – and of human and non-human actants – highlight the importance of the machinic city as symbolic of relational agency in urban space against the vision of a technocentric model of urban living. As contemporary urban life is increasingly mediated through several machines of both a technical and non-technical nature – we must investigate how human-machine assemblages might generate meaningful social encounters in the city that are not tied to the mechanistic rhythms of the technical machine.

1

A Machine To See With

A participatory account of performance art in the city

Walking through the city, your mobile rings. You pick up your phone and answer. You are expecting this call, but the voice on the other side is unfamiliar. It is unclear if it is a recording or a real person, yet it is reassuring. It prompts you to partake in an experience that you earlier consented to, although you are not sure about the aim or the outcome. The voice tells you to remain alert, to avoid talking to anyone and to go to a specific location in a few hours' time. The voice is intense and mysterious. From this point onwards, you are engaged in a narrative that will challenge your perception of the city and how you interact with it (and within it) through a digitally mediated narrative conveyed to your mobile phone. The following section is a description of my experience as a participant in Blast Theory's performance art project *A Machine To See With*, which took place during the Brighton Digital Festival in September 2011. The extracts that follow are part of the script (Blast Theory, 2011a) that was specifically adapted for Brighton's urban space and conveyed to me through an automated recording narrated by Blast Theory's artist Matt Adams.

It's ten past seven in the evening and the day is bright and clear. I am in front of the derelict Astoria theatre building (see Figure 1.1) on the outskirts of central Brighton after following the initial prompt from the voice.

To confirm you are standing outside the abandoned Astoria Theatre on Gloucester Place and ready to begin, press 1.

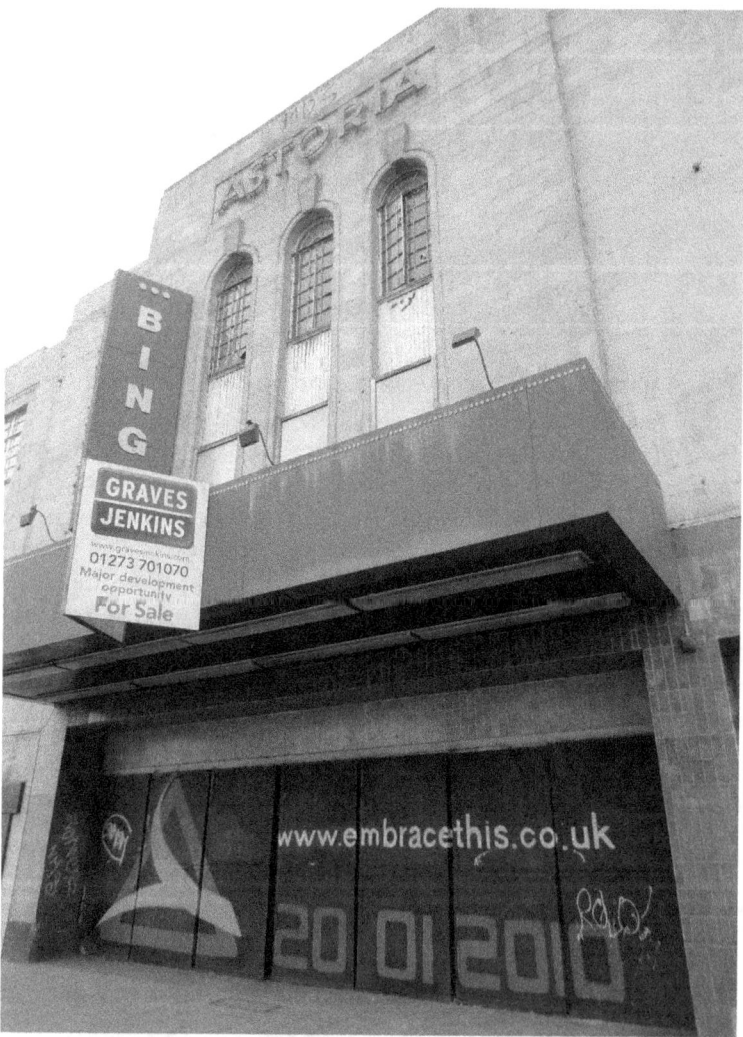

Figure 1.1 *A Machine To See With* – Astoria theatre

What's your name? I want you to record it for me after the tone.

OK. Your answer has been recorded [...] I don't know what your name is because this is a recording and I could be thousands of miles away. I could be in Delhi or Derry or Denver.

You agree that you will take responsibility for your own safety and actions during this time [...].

If the police are called they will not take any notice of your excuses. If you get caught you just deny that you knew you were breaking the law, just tell the authorities that re-distributing capital from where it is not being used to where it will get used is a service. Get ready to think on your feet.

Things will NOT go as planned. This is just a recording. You're going to have to use your initiative to get through this.

It's time to initiate your surveillance system. Your eyes are a machine to see with. Your ears are a machine to listen with. This environment is not what it first appears. (Blast Theory, 2011a)

At this stage, it is not yet clear what I am going to be asked to do, but it looks like it involves something challenging and outside the comfort zone of a law-abiding citizen. As I start walking while following the directions from the voice, I feel like I am the main character in an action movie. However, I am also the cameraman and spectator of my own movie: as I focus on the visual prompts suggested by the voice I 'film' them with my own eyes and subsequently I play back the film to myself, reflecting on it as I follow the route defined by the narrative.

On the right, you pass the boarded-up side entrance to the theatre. On your left, through the green painted bars, is the leafy yard of solicitors' offices.

Around you a constellation of cameras, booms and cranes hover. As you tilt your chin, they tilt with you. As you walk, they glide – surround you.

Do not draw attention to yourself. Everything around you is just pretend, it's all made up.

The voice suggests that I am being watched all the time. I don't see anything unusual, but the mention of an invisible surveillance apparatus heightens my awareness of my own presence in the city. Am I drawing attention to myself? Am I walking too fast? Or too slow? Guided by the voice, I get to the entrance of a leisure centre.

When you're in the toilets in the swimming pool and locked in a cubicle, call me back.

You are hidden in a cubicle, tightly framed.

The toilets are publicly accessible despite being located behind the main reception, but nevertheless I felt like I shouldn't really be here. Do I need to pretend I am using the cubicle for its intended purpose? No, I decide. For the next five minutes, the voice quizzes me on my leadership skills and my ability to remain calm in a stressful situation. It also states that it is able to categorise my behaviour through a simple multiple-choice test answerable through the keypad on my mobile phone.

Let's learn something about you.

Most psychologists now believe that the apparent complexity of human personality is just an illusion.

In reality, people vary on just five fundamental dimensions. Understand these dimensions and we gain an important insight into your behaviour and thinking.

I'm going to give you five statements and I want you to give your response to them swiftly and honestly. Don't think too hard. Just give me your reply as a number between 1 and 3, where 1 is Agree and 3 is Disagree.

[First Statement] I see myself taking the lead in a stressful situation. Now press 1 to agree, 3 to disagree and 2 if you neither agree nor disagree.

What the voice doesn't tell me is that – regardless of my choices – it will confirm that I am destined to be the leader of a highly transgressive act: a bank heist.

Your answers indicate that you're someone who doesn't take things lying down. The banks have got away with things long enough. You will be the one to set things right. Keep on your toes and be ready to act quickly if things go wrong.

Now it's time to get ready to leave. I want you to take out all your money; every single note. I want you to look at it, count it and then hide it, on your body somewhere. Somewhere they're not going to find it.

You have 1 minute to hide the money before I call you back.

I exit the cubicle and wash my hands (pretending I am using the toilets for their intended purpose) and leave. I don't think I raised any suspicion so far from bystanders or any public or private surveillance system. My next destination is the top floor of a multi-storey car park, where I will be prompted to partner up with a stranger (another participant) to execute the bank heist.

Go into the car park and up to the 5th floor. Once you're on the 5th floor, tucked out of sight, call me back.

Parked on the roof of the car park is a silver BMW 3 Series [...]. If there's anyone around, keep your distance for now. Find a place where you can watch the car unnoticed – study it.

As I make my way up to the top floor of the car park, my awareness is heightened. I stand behind a pillar trying to remain inconspicuous. I notice a guy sitting on the concrete parapet of an access ramp. Turns out he is a participant. A lady goes past me, but she is just fetching her car. The guy walks towards the BMW. There is another person in the car already and they seem to know each other. I walk to the car, and the guy – perhaps alert to my presence – walks back towards the parapet.

Ok, your partner's already there. Now pay attention to what I'm asking you to do. Mistakes at this point will be costly. Don't give them reason to doubt you. Ready?

Approach the car, passenger side. Knock on the window – three taps. If they trust you, they'll let you in. Approach, three taps, get in.

I meet participant Nick at the car. He said the other guy – Tony – is a friend whose foreign mobile phone is not connected to the local mobile network, and therefore they decided to take part together. Tony joins us, and we are now a trio of potential bank robbers (although the narrative is scripted for two partners rather than three).

Right, you're going to rob Barclays Bank on North Street. You will have one minute to agree with your partner how you're going to do this.

OK. It's time to move.

Now, both get out of the car. Close the door behind you but don't bother to lock it.

You will soon split up to scout the bank.

You will take a position with a view of the bank on level 4 while your partner does a recce around the far side. Along one side are six cashier's desks facing a line of ATMs on the other side. There is a counter towards the back behind bulletproof glass. Beyond this, an unmarked door leads to the offices and vault.

Now, get moving. Head down the stairs to the street. Walk along this side of the bank down to the main road. On the corner next to the bank is a 99p shop. Look out for your partner. They will meet you again outside the 99p shop.

Nick has his phone on loudspeaker, so Tony can also listen to the narrative. We split up and reconvene in front of the 99p shop opposite the bank.

Now stand facing your partner. Look them in the eye. If you're both ready then press 1 together.

At this point the narrative gives different prompts to me and to Nick and Tony. I am prompted to discreetly betray them after a countdown of ten. At the same time, Nick and Tony are prompted to execute the bank heist. I move swiftly away from them as they walk towards the bank.

Now: big change of plan. You're going to dump this other person in three minutes. I need you to act very quickly and discreetly when I give you the word. You will turn and walk fast directly away from them as soon as they start to approach the bank. Use your judgement. Keep an eye on them and take your chance to get away without being seen.

If your partner speaks to you or signals to you, just shake your head and keep going.

As I move away, I look back and see Nick and his friend aborting the bank heist as they approach the entrance to the bank and moving swiftly towards a side street after being told to do so by the narrative.

I need you to be inside the bank by the time I get to 1. I'm going to count down from 10. Now walk straight for the front doors of the bank. 10, 9, Speed, 7, 6, 5, 4.

Stop. Stop. Stop.

Do not walk any further. Get out of there as quickly as you can. Don't go back the way you came. Avoid your so-called partner at all costs and get out of sight now.

It all fell apart. That robbery was an invention that could never hold. And it's a long time since the bankers were concerned with robbers. That battle is over. Best to swivel at the door and walk away. Let's get out of here.

The narrative tells me to go to the nearby Victoria Pub and call back. As I arrive there, I am spotted by my partners in crime. They look at me and laugh as I mention I was told to betray them. I am now told by the voice to move towards the end point of the performance (a leisure arcade). I also get a message on my phone (which is roaming) warning me that my credit is low.

You know that point in a film where it dawns on you that it can only end in one of two ways? And either option feels familiar and less exciting than it should.

They either get together or they don't. They either win the battle or they lose. They either get away with the loot or it all falls apart.

My phone credit runs out on my way to the end point. Ironically, the last thing I hear from the voice is: 'the end is up to you'. I missed the following narrative prompts, but Nick and Tony listened to them:

You're standing outside the Regency Leisure Arcade. Take a deep breath. Suck it in. You are here for a reason, try to stay calm.

I want you to wait here until you see someone you can connect with. It can be anyone. A member of the public walking past. An employee of the arcade. Someone else taking part in A Machine To See With. You will know them when you see them.

And you will give that person some money.

Think about how you're going to give it. Will you do it silently with no explanation, press it into their palm and walk away? Or is it better to say something: one tiny statement to cement this moment between the two of you? Choose how you're going to do it.

Now, if you're going to do this, get some money into your hand. Do it as subtly as you can.

I meet up with Nick and Tony again at the Regency Leisure Arcade and interview Nick. He knew five other people taking part around the same time as him. They all enjoyed it. Another participant joins the conversation. She said she got too excited at the start, dropped her iPhone and the screen was smashed. She shows her phone to us, but she doesn't seem too upset (she was actually laughing). Later that day I made some notes of my overall experience, starting with an overview:

Interesting experience. Quite unusual. Uneasy at times, but not uncomfortable. Quite the opposite: at certain times I felt comfortable with the voice guiding me around town. I heard the same from other participants.

Reflecting on participation through performance art

After my participation, I made a list of my impressions for further analysis, which subsequently helped me during my observations of other participants and interviews with them. The following paragraph is an abbreviated version of these notes.

The encounters with other participants were unpredictable. The voice of the narrative asked my name (suggesting empathy) but it subsequently stated that it didn't know me because it was a recording. There was a clear cinematic influence in the narrative, including several allusions to a network of cameras capturing every single moment of my participation. The uncanny psychological test that took place inside a public toilet cubicle in the leisure centre was a claustrophobic experience. It was strange to be told that I was assigned a leadership role in the planned bank heist. The experience of being guided through the city by the narrative's voice felt like taking part in some ad hoc guided city tour. There was a build-up of intensity as I approached the car park. It was hard to distinguish between participants and bystanders, and there was a mutual game of surveillance between participants (where we were all paranoid about being surveilled by each other). The aborted bank heist triggered reflexivity on the whole meaning of the performance. I was a victim of technological failure – or to be more precise – technological unpreparedness, as I ran out of credit while using my mobile phone on roaming during the performance. Although I didn't really get to the end of the performance, by speaking to other participants who did, I was made aware that the narrative prompt to give money to a stranger in the leisure arcade was the most challenging aspect of the event.

I was aware that the bank heist was a fabrication before taking part in the performance (unlike most participants), and therefore I was expecting my participation to be closer to the experience of an ad hoc tour of the city (as I mentioned above). Or in other words, I wasn't expecting the performance to be as exciting and engaging as it actually was. Yet the embodied experience of navigating the city, combined with an ambiguous and unusual cinematic narrative while interacting with other participants unknown to me, bystanders and urban actants (traffic, weather, lift, staircases, public and semi-public toilets, crowds and so on) made it into a very engaging and enjoyable experience that is hard to describe in words. Other participants expressed the same to me, regardless of the diverse ways in which they interpreted and engaged with the narrative prompts.

This type of performance draws from a lineage of aesthetic machines that emerged in the avant-garde art movements of the twentieth century in parallel with the evolution of the mediated city and its associated communication technologies, from traditional photography to performances mediated by sophisticated assemblages of software and hardware. However, there are some noticeable differences. For example, the Futurist performances from the earlier twentieth century were marked by an emphasis on the superiority of the machine over human being, driven by radical manifestos and the belief that they could transform society. In contrast, contemporary performance art projects are usually more concerned with exploring hybrid human-machine assemblages rather than making claims about the superiority of the latter; they are not defined by radical manifestos and they do not claim to be able to transform society. Dixon (2007: 64) suggests that the more introverted nature of contemporary performance is algorithmic in nature: 'The introversion of the computer paradigm may offer a clue as to why there are no manifestos for digital performance, in contrast to the scores there were for Futurist performance. Digital performance artists generally lack the aggressive, extrovert bravado of the futurists, their fiery rhetoric and grandiose claims.' Yet this does not limit the ability of contemporary performance art to generate a meaningful, intense and personal experience for each participant, as I will discuss later through case studies.

My general argument in relation to participation in performance art projects is that it should not be pre-empted, regardless of how structured and scripted a particular project might appear to be. While the artists behind such projects might seek a specific participatory effect or outcome, generally associated with a particular trajectory in public space, it is up to the participant to interpret the narrative of the performance through their own awareness of how it engages with urban space and its multiple actants. The outcome of performance art manifests itself through emergent interactions between participants, bystanders and mediated urban space, and through the affordances of a hybrid space (combining virtual inputs and physical space) with no fixed boundaries. The aesthetic machine of performance art is relational by nature, assembling with established cultural, economic and social practices while also reconfiguring these practices. Through a participatory process that involves reflection, embodied encounters and emergent social interaction, performance art questions the role of pervasive technologies in the contemporary mediated city and invites us to think about how much we trust (or not) these technologies. It also questions the ability of such technologies to pre-empt social interaction in the city, or to have a dominant role in everyday life encounters.

When technological actants are exposed to the relational nature of performance art in public space, they are subject to failure, misunderstanding and interference. As the analysis of my observations of *A Machine To See With* revealed, technology failures were not always counterproductive, as they also enabled positive, fun and enlightening outcomes for participants and even bystanders. These failures symbolise the resistance against the rhetoric of the digital sublime and its 'guarantees of instantaneous worldwide communication, of a genuine global village [which] are in essence promises of a new sense of community and of widespread popular empowerment' (Mosco, 2004: 24, 25). The digital sublime – as the logical continuation of other forms of technological sublime and its mythological seduction (Mosco, 2004: 22), is driven by buzzwords such as smart city, big data and the Internet of Things. In a world where abstract and virtual machines (such as the information flows of the Internet) are an intrinsic component of everyday social interaction, 'it is vitally important that we understand how matter matters', as Barad (2003: 83) states. However, my contestation of the digital sublime is not carried out from a human-centred perspective, but by situating both human and machine(s) as relational actants on a non-hierarchical structure that should have a positive outcome for human beings.

The machinic assemblage of the (aptly named) performance art project *A Machine To See With* is unstable by nature. It assembles human beings, technical machines and urban space through an artistic narrative that is linear and that defines a clear spatial trajectory, but despite this it triggers unexpected outcomes: participants get lost during the performance, start conversations with complete strangers, wonder if they are being followed and surveilled (they aren't), and partake in meaningful and enlightening social experiences. Performance art does not foreclose difference or pre-empt meaning, and neither does the machinic city. The ability of performance art to remain indeterminate, open and to instigate reflection foregrounds its important role in a world where social relations have been so heavily mediated by digitally enabled interactions that are pre-emptive, mechanical and deterministic in nature.

Tracing relations

The unstable frame of performance art presents a challenge for investigating and tracing the relations between its multiple actants. A useful framework for investigating these relations is provided by

Actor-Network-Theory (ANT), which focuses on tracing associations between actants (Latour, 2005: 3).

As Latour (1997) points out, what matters in ANT is the intensity of connections between actants, rather than their scale in relation to each other – which suggests a hierarchical structure between actants – or the distance between them – which suggests that proximity is directly proportional to the intensity of the interaction. The fact that performance art projects can be equally influenced by actants that are nearby and visibly present (such as bystanders and urban actants) or thousands of kilometres away and not visible (such as remote servers) illustrates Latour's argument.

An actant is defined as 'something that acts or to which activity is granted by others' (Latour, 1997). Tracing actants' agency and the relations between them is particularly challenging in performance art projects in public space, as the observer (or researcher) does not hold a privileged point of view detached from the subject of observation. Therefore the observer must 'move around the work', as there are no 'a priori limits on knowledge' (Latour, 1997). ANT distinguishes between two types of actants: intermediaries and mediators. An 'intermediary' 'transports meaning or force without transformation' – or in other words, they are simple conduits of agency – while 'mediators' 'transform, translate, distort, and modify the meaning or the elements they are supposed to carry' (Latour, 2005: 39). These roles are interchangeable, as Latour illustrates by providing two different scenarios for two distinct actants (namely a computer and a conversation):

> A properly functioning computer could be taken as a good case of a complicated intermediary while a banal conversation may become a terribly complex chain of mediators where passions, opinions, and attitudes bifurcate at every turn. But if it breaks down, a computer may turn into a horrendously complex mediator while a highly sophisticated panel during an academic conference may become a perfectly predictable and uneventful intermediary in rubber stamping a decision made elsewhere. (Latour, 2005: 39)

In the quote above, Latour describes the mediators (reconfiguring or distorting meaning) as the computer that breaks down and the passionate conversation that is not pre-empted, and the intermediaries as the computer that works flawlessly and the mind-numbing academic conference panel. The predictable flow of events is disrupted through a performative process, transforming the intermediaries into mediators and demanding reflection: what is wrong with the (usually predictable) computer and who has the most persuasive argument in the conference? Latour's example illustrates how performance is capable of interfering with even the most logical exchanges, such as electronic and algorithmic processes. In mediated performance art projects, these interferences can become performative artistic strategies, through the reappropriation of functional technologies or through the questioning of the role of technology in our everyday lives.

ANT provides a good framework for researching complex subjects such as performance art in urban space, where highly mobile actants (participants and bystanders), remote actants (the servers relaying the narrative prompts to participants) and multiple unexpected actants (bystanders and the unruly urban environment) are all assembled together. ANT eschews conceptual shortcuts and overarching arguments that interpret the social as a stable system defined by a limited number of actors, dualisms and pre-emption of meaning. Performance art operates instead as an unstable system and is subject to a multiplication of outcomes, where 'each of the points in the text may become a bifurcation, an event, or the origin of a new translation' (Latour, 2005: 128).

Therefore, any investigation of the outcomes of performance art will benefit from close observation, where it is not possible to fulfil the role of a fully detached observer. My participatory account of *A Machine To See With* is just one of the components of the research that I conducted on the performance. I benefited from Blast Theory's willingness to facilitate my research. During my stay in Portslade, I was invited to stay as a guest in Blast Theory's in-house guest accommodation in their studio in Portslade (just outside Brighton). I had access to their studio archive, I was able to observe a project meeting on a particular aspect of the performance and I was invited by the artists to become a tester of the performance prior to its premiere. By staying in their studio I was also able to observe their everyday work process (including spontaneous meetings and conversations) and to arrange interviews with artists and collaborators at short notice. In doing so, I was conscious of what Latour and Woolgar (1986: 44) define as the role of the inside-outside observer, a performative role that involves striking a balance between being neither fully detached nor fully immersed, where the researcher must steer 'a middle path between the two extreme roles of total newcomer (an unattainable ideal) and that of complete participant'.

Blast Theory – a trajectory of digital performance

Before I analyse in more depth the participatory output of Blast Theory's *A Machine To See With*, I will situate it in relation to the group's extensive body of performance art (in both indoor venues and urban space) and outline why their work is capable of stimulating reflection on our digitally mediated contemporary lives. Blast Theory has an extensive background in performance art and theatre that spans over two decades. They have won several awards, including a Prix Ars Electronica Award in 2003 for *Can You See Me Now?* (Blast Theory, 2001) and an Interactive Arts BAFTA Award in 2005 for *Uncle Roy All Around You* (Blast Theory, 2003). Blast Theory's performances have been investigated by several research projects, in particular in the field of performance studies. Gabriella Giannachi (2004) argues that Blast Theory's work is at the fore-front of digital performance, while Steve Dixon (2007) concludes his comprehensive historical analysis of digital performance with an enthusiastic account of his personal experience of taking part in Blast Theory's *Uncle Roy All Around You*, which he describes as an avant-garde performance. *A Machine To See With* is part of a long lineage of Blast Theory works that instigate participants to reflect on their use of digital communication technologies in urban space. Blast Theory state that they create 'interactive art to explore social and political questions, placing audience members at the centre of [their] work' (Blast Theory, 2019).

Blast Theory's innovative performances make use of assemblages of repurposed digital communication technologies (such as mobile phones, video game controls, network communication protocols and automated call centre systems). By interfering with the normal modes of operation of such technologies and combining them with engaging and sometimes ambiguous narratives, Blast Theory's performances facilitate reflection about the normalisation of digitally mediated communication technologies. As Thrift (2004: 13) points out, our acceptance of the mediation of social processes through computing is mostly unconscious, as computing devices 'augment rather than … monopolise attention' and computing becomes 'fitted to activity-in-context like a glove is fitted to a hand'. Blast Theory addresses this paradigm in their projects by enticing participants to reflect on how digital communication technologies mediate trust and reconfigure patterns of social interaction and engagement with public space.

In the following sections I will analyse a selection of Blast Theory performances from the last two decades that use similar artistic strategies and technologies to those employed in *A Machine To See With*. *Desert Rain* (Blast Theory, 1999) – which initiated a long-term collaboration between Blast Theory and the Mixed Reality Laboratory (MRL) in the University of Nottingham – reflects on the potential of the media machine. *Can You See Me Now?* reconfigures surveillance and tracking technologies into an embodied experience that unfolds through game play. Finally, *Uncle Roy All Around You* addresses the theme of trust in strangers in public space through a transgressive fictional narrative that involves collaboration between online and street players.

Building hybrid environments

The collaboration between Blast Theory and the MRL was born out of a chance encounter in 1996 while Blast Theory was experimenting with 'video projection into water spray as part of a residency at Nottingham Trent University' (Benford and Giannachi, 2011: 9). *Desert Rain* (see Figure 1.2) took over two years to develop and involved a multidisciplinary production team, actors, a control room and a mix of props and sets similar to those employed in TV and film productions. It was a site-specific project consisting of an experimental theatrical set inside a disused warehouse that encompassed a 'combination of performance, installation and computer game' (Koleva et al., 2001: 38). The

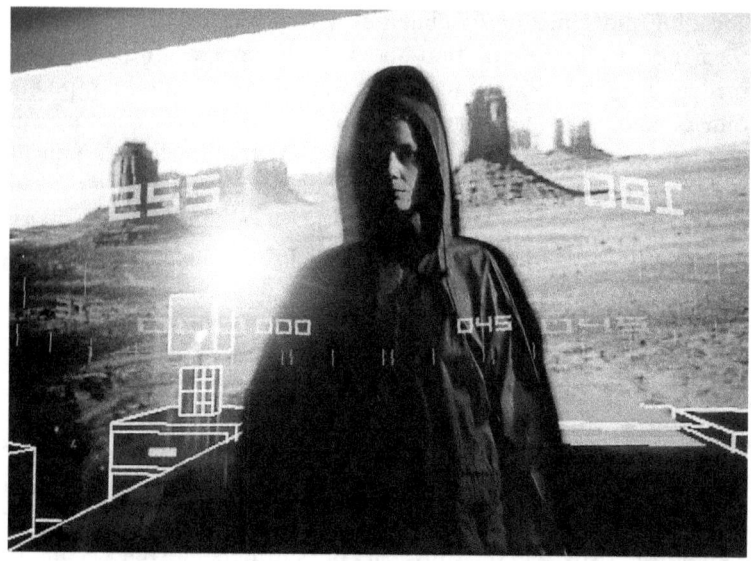

Figure 1.2 Blast Theory – *Desert Rain*

performance employed the technique of projecting a virtual environment onto a water curtain. *Desert Rain* was inspired by 'Jean Baudrillard's assertion that the Gulf War did not actually take place because it was in fact a virtual event' (Koleva et al., 2001: 38); or in other words, it was experienced by most people through the perspective of the media machine of mass media corporations. Blast Theory explored Baudrillard's critique of how the virtual event can become an unequivocal representation of real events to sustain a particular ideology.

Desert Rain temporarily transported the participant to an alternative reality consisting of two distinct environments: a virtual maze projected onto a screen followed by a custom-built physical environment through which the participant moved towards the end point (a simulation of a motel room). The first environment consisted of individual cubicles with walls made out of fabric, where participants had a view of a virtual world projected in front of them onto a water curtain and had to navigate it using a pressure-sensitive footpad that acted like a navigational joystick. Their objective was to find their allocated targets. Participants also wore headsets through which they could hear ambient sounds and communicate with the control room and other participants (Koleva et al., 2001: 39). Once participants successfully navigated the virtual environment, they were subjected to an unexpected and disorienting experience: one of the actors in the performance walked through the water curtain towards them and handed them a swipe card. This experience symbolised the transition from the virtual environment back to the real world.

Once participants were handed the swipe card, they walked through a narrow corridor that led towards a ramp covered in sand, which in turn led to an enclosed space simulating a motel room with a television set controlled by the swipe card given to them earlier. By swiping the card, they got to see a short video clip of their target (Koleva et al., 2001: 40). The targets were people who experienced the Gulf War through very different perspectives: an actor, a soldier who took part in the war, another soldier who was bedridden and watched the Gulf War on TV, a peace worker, a journalist in Baghdad at the time the war started and an actor who played a soldier in a TV drama about the Gulf War (Koleva et al., 2001: 38, 39).

Desert Rain combined several artistic strategies: references to popular culture events, the use of complex assemblages of digital media and communication technologies, heavy symbolism (through both imaginary references and props) and an ambiguous narrative. The water curtain was a technical achievement, but it also symbolised the 'falling of the bombs that caused the casualties' and a 'ritual act of symbolic purification' (Benford and Giannachi, 2011: 129, 130). The use of ambiguity and symbolic content are also key artistic strategies in *A Machine To See With*. For example, the participant was not given a reason for the bank heist, and the BMW car in the car park could be interpreted both as a symbol of oppressiveness and confinement or power and freedom. Both *Desert Rain* and *A Machine To See With* were moderated by a control centre; however, in the latter the artists had less control over participants. If the participant encountered difficulties in *A Machine To See With*, they had to ring a specific phone number so that the artists could remotely reset the narrative for them. In my observations, I noticed that the artists' lack of full control of the performance enabled some of the most interesting and unusual patterns of participation, as I will describe later.

Playing in the city

Can You See Me Now? (see Figure 1.3) is described by Blast Theory (2001) as 'one of the first location-based games [where] online players compete against members of Blast Theory on the streets'. The street players (runners) – a role fulfilled by Blast Theory's associates – moved through the physical space of the city chasing online players – connected through the World Wide Web – whose position in the virtual world was displayed on a digital map of the city on the runner's portable computer. *Can You See Me Now?* consisted of an exchange where surveillance happened simultaneously in urban space and a virtual representation of this space, and which enabled collaboration between a large group of online players dispersed around the world: 'With up to 100 people playing online

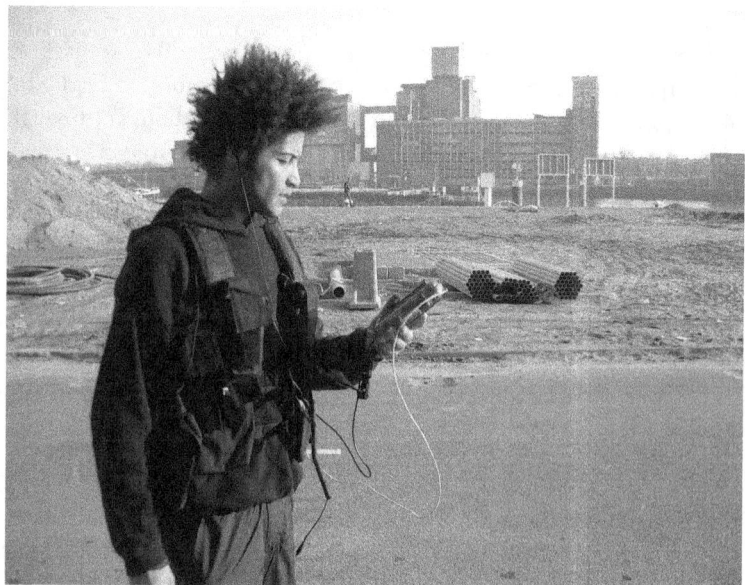

Figure 1.3 Blast Theory – *Can You See Me Now*

at a time, players can exchange tactics and send messages to Blast Theory. An audio stream from the runner's walkie talkies allowed you to eavesdrop on your pursuers' (Blast Theory, 2001).

It consisted of a performance art project that combined simple game play (akin to a game of hide-and-seek) with online surveillance and embodied interaction. While participation in *Can You See Me Now?* unfolded through play, its narrative also sought to generate meaningful social exchanges by prompting online players to reconnect with a 'lost relationship'. At the end of the performance, the narrative associated this relationship with a nondescript location in the physical space of the city, as described on the performance's webpage:

> As soon as a player registers they must answer the question: 'Is there someone you haven't seen for a long time that you still think of?'. From that moment issues of presence and absence run through the game. This person – absent in place and time – seems irrelevant to the subsequent game play; only at the point that the player is caught or 'seen' by a runner do they hear the name mentioned again as part of the live audio feed from the streets. The last words they hear is the runner announcing their catch, referring to them by the name of the person they haven't seen for a long time. (Blast Theory, 2001)

At this point the street player took a photo of the location where the online player was caught and uploaded it to the event's website. This created a connection between each online player and the city, where 'each [online] player is forever linked to this anonymous square of the cityscape' (Blast Theory, 2001) These photos taken by the street runners were charged with affect and meaning due to the narrative prompts and the dialogue between street and online players.

In *Can You See Me Now?* meaningful interaction emerged between online participants and street players despite the lack of face-to-face encounters. Blast Theory state that the starting point towards developing the narrative of *Can You See Me Now?* was to think about how we move through the city while being connected to a network, where players are simultaneously online and in the physical space of the city. In doing so, it 'plays around with proximity and presence – absence and distance' (Adams in Benford and Giannachi, 2011: 56). It reflects on the condition of being always connected to others through the communication networks of the contemporary mediated city, foregrounding the fallibility of technology, especially when trying to create a level playing field for both street and online players.

Adams (in Benford and Giannachi, 2011: 57) describes an account of technological failure in *Can You See Me Now?*: 'When a runner is moving around in the city, their GPS reports them to be roughly where they are, but because there could be an error in the GPS, they might appear to be in the middle of a building next to their location.' Adams describes how they dealt with this by 'pushing' the street player's position 'to the nearest available space' (in Benford and Giannachi, 2011: 57). To ensure a level playing field for street and online players alike, Adams describes how they added virtual obstacles for the online player: 'if there was a very steep hill, we put in obstacles in the online players' version of the maps, so that they would be slowed down. These processes were invisible to the users but they formed an underlying structural map of the entire experience' (in Benford and Giannachi, 2011: 57). As Benford and Giannachi (2011: 63) point out, the weaving of computers into the fabric of the real world through hybrid experiences is far from being seamless, as '[the] threads all too often become visible to participants'. The misalignment of technical apparatus and the physical space of the city was also evident in *A Machine To See With*, where contingency measures were put in place to safeguard participation in case of technical failure and where small delays in the transmission of instructions could affect the participant's ability to follow the trajectory defined by the narrative.

Ambiguous narratives and transgressive prompts in public space

In *Uncle Roy All Around You* (see Figure 1.4) online and street players were paired up to locate a fictitious character named Uncle Roy during a performance that lasted for approximately an hour. As in *Can You See Me Now?* the game structure of the narrative concealed a prompt for meaningful interaction that was unveiled at the end of the performance: committing to support a stranger

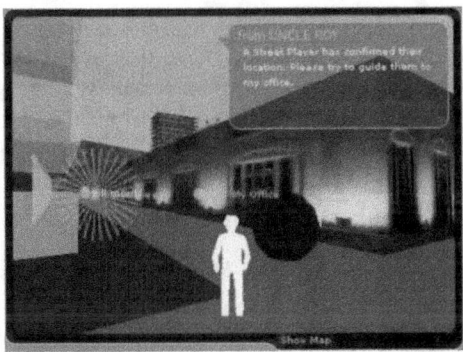

Figure 1.4 Blast Theory – *Uncle Roy All Around You*

(another participant in the event) in times of crisis for a full year. *Uncle Roy All Around* and *A Machine To See With* share similar artistic strategies, such as narrative prompts to perform transgressive acts without a clear purpose, an experimental assemblage of mobile technologies and narrative prompts that suggest that participants are constantly being surveilled. These factors triggered (in both performances) instances of bystanders being drawn into the performance as actant-mediators. They also have in common the desire to instigate reflection on how trust develops when it is mediated through mobile technologies in hybrid spaces. *Uncle Roy All Around You* was first performed at the Institute of Contemporary Arts (ICA) in London in 2003. The online player, sitting in front of a computer terminal inside the ICA, could see the location of street players (but not their semblance) on a virtual map of the streets of London. The street player had to leave all their possessions at the front desk in the ICA. They were then given a handheld computer and told to follow the instructions on screen as they walked through the streets of London. Throughout the game, street players had to report their location (through the handheld computer) and in exchange they received information to help them locate Uncle Roy. The game included actors, a limousine and an office located in an unmarked building where Uncle Roy was supposed to be (Blast Theory, 2003).

Dixon's (2007) account of his participation as a street player in *Uncle Roy All Around You* in his book *Digital Performance* foregrounds its reflective potential. Dixon (2007: 663) refers to John Cage's argument about the potential of art to 'wake [us] up to the very life we're living' while stating that Blast Theory has 'always tested and pushed the boundaries between technology, art, life and performance'. His account illustrates the blurring of fiction and everyday life that unfolds through the unpredictability of the narrative's unusual and transgressive prompts:

> Get sent to a sinister-looking parking lot and *Uncle Roy* texts you to 'act like a criminal, move in and out closely between the cars, brush against them, if you're seen, get out quickly.' Wonder if the suspicious NCP [car park] attendant is an actor or not (he clearly isn't). Brush along the cars and suddenly a car alarm goes off. Run out of the parking lot, panicking now, messages flashing on the screen. (Dixon, 2007: 665)

Dixon's description of the moment his handheld computer broke down reveals how the failure of the technological assemblage of the performance triggered in him both an emotional response and uncertainty about the boundary between the game and real life:

> Wander around in confusion as a large man approaches, very formally: 'Uncle Roy informs me you have a problem.' He fixes the computer, 'you've been allocated a little more time.' Find the next location, another clue and destination to go to, then the computer's down again. Panic. Be suddenly angry, then angry at yourself for being angry (this is just a game) then wonder 'is this part of the game?' (it isn't). (Dixon, 2007: 666)

As in *A Machine To See With*, the narrative tests the participant's ability and willingness to engage with and trust a stranger, at the moment that the participant is prompted to enter an unknown car:

> Get into the back seat. Once inside, a man (not the large one, another) gets in through the other door, sits down. He says, 'Would you trust a stranger?' Feel your heart miss a beat, and wonder what this means (you remember Blast Theory's *Kidnap*), then talk to him as the limo drives slowly through the streets – about trust, about people, about the one *you* loved and lost – he wants details, name, specifics, the whole story. (Dixon, 2007: 668; original emphasis)

Kidnap (Blast Theory, 1998) is a performance by Blast Theory in which they kidnapped two participants with their consent. The participants were selected through a lottery system that they voluntarily took part in and were kept in captivity for forty-eight hours. Dixon's awareness of the participant experience in *Kidnap* triggered the anticipation in him of an unpleasant yet unrealised encounter; or as Massumi (2003: 8) states, a 'known but not yet actually afforded outcome'. This reveals the potential of performance art to extend its impact beyond the duration of the narrative. It also reveals the potential to generate affect and reflection, as Dixon's conclusion of his account clearly states:

> Go home, reevaluate yourself, the one you once loved and lost, the nature of memory, time's winged chariot, cities and surveillance, 'virtual' realities, the fallibility of computers, the boundaries of bodies and space, the nature of life and its relationship to performance, the meaning of art. Cry like a baby. Realize, again, just how new and unprecedented such work is, and how timeless and humbling is the experience of great art. (Dixon, 2007: 669)

Uncle Roy All Around You and *A Machine To See With* provide an alternative approach to the perceived role of mobile and pervasive technologies as 'tracing the action of the subject in the world' (Tuters and Varnelis, 2006: 359). Instead, they enable participants to trace their own performance and its social impact rather than letting technology trace it. In doing so, they enable the space of the city to be transformed into what Massumi defines as 'a *social laboratory*: a performative platform for provisional group definitions of potential' (2003: 10; original emphasis). In this social laboratory, the simple experience of being temporarily liberated from the guidance of mobile and pervasive technologies generated a sense of anxiety and displacement in participants, as Adams (in Benford and Giannachi, 2011: 56) points out: 'Being lost or getting lost was wired into the player experience. [Participants] felt uncertain about where they were and whether they were going in the right direction. This threw back onto them an anxiety about place, which was a crucial part of the game experience.'

The ambiguous narrative of *Uncle Roy All Around You* – as in *A Machine To See With* – heightened this anxiety and also challenged the participant's sense of trust:

> Some [narrative prompts] are relatively direct and useful, while
> others are misleading to the point of being mischievous, encouraging
> players to follow diversions, drawing on the history of the local envi-
> ronment, implicating passers-by in the game, heightening the sense of
> being watched and also casting doubt on the intent and personality of
> Uncle Roy, especially the extent to which he can be trusted. (Benford
> et al., 2004)

It also drew bystanders into the performance as unintended actant-
mediators, as Matt (in Benford and Giannachi, 2011: 59) points
out: 'People came back and said that they had been amazed by the
acting of the tramp. They didn't actually believe us when we said
that there was no actor playing a tramp. People just folded everyday
experiences back into the fictional experience and intermeshed
them.'

Benford et al. (2004) highlight the open-ended potential of the
performance that emerges from the many (interrelated) levels of
ambiguity present in *Uncle Roy All Around You*, namely ambiguity
of information ('present[ing] information in a way that demands
interpretation'), of context (mixing game/performance and virtual/
physical environments) and of relations (between players, bystanders and 'Uncle Roy'). Such ambiguities can also emerge in the configuration of systems of trust in the contemporary mediated city
as we negotiate assemblages of mobile and pervasive technologies,
urban space and interaction with strangers.

Another interesting aspect of *Uncle Roy All Around You* is the
ability and willingness of some participants to engage with the
narrative prompts in a playful and tactical way – such as giving
misleading information about their location – to enable them to
complete the performance in a more efficient and quicker way:

> [Street players] would ... sometimes declare themselves to be ahead
> of their actual location, perhaps to get information in advance [...]
> Conversely, they would sometimes re-declare their position to be
> somewhere where they had previously been, perhaps to revisit a clue
> or as a result of pressure from online players who had missed it.
> (Benford et al., 2004)

The playful and strategic interaction of participants in performance
art projects generates multiple participatory outcomes that are not

necessarily aligned with the narrative of the performance or supported by the artists, as my encounter with participants Nick and Tony in *A Machine To See With* reveals. I will discuss this process in more detail in Chapter 5 by referring to Rancière's (2009a) critique of the emancipated spectator and Eco's (1989) concept of the open-ended work. The performance art projects that I described above depend on custom assemblages of hardware and software, yet their persuasive power and ability to generate reflection is not a direct outcome of their procedural rhetoric, to borrow Ian Bogost's (2007) definition. Instead, the persuasive and reflective power of digitally mediated performance art emerges through an assemblage of computer technologies, artistic narratives and the city as a collective of actants. Therefore, it is well situated to provide a balanced account of the impact of digital media on contemporary urban living, where no specific machine – human, technical, urban – is prioritised. In the next chapter I provide a detailed breakdown of the several actants that constitute *A Machine To See With* to illustrate its persuasive and reflective potential. This task will be undertaken by dividing the actants into three main categories – design, technology and city actants – and analysing their impact as they assemble with the human-machine in the performance.

2

Probing the machine of performance art

Unpacking *A Machine To See With*

A Machine To See With consists of a complex assemblage of actants. During its performance, actants move dynamically between the states of intermediary (a mere conduit of agency) and mediator (capable of reconfiguring agency), and in the latter state they reshape the flow of agency as the performance unfolds (Latour, 2005). By breaking down *A Machine To See With* into three main categories of actants – design, technology and city actants – I am able to define the role of each actant in the different phases of the performance (planning, design, production and performance). This process is informed by insights from the commissioners of the performance, the artists, their collaborators and the participants.

Prior to my field research, I was able to identify some of the actant-mediators in *A Machine To See With* and make the necessary preparations to observe them. However, several other actant-mediators emerged through my observations of several iterations of the performance, my own participation, and the interviews that I conducted with participants, artists and collaborators. Design actants emerge from the process of planning, designing and producing the performance. Technology actants encompass the hardware, software and communication protocols that enable the performance, including remote servers, automated call centre software and the participants' mobile phones.

While design and technology actants can be easily singled out, the city actants are harder to pinpoint. The latter include a combination of actants determined by the narrative – such as the BMW car and the city locations for each part of the performance – but also a large group of unexpected actants – such as seagulls, rowdy teenagers, sea fog and bystanders – who were drawn into the event either by prompts from the narrative, by pure chance or through the participant's interpretation of the narrative. While the design actants provide the framework for the performance to unfold, the emerging and unpredictable interaction between technology and city actants reconfigures the performance and ensures a different outcome each time it is performed.

Design actants: the commissioners

A Machine To See With was born out of a joint locative cinema commission awarded to Blast Theory from three cultural institutions across the United States and Canada: ZERO1: The Art and Technology Network (San Jose, United States), the Banff New Media Institute at the Banff Centre (Banff, Canada) and the Sundance Institute's New Frontier Initiative (Park City, United States). The commission organised an international competition with an open call for submissions in 2009, which aimed to '[bring] attention to narratives of place and space and [seek] new forms of description and experience' (ZERO1 San Jose Biennial, 2010). The commission's jury criteria – based on the proposed concept of locative cinema – stated that the submissions should engage people through a placed-based experience and a combination of technologies, including mixed reality as an indicator of the blurring of boundaries between fiction and reality (ZERO1, 2009). Shari Frilot – senior programmer of the Sundance Film Festival – emphasised the importance of supporting 'artists and filmmakers who are moved to invent new ways of cinematic storytelling that adapt to the new landscape', stating that Blast Theory's work 'exemplifies an artistic vision that is located at the crossroads of art, film, and new media technology' (ZERO1, 2009).

As part of the locative cinema commission, Blast Theory took part in a residency at the Banff New Media Institute, where they developed the first iteration of the performance and afterwards it was performed at events organised by the other partners in the commission. Compared to budgets usually allocated to traditional filmmaking, the financial grant allocated by the commission was quite small: '$4,500 [US dollars] for the art commission with an additional $5,000 available for production and residency costs' (ZERO1, 2009). This played a part in Blast Theory's decision to work with a linear narrative form, as artist Matt Adams (in Dias, 2012a) points out: '[*A Machine To See With*] was made on a shoe-string financially, and so we had to make a number of concessions very, very early on ... We didn't really begin with an aim to make the work as linear as this.'

The Brighton performance of *A Machine To See With* that I researched was commissioned by Lighthouse, a digital culture agency with charity status supporting works by artists and film-makers. It was part of their 2011–2012 theme – Beyond Cinema – and became one of the events of the Brighton Digital Festival 2011, a month-long festival in Brighton that included several events focused on digital media (Lighthouse, 2011). The Brighton premiere of *A Machine to See With* was also supported by PARN (Physical and Alternate Reality Narratives), a project funded by the European Union's Culture Programme (2007–2013) with a focus on exploring contemporary narrative practices in immersive situations through the embedding of 'media, objects, texts, interactions and their arrangements' in physical space (PARN, 2013). Lighthouse, PARN and the original commissioners of *A Machine To See With* all share the aim of engaging people through an assemblage of fictional narrative and urban space.

Design actants: artistic vision

According to Blast Theory (2014), *A Machine To See With* was inspired by three main themes: cinema, the tyranny of choice and consumerism, and the financial crisis. In order to fulfil the objectives of the locative cinema commission, Blast Theory began by developing three questions related to cinema to guide their process: 'Where does cinema operate, between the screen, the eye and the mind? What does it mean as screens get smaller and move closer? How does location – or context – act in relation to the screen?' (Adams in

Lighthouse Arts, 2011). Adams argues that the first two questions address the difficulty in translating the experience of cinema from a large screen indoor experience to small single screens in public space: 'Cinematic in my mind is something that is about scale, breadth, grandeur and immersion, and all these things are badly broken as soon as you are dealing with some poxy little screen and you are in the street with noise and you can't control it' (Adams in Lighthouse Arts, 2011).

The third question situates cinema's screen in relation to urban space. Adams emphasises the importance of context over location: '[Context] is a much fuller term that incorporates the fact that we are in cultural and political sets of relationships as we move around [and] not just in spatial and geographical ones' (Lighthouse Arts, 2011). The experience of mobility in the city involves, as Adams argues, the 'constant engagement with visual images that absolutely overwhelm and are inscribed in our imagination' (Lighthouse Arts, 2011). Fictional narratives that are played out in public space benefit from the influential power of the media machine to trigger our imagination through well-known symbolic references and tropes. Adams (in Lighthouse Arts, 2011) illustrates this by referring to the ubiquitous presence of the 'yellow school bus' in American movies about schools: 'When we think about a yellow school bus, we all understand what [they] look like, how they operate and what they do. They have a whole set of properties for us, even though most of us would never have clapped eyes on one.' The narrative text in *A Machine To See With* includes several cinematic references to phone call scenes in well-known action movies, as Blast Theory artist Nick Tandavanitj (in Dias, 2012a) points out:

> When we talked about *A Machine To See With* we had a whole set of cultural references which were things like: the Clint Eastwood movie *Dirty Harry* where he is led on a chase through the use of phone boxes; and *Matrix*, when the phone is delivered in an envelope and then he [Neo] is instructed to crawl beyond the desk and out onto a window ledge; all those seminal cinematic moments in people's experiences of using phones and mobile phones within the cinema.

Blast Theory also utilised film noir references from the movie *Chinatown* (1974) and from Richard Stark's book

The Jugger (1965), which has a bank heist theme. Adams (in Lighthouse Arts, 2011) states that Stark's book was appropriated by Jean-Luc Godard, who adapted it into a movie called *Made In USA* (1966). He cites Godard as an inspirational influence in the development of *A Machine To See With*, due to his ability to challenge the perception of the viewer, as he walks the 'delicate line between immersing [viewers] into all of those cinematic pleasures of the genre while constantly undermining you, pushing you ... into different forms of contemplation; breaking your identification to ... great effect' (Adams in Lighthouse Arts, 2011).

In the early design phase of the performance, Blast Theory experimented with embodied interactions that were inspired by cinematic language, and eventually realised that they didn't need a screen, as Adams (in Lighthouse Arts, 2011) states: 'We started to do things ... where this cinematic imagination is engaged, all these tropes and genre clichés are invoked ... starting to follow someone down the street, staking out a building [and] putting someone under surveillance. So we just played with those things and reflected on what way that invoked a certain atmosphere ... and it very quickly became clear that we didn't need a screen.'

The decision to do away with the screen had two main outcomes: it enabled the performance to be mostly inconspicuous in public space, and it transferred the responsibility of framing the film – a task usually accomplished by the cinematographer – to the participants' own imagination, where their eyes became a 'machine to see with' guided by the narrative prompts. In this process, cinema's traditional sensorial apparatus – the sense of being part of a crowd sitting in front of a large static screen, the darkness and smell of popcorn, disruptive punters – is replaced by a human-machine cinematic apparatus consisting of the participants, cinematic language, public space, fictional narrative and information technologies. Adams (in Lighthouse Arts, 2011) mentions a quote from Chris Hedges' book *Empire of Illusion* (2009) that refers to this apparatus and that served as inspiration in the design process: 'We try to see ourselves moving through our life as a camera would see us, mindful of how we hold ourselves, how we dress, what we say. We invent movies that play in our heads.'

The second main theme of *A Machine To See With* is the tyranny of choice and consumerism. Blast Theory has explored the tyranny of choice theme in previous works, such as in *Ulrike and Eamon Compliant* (Blast Theory, 2009), where the participant is asked to assume the guise of one of two well-known terrorists, as the narrative text uncannily prompts the participant to assess their ability to commit a murder. Adams (in Lighthouse Arts, 2011) states that Blast Theory's inspiration to address the tyranny of choice is inspired by philosopher Phillipa Foot's trolley dilemma from the late 1960s: 'A trolley is running out of control down a track. In its path are five people. You can flip a switch, which will lead the trolley down a different track to safety. Unfortunately, there is a single person tied to that track. Should you flip the switch?' Adams (in Lighthouse Arts, 2011) points out that the trolley dilemma inspired them to challenge the participant in their performances to make difficult ethical choices: 'It suddenly made it clear to us that when you put the member of the public as a protagonist in the work, if you can give them interesting and awkward moral questions like this to enact, rather than just: "Hypothetically, what would you do?" … Even in the realm of a fictional experience, it is an interesting and unusual position to be placed in.'

In *A Machine To See With*, the tyranny of choice emerges in the narrative at different stages: when the participant is prompted to choose between different options and outcomes by pressing buttons on their mobile phone's keypad, such as during the pseudo-personality test inside the toilet cubicle; when they are asked if they want to partner up for the bank heist; and when they are prompted to answer (by also pressing buttons on their phone's keypad) if they and their partner in crime will react violently or not to specific events during the fictional bank heist.

The tyranny of choice and consumerism theme in *A Machine To See With* addresses what sociologist Eva Illouz (2008) defines as the process of smoothing the individual through the promotion of a culture of self-help governed through consumption (through the capitalist machine) and therapeutic discourse. In this process – according to her – self-knowledge becomes the 'new language of the self'. Illouz (2008: 3) argues that psychoanalysis is employed on the premise of emancipating the self by enabling individuals to 'search and speak the truth about themselves [although] the self is made to work seamlessly for and within a system of power'. Key to Illouz's argument is the ability for external parties to control and manipulate emotion through what she defines as emotional styles. She describes these as 'the combination of the ways a culture becomes "preoccupied" with certain emotions and devises specific "techniques" – linguistic, scientific, ritual – to apprehend them' (Illouz, 2008: 14).

In *A Machine To See With*, emotional styles are present through narrative prompts on three occasions. First, during the pseudo personality test, where the questions seemingly probe the participant's ability to be the leader in the bank heist. Regardless of how they answer the questions, participants are told that they are in fact highly suitable to lead the task. Second, when participants are waiting outside the bank prior to the countdown for the bank heist and the narrative prompts them to reflect on how their partner will react during the heist: in an aggressive and uncontrolled manner or in a calm and pragmatic way by following the (non-existent) heist plan (Blast Theory, 2011a). This is followed by the staged betrayal of one partner by the other after a prompt from the narrative, which left many participants confused as to what exactly was happening. Finally, emotional styles are present when the narrative prompts the participants to redeem themselves from any feelings of guilt triggered by the botched bank heist, ending with the prompt to give money to a stranger (as a symbolic gesture of redemption).

The third main theme of *A Machine To See With* is the financial crisis, inspired by the sense of impotence and disempowerment experienced after the 2008 global financial crisis, as Adams (in Lighthouse Arts, 2011) summarises: 'We are still experiencing the lesson of the limits of the democratic power in the age of global finance, and for me I feel profoundly quite disempowered by that ... And so you can't make work [where] one deals with banks, bank robbery, and more so fundamentally deals with agency and power ... without in some way accepting that it is in that context.'

This theme exposes the assemblage of capitalist, media and computer agency, represented by 'the rapid proliferation of global computer-based networks and the digitization of a broad array

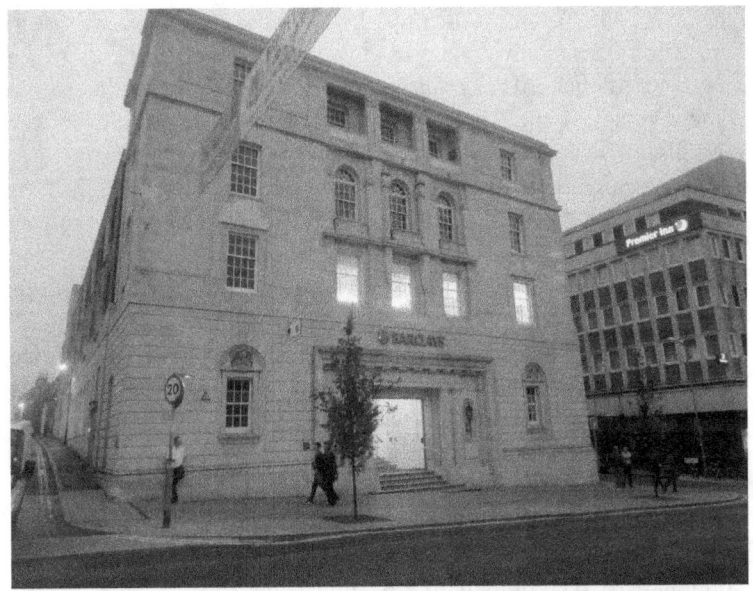

Figure 2.1 *A Machine To See With* – Barclays Bank

of economic and political activities' (Sassen, 2006: 327). This assemblage enables 'money [to take] on a mediatic form' (Lash, 2010: 30), which questions the relevance of bank heists when most money transactions are mediated through digital communication networks (see Figure 2.1). This is addressed in the narrative after the aborted bank heist: 'It all fell apart. That robbery was an invention that could never hold. And it's a long time since the bankers were concerned with robbers. That battle is over. Best to swivel at the door and walk away. Let's get out of here' (Blast Theory, 2011a).

Design actants: the voice

The narrative's voice is an important actant in *A Machine To See With* as the point of contact between the artists and the participants while guiding the process of cinematic framing of the city. The artists experimented with several voices before deciding to use Blast

Theory's Matt Adams' voice for the Brighton premiere. This decision was taken to invoke a specific cinematic motif, as Adams (in Dias and Adams, 2013) points out: 'We ultimately decided to use a male voice for the Brighton premiere because the quality of the masculine voice-over is a cinematic motif that we really wanted to invoke; going all the way back to those classic film noirs such as *D.O.A.* [from 1950] and other movies of that period, that sense of the voice looking back on experience and framing it.'

The desired effect of reflecting on previous experiences is evident on many occasions during the performance, such as when the voice probes the participant to reflect on the aftermath of the aborted bank heist as described above. The ambiguity of the narrative is reinforced by the voice, as it attempts to empathise with the participant despite being a recording, leaving the participant to wonder if the performance is being mediated by human beings or machines. This process is symbolic of how our everyday lives in urban space are mediated by systems of trust where it is difficult to draw a clear boundary between human and machine agency.

Blast Theory artist Nick Tandavanitj (in Dias, 2012a) illustrates these disjunctions through an account of his experience of hearing a railway platform announcement with a recorded message stating: 'I am sorry for the late arrival of this train.' Tandavanitj points out that the technological apparatus (composed of loudspeaker and recorded message) is embodying a human being: 'It was like this disjunction, because I thought, "You're not saying 'we', it's not a recording speaking on behalf of the company, it's saying 'I'". So at the point he was saying, "I'm sorry", the person wasn't there, and it wasn't aware of what train it was or why it was late. But you are listening to a machine say, "I am sorry", so it's embodying the person' (Tandavanitj in Dias, 2012a). In both *A Machine To See With* and the train announcement, the recording of the human voice is encoded and automated by a technological apparatus that emulates human empathy, trust and authority. In *A Machine To See With* this is done through an intentionally ambiguous narrative, prompting reflexivity on the issues arising from technologies that replace human agency.

Design actants: testing and promotion

Blast Theory made use of several technologies to help them adapt the narrative to the particular features of the city of Brighton. Google Maps was used in the process of plotting the trajectory and the points of interest of the narrative. This followed a process adopted in previous performances of *A Machine To See With*: prior to arriving at the location of each performance, Blast Theory used Google Maps and its Street View function (enabling a street-level view) to sketch the initial route and to search for specific types of building and city amenities needed in the performance (a bank, public toilets, a car park and so on). Once they arrived at the location, Google Maps was once more used to fine-tune the trajectory defined by the narrative.

One of the on-site tasks carried out during the Brighton performance was testing the strength of the mobile phone signal for every United Kingdom mobile phone operator inside several public and private toilets across the city. This task was undertaken to ensure that the participant's mobile phone signal strength wouldn't drop during their experience of the pseudo personality test inside the toilet cubicle. The data collected was plotted onto Google Maps and informed a discussion during a project meeting that I attended as a guest. On a Google Map of Brighton projected onto a large screen, artist Nick Tandavanitj plotted icons, repositioned existing ones and added notes to the map, shaping the six predetermined routes of the performance (see Figure 2.2) according to the information collected during the testing. In a similar way to how an editor would stitch together different shots to assemble a rough cut of a movie, Blast Theory edited a 'rough cut' of the cinematic experience of *A Machine To See With* by plotting each of the six possible routes of the performance onto the Google Maps interface.

This task illustrates the repurposing of Google Maps as a design machine that can be deployed for creative purposes rather than for the purpose of navigating urban space efficiently. Google Maps and its companion Street View constitute a comprehensive database of thousands of cities across the world, combining real world data and computer-generated data (McQuire, 2016: 66). This database can

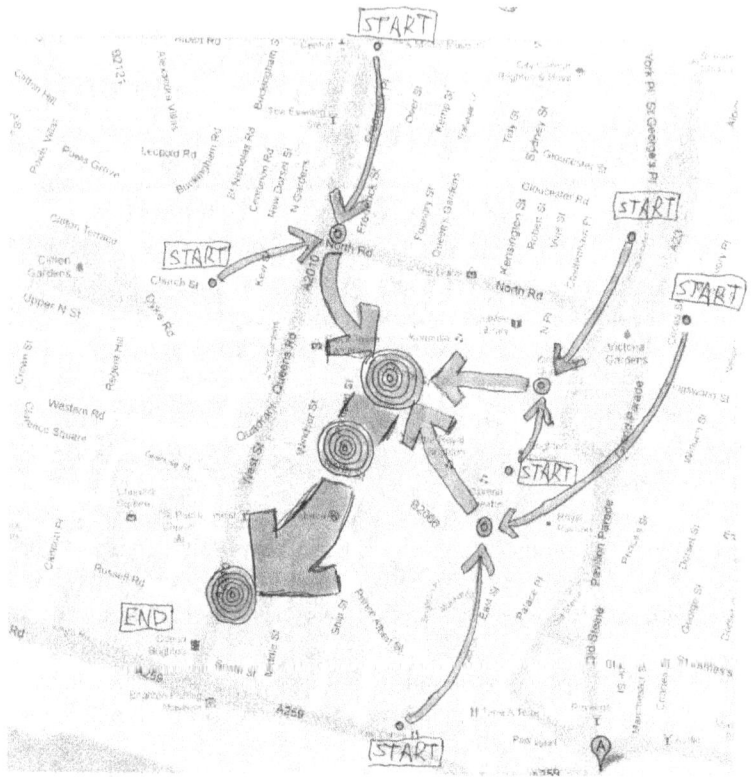

Figure 2.2 *A Machine To See With* – Brighton route map

be redeployed towards producing original aesthetic artefacts. The cinematic potential of Google's Street View draws from classical references of 'machine-driven cinema' and from the technique of montage, such as in Dziga Vertov's *Man With a Movie Camera* (1929), which predates Google's Street View by several decades. While Vertov's film stitches together specific shots from several cities, Google's Street View presents 'the simultaneous availability of all "shots"' (McQuire, 2016: 75). These shots are arranged instead 'according to the dictates of the GPS data gathered in the process of image-capture' (McQuire, 2016: 76).

Blast Theory conducts extensive testing for each performance, and in *A Machine To See With*, several machines – most notably the urban, cinema, media and information machines – were assembled through a well-rehearsed and detailed process to create a seamless experience for the participant. To aid in the development and deployment of the performance across multiple cities, Blast Theory (2011b) developed a manual that mentions the need to conduct tests with the public. I was invited to observe a public test screening two days prior to the premiere of the Brighton performance of *A Machine To See With* and also to take part as a participant in a focused test on the car park section of the narrative the following day. As a result of these tests, some sections of the narrative were re-recorded the day before the premiere to fine-tune the desired participatory outcome.

During the public test screening, participants took part in the performance and were subsequently interviewed by Blast Theory through a structured questionnaire. This process allowed the artists to make subtle adjustments to the narrative prompts for interaction, aligning the pace of the instructions given over the phone with the pace of the average participant. It also gave them an insight into the different participant interpretations of the event and of specific encounters (such as the partnering up interaction in the car) and to probe the efficiency of Blast Theory's marketing strategies (including direct mailing lists and press releases). The public test screening was immediately followed up by an ad hoc meeting between Blast Theory artists and staff, where the most important issues were flagged, and tasks were assigned to deal with them.

During the focused test that was conducted in the car park on the day before the premiere, artists Nick and Matt provided phones that were set up for the test to me and Blast Theory intern Sandra, who was helping on the project. The focus of the test was to review the section of the narrative that unfolds in the car park towards identifying a solution for two specific issues flagged during the public test screening. First, the possibility of more than two participants approaching the BMW car together at any given time, as this was not a desired artistic outcome. Second, the need to find a better location for the BMW car so that it could be spotted more easily, while at the same time enabling participants to surveil the car discreetly before approaching it. The changes made to the narrative after the test didn't prevent the unintended outcome of more than two participants approaching the car together at the same time, as I described earlier through my account of my own participation.

The promotion strategy focused on emphasising the cinematic aspect of the performance without mentioning the specific theme of the narrative (bank heist) and the operational mode (partnering up with unknown participants).

The Brighton performance of *A Machine To See With* was promoted through Blast Theory's own social media channels, through the umbrella event (Brighton Digital Festival), and through word of mouth (through staff, associates, acquaintances and participants' contacts). The promotional imagery emphasised the cinematic theme of the performance. To promote *A Machine To See With*, Blast Theory conducted a photo shoot using the surrounding industrial area near their studio as a backdrop, and an actor dressed in a sharp suit as the protagonist. In one of the promotional photos he moves briskly down an iron ladder attached to a concrete embankment, suggestive of action movies and a chase scene.

On the promotional postcard for the Sundance Film Festival performance of *A Machine To See With* (see Figure 2.3), the title of the event is layered over a close-up shot of the actor against an industrial backdrop as he stares directly at his mobile phone while holding it at eye level. The postcard makes use of a simple and bold colour palette (mostly black and red). A caption above the title states: 'This movie is real and you are playing the lead.' The promotional poster for the Brighton performance uses the same photo and visual style, with the inclusion of a quote that makes a direct reference to the content of the narrative: 'Have you ever wanted to rob a bank?' The promotional material does not represent accurately the actual participatory experience of the performance, but through its use of cinematic language and bold quotes, it suggests a challenging and action-packed experience.

Technology actants: unpacking the components

The technology assemblage of *A Machine To See With* draws from previous Blast Theory projects as mentioned above, most notably

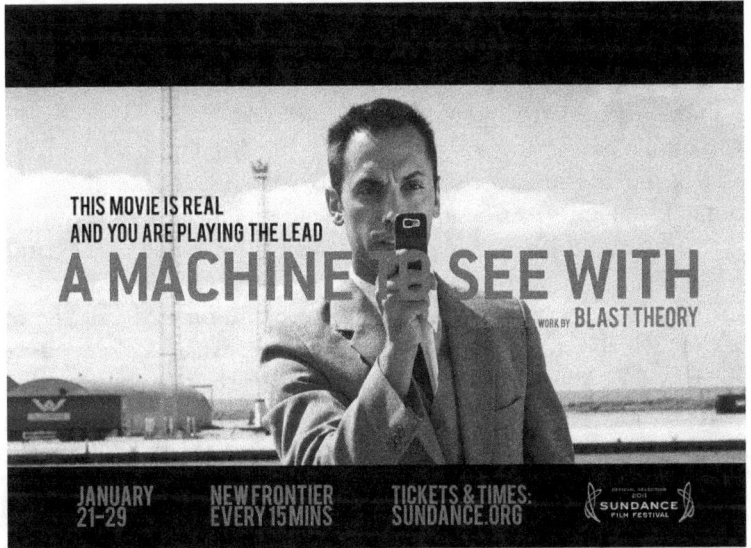

THIS MOVIE IS REAL
AND YOU ARE PLAYING THE LEAD

A MACHINE ᴛᴏ SEE WITH

ᴡᴏʀᴋ ʙʏ BLAST THEORY

JANUARY
21–29

NEW FRONTIER
EVERY 15 MINS

TICKETS & TIMES:
SUNDANCE.ORG

SUNDANCE
FILM FESTIVAL

Figure 2.3 *A Machine To See With* – promotional postcard

Ulrike and Eamon Compliant. In both works, a sequence of calls relayed to the participants' mobile phones guided them through the city as they assumed the role of a fictional character. In both performances, the narrative had to be flexible enough to deal with communication failures, such as mobile phone interference or sudden loss of connection. There were four main components in the technology assemblage of *A Machine To See With*. First, the participant's mobile phone, which enabled them to access the narrative and interact with it via standard phone calls and the mobile phone's keypad. Second, a database server, which consisted of a remote computer server with a database that contained all the narrative's recordings, and that controlled the relaying of the narrative text according to input from participants. Third, the automated call centre server, which consisted of a second remote computer server in a separate location. This second server contained open source automated call centre system software (Asterisk) that sent and received phone calls, mediating the connection between the database server and the participant. Fourth, the control room, which was located near the venue of the performance and where the artists and technicians monitored the participants' trajectory, providing feedback if necessary. In this room, the artists and technicians were able to reset the narrative to any specific point in case of system failure or if the participant got lost or delayed.

To take part in the performance, the participant booked a time slot by purchasing a ticket (at the box office, over the phone or online). The information about their chosen date and time of performance and their mobile phone number were stored in the database server. A few hours prior to the participant's allocated time, the database server sent a message to the automated call centre server, which triggered a phone call to the participant reminding them of their starting time and place. During the performance, the participant's input (either by calling the server or pressing keys on their mobile phone's keypad) was relayed via the automated call centre server to the database server, which in turn relayed the correct sequence of the narrative back to the participant via a reversal of this process.

The database server was programmed to deal with planned contingencies, such as the delay of a participant in choosing options or their failure to call the system back in reasonable time when prompted to do so. However, it wasn't programmed to deal with more complex deviations from the planned trajectory defined by the narrative for each of the six participant routes. The open source software (Asterisk) used in the automated call centre server employs a technology called Voice Over Internet Protocol (VoIP), which is the same technology employed in some of the most common apps – such as Skype, WhatsApp and Facebook Messenger – to make phone calls over the Internet. VoIP is susceptible to fluctuations in call quality because it usually uses a communication protocol called UDP (User Datagram Protocol) that is 'lossy': when the communication lines are too busy, it maintains the flow of information by dropping some of the information transmitted, which in turn impacts negatively on the quality of the voice call. As I will describe later, this communication failure could be detrimental to participation, but it could also enable unexpected participatory affordances that enriched some of the participants' experience of the performance.

Technology actants: the state machine

While the participant's mobile phone in *A Machine To See With* relied on established communication protocols and technologies, the three remaining technological components – the database server, the automated call centre server and the control room – relied on the state machine, a system developed by Blast Theory's collaborator – the Mixed Reality Laboratory – and employed in several other Blast Theory projects. It consisted of customised software assembled into a modular structure that connected the servers (running each performance) to the participant's mobile phone. The modular nature of the state machine allowed it to be reconfigured for different performances by customising its programming rules. Described as the foundational structure of the performance's interface in the technical manual for *A Machine To See With* (Blast Theory, 2011b), the state machine consists of modular code and procedural programming, where clear and logical computational steps are carried out in response to prompts from the user or from other computational devices. By planning for multiple scenarios, the state machine can adapt to unpredictable participatory outcomes. Its name refers to a change in state of the performance. Once the state machine identifies this change, it is capable of triggering actions in response, such as relaying a new section of the narrative to the participant.

The state machine has three main components: player states, call triggers and call script. On receiving a call from the participant at any stage during the performance, the state machine records their player state in the performance; this might be a location reached by the participant or their answer to a narrative prompt (Blast Theory, 2011b: 5). Subsequently, the state machine sends a call trigger that activates the correct response stored in the database server that relates to that specific player state (Blast Theory, 2011b: 5). This is done through the third component – a call script – which is an executable action that might have several purposes: relaying a section of the narrative to the participant, recording the participant's input (such as their name) or updating the participant's current location or answer to a specific question (Blast Theory, 2011b: 5).

A call trigger is also used to call participants at programmed times, such as their starting time, and also to make a repeat call to a participant if they have taken too long to respond to a request from the narrative (Blast Theory, 2011b: 5). The technical manual for *A Machine To See With* mentions the lengthy work involved in adapting the state machine to each different venue for the performance, which includes: 'planning routes and rewriting/recording calls, but also … data entry, any technical integration of ticketing procedures, set up of the call centre server and VOIP provider' (Blast Theory, 2011b: 2). The state machine enables Blast Theory to control certain aspects of the performance remotely, such as: 'manually registering participants with the server, following progress through calls and monitoring server performance' (Blast Theory, 2011b: 2).

The remote capabilities of the state machine enable it to deal with issues such as calls dropping out, bad audio quality across multiple handsets, call scripts behaving unexpectedly and calls not being sent from the system. However, due to the Brighton performance of *A Machine To See With* being controlled remotely and the fact that the database and call centre servers were in two separate countries (one in Ireland and the other in the United Kingdom), there was an issue with latency (delay in transmission of messages). Even a few milliseconds of latency during the transmission of information between the two servers could lead to the participant misunderstanding the narrative or missing one of its prompts, an issue that was highlighted by some of the participants I interviewed. I observed two occasions during which Blast Theory artists had to interfere remotely to solve participation issues. First, to manually register a participant who was taking part in my research at the last minute. Second, to restart the initial phone call to a participant who failed to receive it. This highlights the possibility of failure of the technical machines mediating the performance and the need for human oversight.

The procedurality of the state machine was perceived by some participants as a positive experience. Participant Clara (in Dias, 2011) described the performance as 'the machine with the options'. And even the perceived limitations of the state machine were not always interpreted negatively by the participants. Participant Paul (in Dias, 2011) stated that he enjoyed 'being governed by a very fickle mobile phone signal [that] sometimes dropped out'. The assemblage of the state machine and the narrative was consistently interfered with by city actants and sometimes by the participant's difficulty in keeping up with the pace of the instructions provided. For example, participant Tim (in Dias, 2011) described his experience of missing a narrative prompt: '[The narrative] said: "Get your money ready", and then it said: "Have you got your money ready yet?" And then I pressed number two, because ... I was seriously getting money out of my bag, but I hadn't got it in my hand yet, and I thought: "Will I stall the question, or then go back to it?" And then it was like: "You won't hear from me again", so I was like: "... I missed that part."'

The state machine on its own constitutes a form of informational interface that is governed by strict computational rules coded to respond to predefined scenarios. However, when it is assembled with the other technical components of the performance and the artistic narrative, it becomes a performative urban interface, which consists of: 'a system based on electronic devices connected to remote or local databases that interfaces with public space and that is governed by non-functional narratives that – intentionally or not – augment, displace and reconfigure patterns of social and spatial interaction in urban space' (Dias and Adams, 2019). Hence the performance, despite being mediated by prescriptive technologies, generates multiple participatory outcomes of a non-deterministic nature.

Technology actants: the mobile phone

Blast Theory deliberately decided to use standard voice calls over a mobile phone as the point of interaction between the narrative and the participant for accessibility purposes but also to achieve a specific participatory mode, as Blast Theory artist Nick Tandavanitj (in Dias, 2012a) points out:

I think the motives [for using standard voice calls] for me were twofold: one was accessibility [...] The other is the quality of voice calls as a medium and all these associations that they bring. The resonances that they have in terms of what it actually means to be on the phone speaking to someone is a whole different set of things [rather than] interacting with an application.

The mobile phone was the point of connection between the participants and the narrative, fluctuating between the role of intermediary – a mere conduit of information – and mediator – as it interfered with key sections of the narrative through its affordances and limitations. An example of affordance was the loudspeaker capability of the phone that enabled participants Helen and James to take part in the performance together from the beginning, against the expected participation mode scripted by the narrative (participants were expected to start on their own). An example of limitation was participant Tim's description above of how he missed a key interaction of the performance as he dealt with the keypad of the phone. The narrative used the phone's expected mode of interaction as a form of bluffing during the bank heist:

> Now: big change of plan. You're going to dump this other person in three minutes. I need you to act very quickly and discreetly when I give you the word. You will turn and walk fast directly away from them as soon as they start to approach the bank. Use your judgement. Keep an eye on them and take your chance to get away without being seen. Just act as if you're getting exactly the same call as your partner. If they press their keypad, just pretend to press your keypad too. They don't know a thing and they don't need to know. (Blast Theory, 2011a)

City actants: urban furniture and performance art props

The city actants include urban furniture and performance art props situated in urban space. While Blast Theory had control over how the design and technology actants were assembled in the performance, they didn't have full control of the city actants, despite their detailed research on the urban environment of the performance and the contingency measures put in place through the state machine and the control room. The BMW car (see Figure 2.4) purchased by Blast Theory and positioned inside the car park was an example of a performance art prop that moved between the roles of intermediary

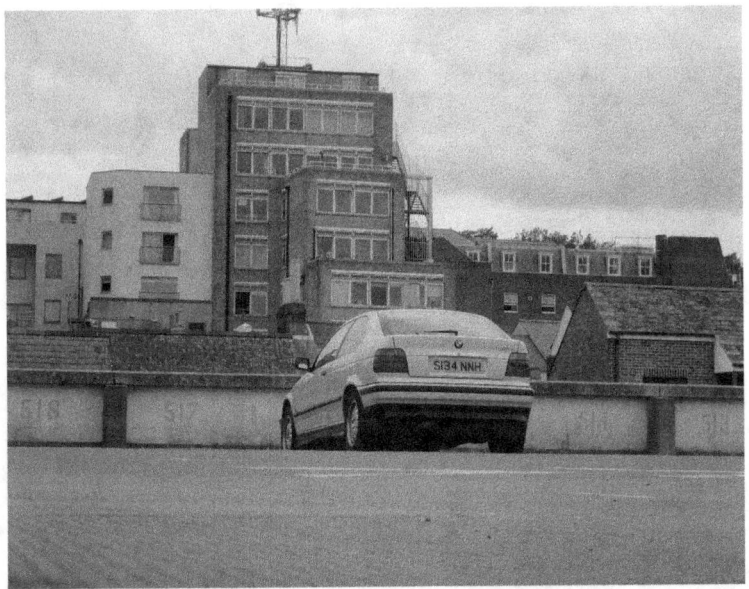

Figure 2.4 *A Machine To See With* – the BMW car

and mediator. For example, it became a mediator of agency by evoking rich cinematic references that triggered the participants' imagination. As participant Tim (in Dias, 2011) described to me: 'I thought maybe [laughs] they would ask me to drive the car or something and I do have a driving licence, but I am not insured [laughs] for a BMW so I kind of felt uncomfortable that maybe that would happen.'

Some of the participants that I interviewed described the experience of entering the confined space of the car to negotiate a bank heist with a complete stranger as one of the most challenging moments of their performance (see Figure 2.5). Participant Marney (in Dias, 2011) described it as going 'against [her] instincts', while participant Jon (in Dias, 2011) thought he might have to break into the car. Participant Sarah (in Dias, 2011) felt out of her comfort zone while 'sitting in a car that doesn't belong to you [and] waiting for someone to knock on your window'. Due to the exposed location of the car on an open-air level of the multi-storey public car park, it was very difficult for participants to remain inconspicuous

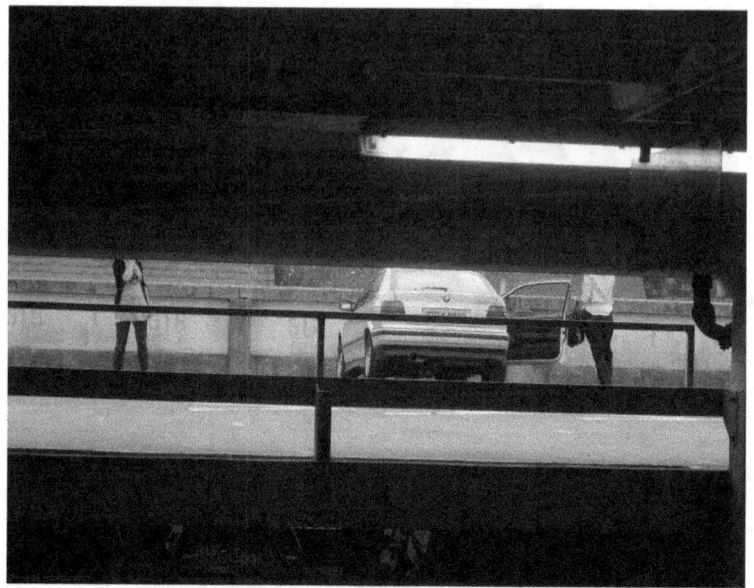

Figure 2.5 *A Machine To See With* – participants meeting at the car

as they approached it, especially when the car park was empty. However, when the car park was full – for example, during busy shopping hours on weekends – a different scenario unfolded: participants struggled to locate the car as they negotiated a constant stream of potentially suspicious people moving around the car park (mostly shoppers). Most participants (including myself) opted to approach the car by walking up the ramp connecting the fourth floor – which was enclosed and dark – to the open-air fifth floor. This provided the best chance to remain unnoticed while trying to reach the car.

Participants entering the car listened to different sections of the narrative depending on the order in which they arrived. The first participant entering the car had to listen to a lengthy narrative about the persuasive strategies to target indecisive voters during Bill Clinton's 1994 United States re-election campaign as they waited for another participant – their partner in crime – to join them. This script section was played on a loop until a second participant joined them in the car or they decided to execute the bank heist on their own. Many participants told me they couldn't understand the meaning of this narrative section. Participant Nick (in Dias, 2011), for example, described it as the 'psychology about Clinton', associating it with the 'psychology in the loo' (the pseudo-personality test inside the toilet cubicle) and stating that neither were coherent to him. Participant Tim (in Dias, 2011) also said that he didn't understand it and described it as boring.

The second participant entering the car never listened to the narrative section about Bill Clinton's campaign. Once both participants were in the car, they listened to the same section of the narrative prepping them for the bank heist. Blast Theory's use of cinematic references and attention to detail is illustrated by their decision to plant a fictional (yet reasonably accurate) map of the bank inside the car. However, the map wasn't mentioned by any of the participants I interviewed; it either went unnoticed or was misplaced (a potential issue that had been highlighted during the public test screening). Many participants mentioned the car park as one of the highlights of the event for them, and the car played an important part towards this outcome. This section of the narrative benefitted from cinematic references, such as car chases and suspicious exchanges inside multi-story car parks. Tim's description of the possibility of the car being used as an escape vehicle – despite its impractical location for such a task – illustrates well the imaginative potential of the narrative and its associated props.

Some of the most unexpected and influential actants in the performance were atmospheric actants, such as wind, fog, dusk and sudden changes in daylight. While it didn't rain during my observations, the wind sometimes affected the quality of the phone calls and obstructed the proper understanding of the narrative. This contingency was dealt with by the state machine through the process of repeating questions if the participant took too long to answer any given prompt. Yet atmospheric actants also played an important role in the construction of meaning through their visual impact, as I noticed during one of my observation days: Brighton's sea fog enveloped the top floors of the car park, creating a mysterious ambience that was accentuated by the emptiness of the car park level where the BMW car was situated and also by the presence of a flock of noisy seagulls that were particularly noticeable due to the absence of street level noise. This temporary yet powerful assemblage of actants added a film noir cinematic effect to the car park, which was one of the inspirations for the artistic vision of the performance as mentioned previously. However, on other days – such as the sunny Saturday evening when the car park was full of shoppers – the ambience was less dramatic and less cinematic.

City actants: bystanders turned performers

In previous performances – such as *Uncle Roy All Around You* and *Ulrike and Eamon Compliant* – Blast Theory employed actors to fulfil specific roles. While there were no actors involved in *A Machine To See With*, bystanders were consistently drawn into the narrative and became actant-mediators, interfering with the participant's experience of the narrative and providing some of the most interesting participatory outcomes of the performance. On these occasions, participants were left guessing if the bystander's actions were intentionally included in the performance. This uncertainty generated a variety of emotional reactions described to me by participants during the interviews: astonishment, suspicion, tension, expectation, curiosity and empathy. The uncertainty was heightened by a series of factors: the fact that most participants didn't know each other prior to the performance, the ambiguity of the narrative and its references to the (fictional) surveillance apparatus directed towards participants. During my interview with participant Paul (in Dias, 2011), he described to me how bystanders were drawn into the performance once participants acknowledged them – prompted by either the narrative, their own imagination or a combination of both:

> The further you get into the ... experience you start to question, you know: 'That chap that stood to the right ... is he going to interact with me? Is he ... going to step into something that I need to deal with, react to, be part of?' Somebody quite passive, kids running past ... are they actively partaking or is it something that I have to respond to? If I respond to it, am I giving them recognition that they are partaking?

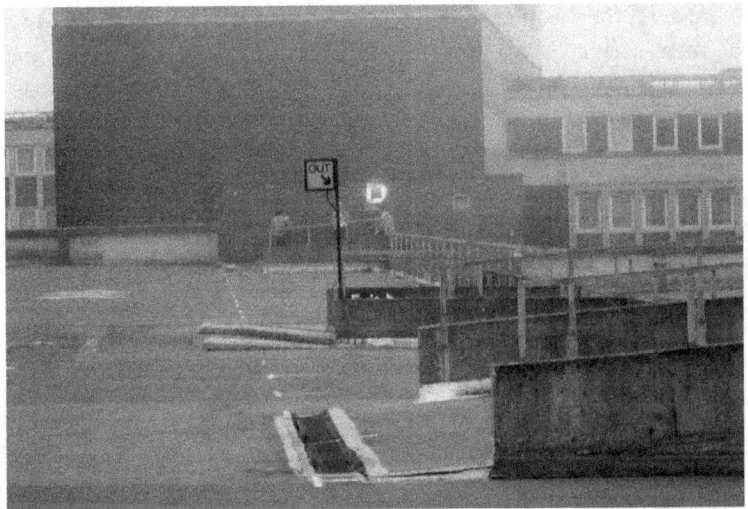

Figure 2.6 *A Machine To See With* – teenagers loitering in the car park

The several bystanders that I was able to observe or that were mentioned to me by participants during my interviews with them performed in many different ways: through playful interactions, as unintended copycats, as chatty strangers or by providing enlightening moments to participants. Playful bystanders sometimes intervened in the performance for their own amusement. On the second day of my observations, I encountered a group of teenagers loitering on the top floor of the public car park, one level above where the BMW car was situated (see Figure 2.6). On that particular day, Blast Theory intern Sandra was stationed on the top floor but at the opposite end to where the teenagers were situated. This enabled her to benefit from a good vantage point to observe and monitor the car to ensure that the performance ran smoothly. I joined her briefly to observe the action around the car during the performance without being spotted by participants. The teenagers seem bemused by our presence, but they were also wondering about the unusual gatherings of people around the BMW car. As participants Helen and James (who took part together as a couple by sharing one phone) left the car along with another participant (their partner in crime) and walked towards the pedestrian access tower nearest the teenagers, they leaned over the railings and started shouting down at them seeking a reaction. The participants seemed unfazed and continued walking towards the access tower. The teenagers' reaction was a mere distraction for the participants that was clearly unrelated to the narrative, yet for the teenagers it was an opportunity to amuse themselves.

Another interesting occurrence was described to me by participant Tim. Influenced by the narrative's surveillance prompts, he suspected that the artists had gone to the length of employing an actor and dressing him with a similar shirt to Tim's, and that it might have been related to one of the narrative prompts, as Tim (in Dias, 2011) stated:

> I thought I was being watched by loads of people, and I probably wasn't at all [laughs]. And then when I got to the finishing point there was a homeless person or just someone sitting on the street wearing a shirt exactly like mine. I was like, what? Maybe that was part of it. Somehow, they must have found a shirt exactly like mine and given it to this guy, and maybe I have to give that guy the money or something.

Participant Dany was also influenced by the surveillance prompts of the narrative. She described to me how an amicable chat with a bystander right at the beginning of the performance left her guessing if she was being played by the narrative, as Dany (in Dias, 2011) described:

> I was waiting, and as you say, looking at the characters and thinking: 'Are they part of this?', you know. And a man came up to me and said: 'I can see you are wearing non-conformist trousers. Have a beer mat. Do you want a beer mat?' And I said: 'No, not really', thinking he was going to just give me some litter ... and then I looked at it and realised it was actually quite a nice beer mat that was specially printed ... And got chatting to this guy, and he's sort of: 'So, I'm just trying to make the world a bit better!' So, one of Brighton's kind of weirdy kind of people, but benign and good ... And then I had a look at this beer mat – once he'd gone – a bit closer, and I thought: 'I wonder if this is part of it?' It had a number on the back: 'I'll just call this number to see' [laughs].

Dany's difficulty in interpreting the bystander demonstrates how this process is mediated by an emergent assemblage of actants: the narrative prompts, unexpected props (in this case, the beer mat), the environment (the bar where Dany encountered the bystander) and the bystander's unexpected interpellation of Dany. The narrative heightened Dany's expectation that she was being surveilled, and left her wondering if she was supposed to trust (or not) the bystander. Dany's interpretation of the event was influenced by the narrative of the performance and its ability to connect unrelated actants and instigate reflection.

One of the most meaningful encounters between a participant and bystanders was described to me by participant Nicholas (in Dias, 2011). Prompted by the narrative to give some of his money to a stranger inside the leisure arcade (see Figure 2.7) at the end of the performance, Nicholas approached a child and her mother who were playing a slot game and put some money in the girl's little purse. He described how the child's mother reacted positively to that and how he felt that this was the most meaningful experience of his participation in *A Machine To See With*. The examples of interactions between participants and bystanders described above

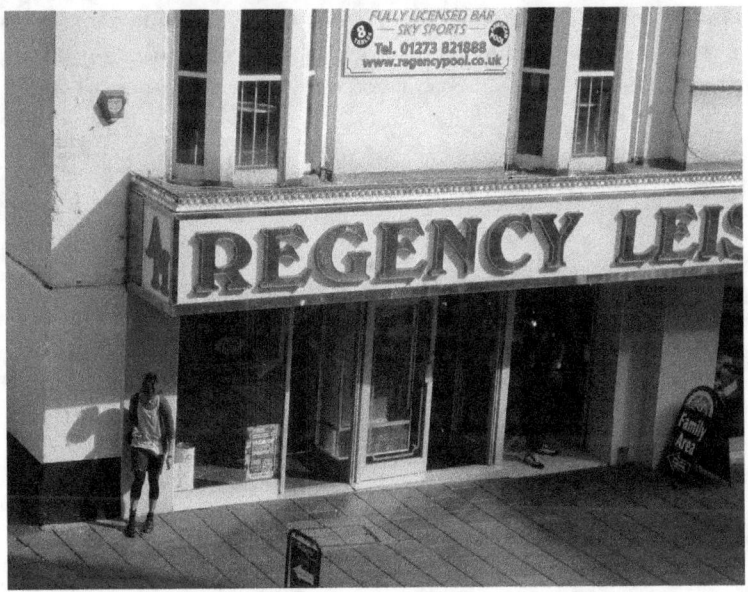

Figure 2.7 *A Machine To See With* – participant at the leisure arcade

demonstrate the potential of the fictional narrative to assemble with city actants and to generate multiple outcomes – or performances. Every iteration of the performance unfolds with a unique cast of human and non-human actants, as the participant plays the role of the protagonist in their own movie.

The task of dividing the actants into the three main categories described above – design, technology and city – helps towards understanding how they are composed, how they work and how they interpellate, assemble and disassemble with other actants. A substantial amount of planning goes into each iteration of the performance, including in-depth research of each city where it is performed, the development of customised software and hardware assemblages and the careful crafting of the narrative to produce the desired effect. Yet as I have demonstrated above, the city (as a collective of actants) plays a crucial part in reconfiguring the performance, at the same time that it provides a stage for the performance with no clear boundaries. In the following chapter I outline the concept of the machine as a performative device and analyse the key machines that enable the potential of both performance art and the contemporary mediated city to reconfigure social and spatial relations. This will be followed by a definition of machinic subjectivity as emblematic of the emergent potential of performance art in the city as an aesthetic machine.

3

Rethinking machines

Another type of machine

I have argued for the importance of the aesthetic machine – in particular digitally mediated performance art – as a form of deliberation on contemporary urban living. This type of aesthetic machine is not situated in opposition to technical machines, nor does it confer a higher degree of agency to its technical components. The aesthetic machine is assembled from several other machines as it traverses other 'Universes of value' (Guattari, 1995: 105). In this chapter I analyse these machines to understand how they operate and how they might assemble with the aesthetic machine. Prior to doing this, it is important to reconceptualise the term machine. Since the seventeenth century, the concept of the machine has been 'limited to its technical, mechanistic and … clearly-delimitable sense' (Raunig, 2010: 19). This coincides with the 'enormous leap in the development of technical apparatuses and equipment … and their dissemination and knowledge' (Raunig, 2010: 20). Its overwhelming influence has in turn generated 'a proliferation of metaphors of man as machine, of the state as machine [and] of the world as machine', referring specifically to the 'utilitarian and functional order' of the machine (Raunig, 2010: 20).

However, the origin of the term machine is not strictly concerned with mechanical and technical processes; it can be traced back to the Latin *machina* and the Greek *mechané*, and 'its more general meaning as "means, contrivance, device"' (Raunig, 2010: 36). This definition is more fitting of the aesthetic machine that is the focus of this book. The title of *A Machine To See With* suggests that it is capable of augmenting human perception, combining technical machines with several other machines and performing on the stage of the machinic city. In my analysis of its design, technology and city actants in the previous chapter, various machines are present without being explicitly referred to, and each of these machines is further constituted by other machine-actants: the capitalist machine (the financial structure of the commissioners and art festivals that finance the aesthetic machine); the performative machine (an assemblage of the narrative machine, the cinematic machine and city actants); the cybernetic machine (including Blast Theory's custom state machine, remote servers and the participants' mobile phones); and the human-machine (including artists, participants and bystanders). In this chapter I analyse these machines towards understanding how they assemble with each other and with the aesthetic machine. In this assemblage, the aim is to understand how the rhythms of the technical machine can cater to the non-mechanical and unstable rhythms of human social interaction, as Mumford (1934: 367) states: 'The problem of integrating the machine in society is not merely a matter ... of making social institutions keep in step with the machine: the problem is equally one of altering the nature and the rhythm of the machine to fit the actual needs of the community.'

This is not an easy task, as the machine in the form of a technical device has always been pitted as a superior and perfect form when compared to the human-machine through the rhetoric of the technological sublime (Nye, 1994). As Nye (1994: xiii) points out, the technological sublime 'is an integral part of contemporary consciousness', where the sublime 'can weld society together' while '[tapping] into fundamental hopes and fears'.

From the synchronisation of time and space enabled by the telegraph to the potential to predict future events through complex computer calculations, the excitement provoked by machines is stirred by their virtual – and yet to be consolidated – potential. This virtual potential is also the basis for our fear of machines as evil and oppressive apparatuses, as portrayed extensively in modern cinema through a series of thematic machines: industrial machines in Charles Chaplin's *Modern Times* (1936), authoritarian machines in *1984* (1956), killing machines in *Robocop* (1987), surveillance machines in *Minority Report* (2002) and cybernetic machines in *2001: A Space Odyssey* (1968).

The alleged superiority of the technical machine manifests itself through its most pervasive form of expression: the informational power of computing and its virtual representation. Computers are key instruments in the cybernetic model of information that is based on Claude Shannon's conceptualisation of information as a mathematical quantity (Hayles, 1999: 18). As Hayles (1999: 18) points out, the decontextualisation of information is key to Shannon's argument: 'Shannon's theory defines information as a probability function with no dimensions, no materiality, and no necessary connection with meaning. It is a pattern, not a presence.' Hayles (1999: 19, original emphasis) argues that Shannon's definition of information as an abstract, free-floating entity foregrounds the significance of virtuality as a condition in which information is perceived as 'more mobile, more important, more *essential* than material forms'. Hayles (1999: 20) suggests that we need to rethink virtuality by recognising 'the importance of the embodied processes constituting the lifeworld of human beings'. The digitally mediated performance art projects that I have discussed so far combine the virtuality of computer processes (such as through remote management of the performance) with the physicality of urban environments, enabling us to reflect on the consequences and limitations of the technological sublime through its failures and shortfalls.

The ability to reflect on our digitally mediated lives raises important questions: how do digital technologies affect our subjectivity? What are the positive and negative social outcomes emerging from them? And finally, how can we be more aware of the processes governing them? I argue that performance art is capable of generating reflection on these important matters, questioning the role and the transformative power of technical machines that are embedded in the urban fabric. However, to understand how the aesthetic machine of performance art operates, we must break it down into its machine-components prior to analysing the relation between these components. This mode of analysis curbs the temptation to situate any of these machines in opposition to each other or in opposition to the aesthetic machine. For example, it is counterproductive to pit the aesthetic machine of performance art as a form of autonomous machine operating against the capitalist machine. By its own nature as a probe into contemporary urban living, the aesthetic machine has to operate in conjunction with the capitalist machine, even if it is being used to critique the latter. By analysing the nuances of each particular machine and their modes of operation, we are better equipped to understand how they might assemble dynamically and reconfigure social and spatial relations in urban space.

This process is always informed by the importance of the concept of the human-machine hybrid as symptomatic of contemporary urban living, which has been the subject of several accounts of metropolitan life. For example, in Simmel's (1950) essay 'The Metropolis and Mental Life', from 1903, he alluded to the machinised citizen and analysed the city as an assemblage of actants subject to the pervasive effect of the capitalist machine and the psychological effect of the newly built environment. The current urban landscape, however, is much more complex than what Simmel encountered in the early twentieth century. Prior to unpacking specific machines that are part of performance art and of the mediated city, I will provide an example of a participatory encounter in *A Machine To See With* that illustrates the importance of machines that don't operate through technical prowess. In this example, performance art unfolds through a technically deficient but socially efficient assemblage of machines.

A case study of a technically deficient but socially efficient machine

Paul was one of the participants that I interviewed in my ethnographic study of *A Machine To See With*. He was familiar with other Blast Theory projects, but nevertheless he approached *A Machine To See With* as completely uncharted territory. The narrative text led him to reflect on many things, in particular the financial crisis and its implications, as Paul (in Dias, 2011) stated: '[There are] certainly a lot of underlying questions that I think it throws up, and I think those questions ... broaden the financial scenario ... at the moment. And I think ... there's a lot of time in it that is quite reflective. I found myself reflecting on my own kind of situation in these last five years.' The performance also enabled him to reflect on the impact of digital communication technologies on his life: 'There is something quite refreshing about that, because of the digital life we live in, everything is actually quite controlled. And we are able to very much manage it remotely. So it's quite nice sometimes for you to have that responsibility quashed, which is out of your control. I quite enjoyed that' (Paul in Dias, 2011). Despite his awareness at an early stage that the bank heist was not going to take place (partly because his time slot for the performance was after the bank's closing time), Paul engaged deeply with the narrative and its surveillance rhetoric, which was heightened by his perception of the synchronicity between the timing of the instructions given and his own pace: 'I almost thought that someone was watching me from a window, because it was so timely' (in Dias, 2011).

At one stage, Paul failed to follow the narrative's directional prompts, which led him to a serendipitous experience that became the highlight of his participation. Unable to locate the car park mentioned in the narrative, he asked a bystander for directions and ended up being sent (unknowingly) to the wrong car park, as he described to me in detail during my interview with him:

> I got the first NCP car park wrong, and I ended up on level 17 in the theatre NCP car park. And it was absolutely amazing because it's a huge exposed top floor, and it's got like a split-level experience going on, and I hid behind a yellow grit bucket, and it smelt of piss. And I was standing there for about twenty minutes looking for this ... silver BMW. But what I did see which was absolutely mind-blowing was ... a huge tower block directly opposite, and it ... just kind of settled in this fog frame, and it had all these ... lights on it, and I just thought: I would not have seen that if I had taken the left turn – the correct turn – instead of the wrong turn. And if that chap that I asked at the NCP car park who took me to that one – I asked him where it was – hadn't given me that information, I wouldn't have seen that. (Paul in Dias, 2011)

Paul's description suggests that the cinematic tone of the narrative influenced his experience, despite the fact that he was in the wrong place (or scene, to use a cinematic term). Paul eventually got back on track after he realised that there was a mismatch between the car park he was in and the one described by the narrative. With the help of the narrative aided by the state machine and from some bystanders, he eventually got to the correct car park:

> I'm constantly playing back this message, and I wasn't really sure ... the narrative said level *five* or six. I think actually floor six is what it said. So, when I recognised that I was on level *seventeen* (strong emphasis and laughs), and there is *no* BMW there ... and I really don't want to be in this piss corner *any longer*, perhaps I've got it wrong. So then I dialled the number again and went through a different direction with the code in, the keypad code in. And I kind of got the lanes associated with the NCP, and I went downstairs, and there was a couple of guys having a fag outside and I asked them: 'Am I anywhere near', and they directed me then in the right direction. (Paul in Dias, 2011)

To sum up his experience: a substantial detour triggered by an assemblage of human and technical failures enabled Paul to partake briefly in an emotionally intense encounter with a series of non-human actants (impostor car park, yellow grit bucket, fog). Yet this encounter is not limited to these actants, as it also includes: a fictional surveillance apparatus, an ambiguous narrative, communication failure, his personal interpretation of the narrative, the (lack of) a silver BMW and two multi-storey car parks (the correct one and the impostor car park), among many others. The complex assemblage of actants mediating his participation reveals the potential of the city as a performative stage. All these actants were assembled across interconnected machines: performance, human, media, urban and several others. Paul's account demonstrates the potential for reflection and serendipity to emerge from the perceived failure of functional machines.

Some of the human and technical failures I observed in *A Machine To See With* led to meaningful, reflective and enjoyable participant experiences. However, such failures can also disrupt a performance to such an extent that the experience might become unrecognisable, counterproductive or lose its purpose altogether. Therefore, we can't pre-empt the outcome of failure in performance – regardless of it being human or machine-driven – without contextualising it. By the time Paul located the right car park and got to the fifth floor of the correct multi-storey car park, he had missed an opportunity to partner up with another participant. This was partially because he was obeying the instructions of the narrative closely, as he describes:

> I've been chasing that point of contact, you know, I've gone to the wrong car park so I kind of corrected it, so I was kind of ... I was up for it ... I crept around probably a little bit too long just as an incentive to start observing. I could see somebody in there through the fog ... or some image of somebody in there. And I wouldn't be able to get too close, because I was asked not to, just to keep my distance; so I'm doing it all and then this person got out, looked around and then disappeared. And at that point ... I thought there might be someone else in the back of the car. So I got into the car and it was empty. (Paul in Dias, 2011)

Paul demonstrated his disappointment about that particular interaction: 'I was a little bit kind of gutted about it because I wanted ... that point of contact, you know' (in Dias, 2011). However, his overall experience was positive, as he described to me: 'I really enjoyed it (pause). It's actually quite a breath of fresh air just to be launched into something' (Paul in Dias, 2011). Paul's experience summarises the potential of performance art, as it generates unforeseen experiences that both reflect upon and reconfigure social interaction in the mediated city.

The performative machine

Performance is a widely used term in contemporary social exchanges. In workplaces, managers compare the performance of their employees against internal and external benchmarks. A well-known athlete, when competing well, is said to have put on a good performance. In times of global recession, financial analysts are always eager to state that specific markets or countries are not performing as well as they should and are driving down the performance of the global economy. As Schechner (2006: 2) states, the term performance 'must be construed as a "broad spectrum" or "continuum" of human actions [including] ritual, play, sports, popular entertainments, the performing arts [but also] everyday life performances'. Therefore, performance art has an important role as a probe to examine the other performances of contemporary urban life. As Goldberg (1998: 9) states, performance art examines 'contemporary viewpoints [through live work that] unites the psychological with the perceptual, the conceptual with the practical [and] thought with action'. It achieves this through provocation, by resisting categorisation and by unnerving – rather than seducing – the audience (Goldberg, 1998: 13).

Performances are defined by three main factors. First, performances generate boundaries that are both physical and virtual (Turner, 1988: 54). These boundaries indicate what is related (or not) to the performance, including 'participants, their roles, the "sense" or "meaning" ascribed to those things included within the boundary, and the elements within the environment of the activity [...] which are declared to be "outside" [the boundary] and irrelevant to it' (Turner, 1988: 54). This boundary is malleable and likely to change as the performance evolves. For example, in Paul's participatory experience of *A Machine To See With*, the boundary defined by the narrative was stretched by Paul's detour to the impostor car park, and the additional cast of several actants (for example, the fog and the yellow grit bucket).

Second, performances are staged, or performed for someone else, and therefore constitute what Goffman (1990) defines as social dramas. He points out that every event in the world is always already performative, and thus an instance of social drama. This involves a mutual performance between citizens – but also between citizens and non-human actants – where each of them fulfils the role of actor and audience simultaneously (Goffman, 1990: 9). Finally, performances are capable of enabling reflexivity. As they act outwards, they generate inward reflection, enabling us to reveal ourselves to our own selves (Turner, 1988: 81). In recent years, this process of outward action and inward revelation has been increasingly mediated by computer-enabled information machines. An example of this process is the current trend of wearable technologies for fitness and health tracking that engage users through gamification, defined as 'the practice of using game design techniques in serious contexts' (Ruffino, 2018: 5).

The gamification of fitness and health is presented 'as a series of practical and operational suggestions about how to involve users ... and how to maximise their performance towards a specific goal' (Ruffino, 2018: 28). In this case, the procedurality of computer code supports a performance that is pre-empted through 'a kind of engagement which ultimately remains static' as 'the next day's engagement will be measured and evaluated through the same criteria as that of the present day' (Ruffino, 2018: 35). This highlights the unconscious assimilation of the patterns of the information machine by the individual, in search of an optimal and unchallenged connection between body and technology. It represents the state of performance as a taken-for-granted process where all the actants flow smoothly in a friction-free environment.

According to Turner (1988: 54), flow represents the state in which 'action follows action according to an internal logic, with no apparent need for conscious intervention on our part'. He argues that when flow is present in a performance (theatrical, sport, play, religious or artistic), a non-dialectical process occurs through a 'centering of attention on a limited stimulus field' (1988: 54). Or in other words, the experience is already laid out for the participant. However, this can be interrupted or diverted by reflexivity, which '[arrests] the flow process' and enables a flow/reflexivity dialectic (Turner, 1988: 55). According to Turner (1988: 74, 75), the process of displacement of flow occurs through a sequence of steps: breach, crisis, redressive action and reintegration. First, there is a breach of a norm-governed social relation. This triggers crisis, which is brought upon by unstable factors driven by liminal characteristics. Crisis is followed by redressive action that seeks a mode of resolution either through a rational process or a ritual. Finally, there is either reintegration of the contesting parties constituting the social relation or acknowledgement of an 'irreparable schism' between them. Turner's framework can be applied to Paul's unexpected participation event in *A Machine To See With*, as he took a detour from the path established by the narrative (breach), and he had to deal with unexpected outcomes (crisis). Subsequently, he reflected on the narrative and sought to rejoin the correct path (redressive action) and finally he managed to find his way to the correct car park (reintegration).

Turner (1988: 25) argues that 'the dominant genres of performance in societies' are liminal phenomena, as they are 'performed
in privileged spaces and times, set off from the periods and areas
reserved for work, food and sleep'. *A Machine To See With* fits into
this category, which Turner (1988: 26) associates with temporary
events of a cultural, celebratory and artistic nature: 'The great
genres, ritual, carnival, drama, spectacle possess in common a tem-
poral structure which interdigitates constant with variable features,
and allows a place for spontaneous invention and improvisation in
the course of any given performance.' Turner (1988: 26) argues that
such events are capable of 'sustaining cherished social and cultural
principles and forms, and also of turning them upside down'.

This potential of displacement through performance may
emerge from 'the rehearsal of ... conventional formulae in non-
conventional ways [where performance assumes] meanings and
functions for which it was never intended' (Butler, 1997: 147). The
non-conventional rehearsal of performance that Butler refers to
includes the input of the participant as a mediator in performance
art. Fischer-Lichte (2008: 7) argues that in performance there is an
autopoietic feedback loop where the participant's elaboration of
meaning in a performance is fed back into the performance itself
(rather than internalised) and in turn it is capable of generating
unscripted outcomes that break the cycle of unimpeded information
flows (which symbolise a static performance). Performance involves
dynamic feedback loops that displace information flows through a
process of distributed agency, generating a form of reflexivity that
emerges from shared experiences.

The performative machine holds abstract potential that is actu-
alised through the act of performing. As it mutates and concretises
into different forms of expression, it remains in a constant state of
becoming. This potential of becoming through performativity is a
defining factor in performances such as *A Machine To See With*,
where the different forms of expression materialise in the shape of
individual patterns of participation – such as in Paul's experience.
Therefore, the outcome of the performative machine expands well
beyond what is immediately visible, functional and in a stable mode
as it assembles with other machines.

The media machine

The raw material of contemporary society is information (Castells, 1996: 61). Information is subject to a process of mediation which involves the knowledge of how to transmit other knowledge through technology, which constitutes 'the main source of productivity' (Castells, 1996: 17). The media machine is defined by the features of the information technology paradigm: the pervasiveness of new technologies (shaping all processes of human activity), networking logic, flexible reconfiguration and technological convergence (Castells, 1996: 61, 62). While the media machine is supported by the materiality of interconnected communication network infrastructures, its power is largely driven by the abstract potential of media. In *Intensive Culture*, Lash (2010: 30) argues that media is the main unit of exchange-value in contemporary society, suggesting that the media machine supersedes the capitalist machine: 'media displace money as the abstract means that define our times'. In this process, as Lash (2010: 30) points out, 'money and the commodity become mediatized [and] the social itself begins to be submitted to the laws of media'. Lash refers to this process as a form of post-social relation, where the decline of the social bond identified by Simmel over a century ago has intensified through technologically mediated communication:

> We have a *post-social relation* now, the communication. This is a relation after the decline of the social bond [...] This is technologically mediated communication, which takes the old social bond, and stretches, shrinks, accelerates and intensifies it to the point of explosion. No one more than Simmel gives us tools to come to terms with this. (Lash, 2010: 33; original emphasis)

What Lash identifies as the post-social relation manifests itself as a media machine that reconfigures social interaction in the city. The media machine is a fundamental component towards conceptualising urban space as relational space through the mobility, scalability and interactivity of technologically mediated communication (McQuire, 2008: 21).

The assemblage of the media machine and the urban machine is driven by the procedurality of computer code and its persuasive power, to the extent that '[i]nfrastructure space has become a medium of information ... with the power and currency of software' or in other words, 'an operating system for shaping the city' (Easterling, 2016: 13). Yet despite the procedurality of computer code, the assemblage of the media and urban machines can be intentionally ambiguous. It can unfold as a form of performative machine where intent conflicts with disposition, as Easterling (2016: 21) points out: 'For each technology in infrastructure space, to distinguish between what the organization is saying and what it is doing – the pretty landscape versus the fluid dynamics of the river – is to read the difference between a declared intent and an underlying disposition.'

For example, in *A Machine To See With*, the declared intent of the narrative is to test the participant's leadership skills and ability to execute a challenging task (the bank heist), while its disposition is to lead the participant on a reflective journey that interrogates the very same assemblage of machines that drives the performance. In this case, the assemblage of the media and urban machines through performance art constitutes a performative urban interface, that 'involves the interfacing (and repurposing) of digital technologies with their surrounding environment and with interface users for purposes other than facilitating efficient urban exchanges with predefined outcomes' (Dias and Adams, 2019).

The capitalist machine

In *Chaosmosis*, Guattari (1995: 29) argues that 'Capital smashes all other modes of valorisation.' Guattari's argument is concerned with the overwhelming impact of capitalist subjectivity on the social machine, which homogenises expression and commodifies desire 'within the context of ... the information revolution...with its greyness' (Guattari, 1995: 22). The media machine is assembled with the capitalist machine through two main paradigms. First, the power and extent of the Internet as 'the central production and control apparatus of an increasingly supranational market system' as representative of digital capitalism (Schiller, 2000: xiv). Second, the ability of the assemblage of the media and capitalist machines to reduce the world to a simulacrum. According to Boltanski and Chiapello (2005: 451), capitalism denies loyalty to the self, criticises resistance as refusal to connect, and interprets the attempt to link the identity of a representation with its original as a failure to acknowledge the 'infinite variability of the beings who circulate in the network, where everything is exchangeable for computer code'.

This enables the capitalist machine to adapt and to resist any attempt to criticise or confront it, as Boltanski and Chiapello (2005: 455) argue: 'If everything without exception is now nothing but code, spectacle or simulacrum, from what external position can critique denounce an illusion that is one with the totality of what exists?' I argue that performance art might offer an opportunity to reflect on the power of the capitalist machine to homogenise expression and commodify desire, but that this is only possible from inside the capitalist machine itself, rather than from a privileged and autonomous position.

The critique of authenticity of expression in art has been defined by the struggles for autonomy and liberation post-1960s (such as the 1968 movement) to address capitalism's rhetoric of the liberation of the individual through consumption (Boltanski and Chiapello, 2005: 441). In *The New Spirit of Capitalism*, Boltanski and Chiapello (2005: 419–42) argue that the renewed artistic struggle for authenticity has been countered by the capitalist machine through two strategies: first, through capitalism's ability to deny any claims of authenticity; second, through capitalism's power to reconfigure artistic strategies seeking authenticity through expressive forms of liberation and autonomy that perpetuate art as a commodity. The influence of the capitalist machine on contemporary aesthetic machines is manifested through its influence on several actants that are constitutive of the aesthetic machine: artists, art critics, art institutions (museums, galleries, art councils), art patrons and finally the process of branding cities as cultural or creative hubs.

The power of the capitalist machine comes from its capacity of abstraction and self-referencing. Boltanski and Chiapello (2005: 4) point out that capitalism is first and foremost an abstract process with an 'imperative to unlimited accumulation of capital by formally peaceful means'. They define the spirit of capitalism as 'the set of beliefs associated with the capitalist order that helps to justify this order' (2005: 10). According to them, the spirit of capitalism 'permeate[s] the whole set of mental representations specific to a given era ... to the point where its presence is simultaneously diffuse and general' (2005: 57).

The spirit of capitalism, as Marcuse (2001: 53) points out, accommodates and dissipates critique into its system. According to him, it imposes social controls onto individuals that obscure 'the distinction between imposed and spontaneous behaviour'. Marcuse pits the artistic dimension – represented by the individuality of the artist – against the economic individual, while arguing that the latter has the upper hand by incorporating the value of individual creativity:

> In contrast to the economic individual, the artist realizes his individuality in a form of creative work which modern culture has extolled as a manifestation of higher freedom and higher value [...] In the fully developed bourgeois society, the market value supersedes the value of individual creativity; when the latter serves to increase the former, it is the market rather than the individual which asserts itself. (Marcuse, 2001: 70, 71)

Marcuse's critique of the market value versus artistic value illustrates the role of art as an individual commodity (such as in the circuit of art auctions), the fetishisation of the art market (such as through the popularity of art biennials) and the paradigm of the celebrity artist. However, as Guattari (1995: 105) states, the aesthetic machine is capable of traversing other 'Universes of value', including the capitalist machine itself. Therefore, I argue that performance art is able to situate itself as neither fully autonomous nor fully commodified by the capitalist machine, and in doing so it is capable of enacting forms of expression that are not fully commodified or homogenised by capitalist subjectivity. Boltanski and Chiapello (2005: 420) suggest that the main task at hand for art is not to demand liberation and authenticity or to confront the capitalist machine, but rather to focus on highlighting – and possibly providing alternatives – to the perils that the capitalist machine poses to authentic relationships (or the social machine).

The capitalist machine may overstate its influence if provoked by claims of artistic autonomy. Yet we must not assume that the aesthetic machine is always already compromised by the capitalist machine, or that the latter pre-empts or disables art's expressive and subjective potential. Performance art constitutes an aesthetic machine that does not pit itself against the capitalist machine but operates within it while generating reflection on the influential assemblage of the capitalist, media and urban machines and enabling emergent modes of subjectivity.

The human-machine

The concept of the human-machine is tightly connected with the evolution of cybernetics post-World War II. In *How We Became Posthuman*, Hayles (1999: 8) argues that at the core of cybernetics is the concept that the organic and the mechanical – or the human and the machine – can be part of the same system. According to Hayles (1999: 2; original emphasis), this process unfolds through three interrelated stories: first, the separation of information from 'the material forms in which it is thought to be embedded'; second, the development of the cyborg as a *'technological artifact and cultural icon* in the years following World War II'; and finally, the story of how a 'historically specific construction called *the human* [gives] *way to a different construction called the posthuman*'. Hayles (1999: 6) argues that the term posthuman implies a subject that is 'sufficiently different from the liberal subject that if one assigns the term "human" to this subject, it makes sense to call the successor "posthuman"'. She suggests that we become posthuman once our subjectivity is informed by a collective of autonomous agents. However, this assemblage manifests itself through *'complex interplays between embodied forms of subjectivity and arguments for disembodiment through the cybernetic tradition'* (Hayles, 1999: 7; original emphasis).

Therefore, the cybernetic machine unfolds through a tension between embodiment and information, where, as Hayles (1999: 6) points out, the human being competes with the 'prediction of a "postbiological" future for the human race'. According to Hayles

(1999: 7; original emphasis), from a cybernetic point of view 'humans were to be seen primarily as information-processing entities who are *essentially* similar to intelligent machines'. This is the fundamental premise of the Turing test, the benchmark for proving that machines are capable of thinking like human beings, which states that: 'If you cannot tell the intelligent machine from the intelligent human, your failure proves, Turing argued, that machines can think' (Hayles, 1999: xi).

The word cybernetics derives from the Greek word for steersman, and as Hayles (1999: 8) points out, it signals the joint operation of 'three powerful actors – information, control and communication'. This assemblage is indicative of the detachment of information from its materiality as the key factor in cybernetics. As Hayles points out, cybernetics evolved through three distinct phases. The first phase was defined by the concept of homeostasis – 'the ability of living organisms to maintain steady states [in] fickle environments' – controlled by the device of the feedback loop, enabling a system to constantly check itself and adjust to different inputs to remain stable (Hayles, 1999: 8). The feedback loop is a key component of the software code that controls the infrastructure networks of contemporary mediated cities. It is also present in most software systems employed in digitally mediated performance art events, such as in the state machine in *A Machine To See With*.

The second phase of cybernetics is defined by reflexivity. In contrast to feedback loops, which are components that can be observed and controlled from an external point of view, reflexivity implies that the observer is part of the system, which displaces and incorporates the movement through which it is made: '*Reflexivity is the movement whereby that which has been used to generate a system is made, through a changed perspective, to become part of the system it generates*' (Hayles, 1999: 8; original emphasis). Hayles (1999: 11) points out that reflexivity implies a system where information is embedded and indistinguishable from the system itself: 'one could say either that information does not exist in this paradigm or that it has sunk so deeply into the system as to become indistinguishable from the organizational properties defining the system as such'.

The definition of reflexivity in cybernetic machines differs from performative reflexivity because of the distributed nature of the latter. In cybernetic machines reflexivity is contained in its enclosed system, while in performative machines reflexivity emerges through distributed agency as they assemble with other machines (which may also include cybernetic machines as components) and displaces information flows through dynamic feedback loops.

Finally, the third phase of cybernetics is defined by emergence, where systems are capable of spontaneous evolution. As Hayles (1999: 11) points out, this is the concept behind artificial intelligence, where 'computer programs are designed to allow "creatures" [non-human actants] to evolve spontaneously in directions the programmer may not have anticipated'. This is symbolic of the ultimate cybernetic conceptual leap, where all life forms in the universe can be translated into informational code (Hayles, 1999: 11). It suggests, as Hayles (1999: 12) points out, the 'fantasy ... that because we are essentially information, we can do away with the body'. Detaching information from its materiality, as Hayles (1999: 19) points out, allows information to be taken out of its context and out of its body. Yet this separation involves a conceptual leap that ignores the fact that 'for information to exist, it must *always* be instantiated in a medium' (Hayles, 1999: 13; original emphasis). Hayles (1999: 288) instead champions 'a dynamic partnership between humans and intelligent machines' where embodiment is neither erased nor detached from the machine-systems that we engage with in everyday life.

This entails that the human-machine operates *through* data and *as* data, as Gabrys (2016: 196) points out: 'The citizen is a data point, both a generator of data and a responsive node in a system of feedback.' Towards this aim, the citizen performs the role usually associated with sensors embedded in the city, through a continuous process of sensing and acting (Gabrys, 2016: 196). Gabrys (2016: 208, 217) describes the dual role of the citizen as both a sensor (capturing information from the urban environment) and actuator (acting upon the information collected) and associates this with read/write urban practices where citizens can 'modify cities ... as they might modify computer code'. This new model of engagement with the city is consistent with the aims of citizen participation initiatives that '[make] the city open to modification [by focusing] on citizens' abilities to add stories to places, to create alternative urban experiences, or to open up other ways of perceiving and engaging with the city' (Gabrys, 2016: 217).

Yet Gabrys (2016: 217) points out that the inputs available to digital participation by citizens are restricted to 'set registers of computational recognition'. Or in other words, participation by citizens is restrained by the procedural nature of computer code and its pre-emptive character. Tuters and Varnelis (2006: 363) suggest that we might be 'at the threshold of a machinic third nature', as sentient objects take centre stage (replacing respectively nature and human beings) while arguing that art should 'get involved in the messy business of this new world of objects'. Yet it is not a matter of objects replacing human beings and nature, but instead a matter of understanding how human beings and objects are assembled in ways that transpose the dualities that are so prevalent in contemporary society – human versus machine, capitalism versus artistic autonomy, control versus chaos – towards new forms of subjectivity.

Gabrys (2016: 209, 210) refers to Stengers' conceptualisation of cosmopolitics as an antagonistic position to the concept of consensual cosmopolitanism (supported by digital media technologies). Key to Stengers' argument is the definition of the idiot as 'someone or something that causes us to think about and encounter the complexities of participation and social life as something other than prescribed or settled' (Gabrys, 2016: 209). The idiot is therefore an actant-mediator that defies the logic of the city as a closed and predictable system, both disrupting such a system and generating reflection on it. Idiot-ness, as Gabrys (2016: 225) states, is a 'distributed condition (or assemblage) that encompasses would-be urban citizens, access protocols, cards, and sensors, as well as urban spaces and infrastructures'. The figure of the idiot foregrounds the complex and unpredictable condition of the human-machine and the inevitability of the assemblage of the human-machine with the cybernetic machine. But it also highlights the ability of the human-machine to produce individual subjectivity that is mediated – but not controlled – by the procedural nature of computer code. Gabrys (2016: 230) argues that idiotic encounters are 'an ongoing condition of engagement', without which we are left with 'an unquestioned common vision of the city' (consensual cosmopolitanism).

The urban machine

The urban machine performs a double role: it is both stage for the performative, media and human-machines and also an assemblage of actants. Some of these actants are easily identifiable, such as buildings and urban furniture, while others emerge through unexpected and unpredictable performances as I have described above. The association of cities with the efficiency of machines through self-contained, totalitarian and hierarchical urban structures mirrors the ideals of the cybernetic machine, exercising control over movement of peoples and goods rather than information. The machine-city ideal can be traced back several centuries, such as in the unrealised plans for the medieval fortified city of Sforzinda, designed by Filarete in the fifteenth century as the 'fictive ideal version of Milan', with a symmetrical form, a distinct centre and a clear hierarchy of 'three different kinds of houses for different categories of people' (Cornell and Nilsson, 2017). Sforzinda was designed to make 'its order more distinct and easier to govern' (Cornell and Nilsson, 2017). While Sforzinda was assembled through a top-down approach (with total control centred around the governing prince), Thomas More's ([1516] 2016) *Utopia*, published in 1516, describes an island-state of the same name where the structure and organisation of its cities is not determined by strict rules of spatial design, but instead by a bottom-up hierarchical social structure. Utopia is perhaps the most fitting and influential example of consensual cosmopolitanism.

More ([1516] 2016: 78) describes how the hierarchical structure of Utopia is based on the leader of a group of families – a Syphogant – while the top of the structure is occupied by the figure of the Prince, who is in charge of Utopia for life, 'unless he is removed upon suspicion of some design to enslave the people'. The whole population leads a spartan way of life and 'wear[s] the same sort of clothes' (More, [1516] 2016: 80). The main role of the

Syphogant is 'to take care that no man may live idle, but that every one may follow his trade diligently [without wearing] themselves out with perpetual toil' (More, [1516] 2016: 81). The hours of the day are strictly divided: six hours for work and eight hours for sleeping, while the remaining hours are 'left to every man's discretion'; however, More emphasises that no one should 'abuse that interval to luxury and idleness' (More, [1516] 2016: 81).

Filarete's Sforzinda and More's Utopia are examples of machine-city structures that emerged prior to the modern association of the term machine with technical apparatuses. Yet they propose future visions of machinist forms of living that are controlled by an assemblage of built space, autocratic and hierarchical modes of power and strict social organisation. The post-industrial revolution machine-cities were also designed with efficiency and control in mind. This was demonstrated by the transformation of the city of Paris through Haussmann's plans during the second half of the nineteenth century. It involved an extensive network of wide, unimpeded streets for circulation underpinned by the desire to cleanse the 'sick body' of the city and 'disentangle it from its dross, the sediment of past and present failures' (Haussmann in Graham and Marvin, 2001: 55).

In the early twentieth century modernist urban planning executed the vision of the machine-city through a series of interlinked sociotechnical processes based on the proposition that 'comprehensive, integrated networks of streets could be laid across whole urban areas in a technocratic way, to bind the metropolis into a functioning "machine" or "organism"' (Graham and Marvin, 2001: 53). The quest for order and efficient circulation of flows in the machine-city sought a level of control that mirrors the cybernetic machine's aim of efficient and unimpeded flows of information between human beings and technical machines. The control of transportation and communication flows was dependent on the synchronisation of time and the rationalisation of space, an aim that was fulfilled by the consolidation of infrastructure networks across entire cities and countries, which 'required the construction of national systems of interconnected highways, rail, communications and energy infrastructure' (Graham and Marvin, 2001: 41).

Architect Le Corbusier – one of the key figures of modernist urban planning – concluded 'that social frustration was a result of the workers' inability to transfer the rationality of the workplace to home life and leisure' (Sadler, 1999: 50). As Sadler (1999: 50) points out, Le Corbusier's solution to this perceived social imbalance was to adopt a god's eye approach to urban planning: '[Le Corbusier's] version of radical change was carried through not by the populace but by the visionary architect-dictator, capable of planning people's lives by first organizing the spaces and places in which they were acted out: factories, offices, apartment blocks, sports halls, and cars.' The enduring influence of the Athens Charter and its rational and functionalist principles can be seen in large-scale urban projects across the world, with varied degrees of success.

The limitations of the urban machine as an autonomous model of urban development and of the functionalist ethos of the Athens Charter (with little consideration to citizens' needs and desires) is illustrated by the demolition of the Pruitt-Igoe housing scheme that was modelled on its principles in 1972. Around the same time (from the 1970s onwards), the urban machine was being reconfigured through a combination of several factors: increasingly transnational flows of investment, capital and technology (supported by the networking power of the media machine), fiscal crises and the easing of restriction on private entry into previously monopolistic infrastructure markets (Graham and Marvin, 2001: 92–7). This led to an increasing number of infrastructure network projects being developed by private corporations based on project-by-project risk assessment, fragmenting the 'more or less coherent and integrated infrastructure networks that were the legacy of the modern urban ideal' (Graham and Marvin, 2001: 97). Contemporary urban planning is guided by these premises and through a combination of high-tech infrastructure, a stated concern for security and environment issues. These cities are being 'conceived by private multinational corporations as gilt-edged gated communities ... each branded as the ultimate techno-eco-utopia' (Wainwright, 2019).

Around the same time as the performative turn of the 1960s and a few years before the urban machine started to become more fragmented, mediated and dominated by market speculation,

Archigram's speculative designs for their 'Plug-in City' projects emerged as an assemblage of the urban, media and cybernetic machines. Their futuristic visions of urban living combined open-endedness, interchangeability and standardisation. As McQuire (2008: 96) points out, Archigram's designs foregrounded 'the new possibilities for decentralized control enabled by ICTs [linking] the modular design logic of an earlier modernism with a more consumer-oriented model. This model, he argues, predated virtual reality systems and cyberspace, which are both symbolic of the process of dematerialisation of information flows: 'The close resemblance between [Archigram's] dream of responsive architecture, and the investment in "virtual reality" systems which emerged in the 1980s underlines the extent to which Archigram's dream soon morphed into cyberspace' (McQuire, 2008: 97). There is a noticeable lack of human-machines in Archigram's conceptual drawings. This might be partly explained by the monumental scale of their projects, but it is also reflective of the secondary role of the human-machine (in its embodied form) in the command and control model of the cybernetic machine applied to urban space.

Archigram's speculative vision might not have materialised into urban built space, but it provided a metaphor for the translation of the media machine into the urban machine through computer code, and vice-versa, as Apprich (2017: 75) states: 'not only had the city become a data space with the massive dissemination of digital and network technologies, but the data space, generated by these technologies, was now represented as a city'. This enabled projects such as *De Digitale Stad* (the digital city) in Amsterdam in the 1990s, a project that was set up for a limited period (ten weeks) 'to test new forms of civic participation by means of electronic media [by involving] citizens in the political process' (Apprich, 2017: 79). The model of the digital city as a platform for civic deliberation defines 'a new model of governance, which makes use of new urban environments' (Apprich, 2017: 143).

However, the urban machine is also the de facto place for embodied encounters, and these encounters can defy or circumvent the logic of the command and control model of the machine-city, as they cannot be simply programmed or predicted by the cybernetic and media machines in control of urban environments. Strategies to facilitate such embodied encounters are perceived as vital in the promotion of cities to bolster their social, cultural and economic status. Such strategies are dependent on the assemblage of capitalist, media and aesthetic machines, illustrated by Richard Florida's (2004) controversial yet hugely popular argument that a city's economic prosperity is dependent on its ability to attract the creative class. Florida's (2004: 8) definition of the term creative class involves those who are 'primarily paid to create' (and thus partake in the knowledge industry), in contrast to the working class and the service class. The branding of cities as cultural, creative, technological and ecological hubs is a relatively recent phenomenon that aims to raise their status and competitiveness at both global and national level. It involves a mix of local initiatives, national strategies, local business support and tourism promotion, a model that is dependent on strategies of promotion and branding of innovation that are not necessarily driven by technology.

For example, the model of the city as a cultural hub, as Steven Miles and Malcolm Miles (2004: 45) point out, can 'be an effective way of promoting economic growth' through 'culturally led urban development strategies' where new institutions may become 'flagships of a cultural turn in urban development' – such as the Guggenheim Museum in Bilbao. The model of the city as a cultural hub can also be nurtured through a focus on cultural events. Stevenson (2003: 99) points out that the spectacle of the urban festival is 'a frequently devised strategy to repackage the city as a tourist destination'. However, as she remarks, this is dependent on the desirability of such cities, which in turn is dependent on the ability of the city to promote itself: 'the development and improvement of urban cultural resources and the production of events and festivals almost always occurs in conjunction with a concern about whether or not the city is perceived favourably by outsiders as a desirable place to live or to visit' (Stevenson, 2003: 99).

The performance of *A Machine To See With* during the Brighton Digital Festival in 2011 benefited from Brighton's established status as a regional cultural hub and a major tourist attraction in the United Kingdom, but also benefited the city itself by reinforcing its status as a place of cultural and artistic innovation. And while its urban footprint was minimal – in comparison to other performances and art

events with clear boundaries and more pronounced visual impact –
it fulfilled an important role: enabling reflection on our relations
with the urban machine and on the importance of embodied social
encounters in the digitally mediated city.

Machinic subjectivity

In *Chaosmosis*, Guattari (1995) argues that we must move beyond
the understanding of subjectivity as a singular and homogeneous
process, or as a matter of 'opposition between individual subject
and society' (Guattari, 1995: 1). Guattari's argument is constructed
on the basis that human subjectivity is assembled through heterogeneous components that include 'technological machines of
information and communication' (1995: 4). Or in other words, the
production of subjectivity is not an exclusive human process, but
neither is it exclusively moderated by technological transformation.
The production of subjectivity is machinic in nature – as it operates through an assemblage of several machine-components – and
'the machinic production of subjectivity can work for the better or
for the worse' (Guattari, 1995: 5). For Guattari, machinic subjectivity should foreground the aesthetic paradigm to avoid shifting
towards objective scientific paradigms and the homogenising tendency of capitalist subjectivity. To achieve this, he argues, we must
grasp [subjectivity] in the dimension of its processual creativity'
(1995: 13).

The concept of machinic heterogenesis – an assemblage of
machines that cannot be reduced to a unitary value – underpins
Guattari's definition of the machine, and also what I describe as the
machinic city. Referring to Maturana and Varela's (1980) conception of autopoiesis (or auto-production) as a means of defining the
autonomy of machines – human, technical or otherwise – Guattari
states that machines always depend 'on exterior elements in order
to be able to exist as such' (1995: 37). Yet rather than merging into
each other, such machines preserve a certain degree of autonomy
and therefore the ensuing machinic assemblage is never homogeneous or consisting of a defined unity. It is the transversal role of
abstract machines – such as the aesthetic machine – that confers a

'power of ontological auto-affirmation' to these machinic assemblages by 'relating all the heterogeneous levels that they traverse' (Guattari, 1995: 35).

Guattari emphasises the importance of the aesthetic machine towards 'extracting full meaning from all the empty signal systems that invest us from every side' through the 'creation and composition of mutant percepts and effects', in particular through their 'performative modalities' (1995: 90, 91). Guattari refers in particular to performance art as an aesthetic machine that can probe the complexity of contemporary life and reveal to us its implications: 'Performance art delivers the instant to the vertigo of the emergence of Universes that are simultaneously strange and familiar. It has the advantage of drawing out the full implications of this extraction of intensive, a-temporal, a-spatial, a-signifying dimensions from the semiotic net of quotidianity' (Guattari, 1995: 90).

The machines I have analysed in this chapter are essential components of the machinic assemblage of performance art and the contemporary mediated city. As the aesthetic machine traverses media, capitalist, human and urban machines, it engenders new modes of subjectivity. The potential of this machinic assemblage is represented by the conceptual figure of the rhizome, defined by Deleuze and Guattari (1988) in *A Thousand Plateaus* as a model that can neither be reduced to a single unit of representation (as, for example, an electromechanical machine), nor defined by clear entry or exit points. The rhizome represents the potential of performance art as it interferes with the urban fabric and reconfigures it at the same time that it is reconfigured. According to Deleuze and Guattari (1988: 12; original emphasis) the rhizome is '*a map and not a tracing*'. Or in other words, the rhizome is an open map ready to be traced over and over again. The act of tracing determines a single path or trajectory, but this can be modified, erased and combined with other tracings. For example, Paul's detour from the narrative's trajectory described above is rhizomatic in nature. His detour consists of an unexpected tracing, that eventually reconnected with the original tracing of the trajectory predefined by the narrative.

As participants in performance art, we partake in an assemblage of machinic subjectivity through a process that is rhizomatic in nature. Guattari's conceptualisation of machinic subjectivity provides a useful framework to analyse contemporary urban living through performance, as the communication technologies mediating social exchanges become increasingly complex. It enables us to contextualise these technologies and to analyse them not as simply machine-artefacts with a specific effect, but as actants that participate in a complex assemblage that is influenced by (among many other machine-actants) geographical limitations, citizens' desires and needs, technological failure and serendipity. In the following chapter, I turn my attention to some of the earlier aesthetic machines that are precursors of contemporary performance art and its influential role in urban space.

4

The aesthetic machine

Aesthetic machines and their discontents

In this chapter I will outline some of the key historical manifestations of the aesthetic machine, from its origins in ancient theatre where the stage and audience were clearly defined, to more recent aesthetic machines where art is embedded in the city, and where there are no clear boundaries between stage and audience. Some of these machines, such as the Futurist movement, sought to foreground the technical machine as an autonomous actant. While this might seem counterproductive in the light of my argument for a renewal of the concept of the machine, it is important to acknowledge that – even in the technocentric bravado of the futurists – we can identify the potential of the assemblage of human and non-human actants towards innovative social exchanges.

The assemblage of the aesthetic machine with several forms of technical machines has generated two types of criticism: first, that this assemblage is inauthentic – or in other words, that it is not aligned with the higher principles, forms and strategies associated with art – and second, that this assemblage obscures and diminishes the human being as it foregrounds the technical apparatus. Both criticisms draw from the ideal of art as an autonomous form and of the human being as the supreme source of (authentic) agency. As I previously stated, Guattari (1995: 106, 107) emphasises the importance of the aesthetic paradigm while at the same time stating that 'art does not have a monopoly on creation' and that we need to 'promote a [non-mechanist] conception [of the machine that] encompasses all of its aspects: technological, biological, informatic, social, theoretical and aesthetic'.

Boltanski and Chiapello (2005: 450) point out that the art critic's denunciation of inauthenticity in art is directed towards the use of what they define as artifices, through a mechanical approach to art and the use of simulated imitation: 'Deeply entrenched in [the critique of inauthenticity] is the denunciation of artifice as opposed to spontaneous, the mechanical in contrast to the living, the sincere in contrast to the strategic, and hence genuine emotion, which arises unintentionally, as opposed to its simulated imitation: a challenge to the "spectacle."' Boltanski and Chiapello (2005: 450) point out that such critique has been directed at theatre (as a form of aesthetic machine) for centuries. However, they note that theatre foregrounds difference (or authenticity) through the very same processes that are refuted by the critique of inauthenticity. The unique interpretation of the narrative by theatre actors and their infinite combinations of facial expressions and gestures is always already a simulated imitation, or a simulacrum. Therefore, aesthetic machines are no less authentic if they incorporate technical apparatuses and artifices.

The critique of inauthenticity in art that makes use of machine-components can be traced back to ancient Greek theatre and the device of the *deus ex machina* – translated as 'a god from a machine' – as Raunig (2010) illustrates in his analysis of theatre machines. The device of the *deus ex machina* combined material components, such as props and actors (fulfilling the role of ancient religious deities), with immaterial components, such as technical knowledge and artistic creation. Euripides employed the *deus ex machina* in several of his plays. It appeared unexpectedly to bring out resolution to increasingly complex and seemingly unsolvable plots through 'the help of a crane-like machine that allowed gods, goddesses and other figures to fly onto stage' (Raunig, 2010: 38).

Raunig (2010: 40) points out that Aristotle criticised Euripides' use of the *deus ex machina* by arguing that the resolution of the plot should be achieved through an artistic narrative rather than through a machine-device. Raunig (2010: 41) highlights the influence of Aristotelian criticism targeted at the device of the *deus ex machina* in the modern development of theatre. As an interrupting machinic apparatus in the aid of narrative closure, the *deus ex machina* was criticised as 'an unartistic act of force that [had] to be covered up more and more' towards creating a seamless illusion, such as in 'the cloud machines of the Italian baroque theater' (Raunig, 2010: 41). However, the *deus ex machina* wasn't simply an artifice, but rather an intrinsic component of the artist's vision, as Raunig (2010: 40) states:

> This general rule in Aristotle's *Poetics* makes the *deus ex machina* of Euripides's tragedies look like an expedient for a mediocre playwright, necessary for disentangling the dramatic knots he has created, but which virtually take on a life of their own. What is overlooked in an interpretation like this, however, is the skilfulness with which these knots are often constructed, so that in the end only a goddess can untie them.

Therefore, rather than constituting a makeshift solution, the *deus ex machina* was a 'purposely and carefully constructed crosspoint and climax of technical spectacle and the invention of intrigues' (Raunig, 2010: 40). In Euripides' plays, the crane-like machine enabling the *deus ex machina* was a primitive technological device that only had a supporting role towards aiding the actors in their role as religious deities. However, electromechanical machines controlled by computers have assumed an increasingly prominent role in theatre productions. This has generated criticism against the perceived clash between actor and technical apparatus, rekindling the critique against the influence of the machine in artistic practices. In this process, the Aristotelian critique of the machine as inauthentic is directed at the machine's perceived attempt to diminish or erase human presence. This is illustrated through Patrice Pavis's criticism of Robert Lepage's theatre production *Zulu Time* (1999), as Dixon describes:

> As Lepage's stage machinery, robots, and video and digital effects swamp the human beings, [Pavis] says, the audience searches desperately but in vain to connect with a speaking, living body. But amid the high-tech tumult, the performer's body is no longer able to 'be itself' as it is 'pulled in' to the machine and thereafter seems to require techno-sadomasochistic paraphernalia to experience any meaning or pleasure. (Dixon, 2007: 648)

Pavis's argument that the performer's body is being pulled into the machine constitutes a defensive stance in favour of the embodied actor rather than the technological apparatus and is devised through a human-centric point of view. Dixon (2007: 650) points out that Pavis's argument constitutes – rather than simply a backlash against 'new technology's incursion into theatre and performance' – proof of the irrevocable change in the 'role and status of the [human] performer' where both 'contemporary performance and the performer [are placed] into a posthuman frame'. Dixon also notes that Pavis's criticism would have been accepted by the Futurist movement in the early twentieth century as praise for their ability to foreground the machine as a protagonist: 'Pavis's dramatic cries about technology having taking over the theater would have sounded like victory to the futurists who called for that precise outcome almost a century earlier. The futurist's prophecy ... for Pavis at least, come[s] true: "technology has got the upper hand on the human for good"' (Dixon, 2007: 650).

Early aesthetic machines in twentieth-century avant-garde art movements

In several avant-garde art movements of the early twentieth century, electromechanical machines became not only artistic props in theatre and performance, but also prominent actants with key roles in the mediation of agency and the generation of innovative aesthetic forms and practices. For example, in relation to Futurism, Dixon (2007: 9) states that: 'Italian futurist performance theory and practice between 1909 and 1920 laid the foundations for fundamental philosophies and aesthetic strategies found within digital performance.' The futurists went as far as suggesting that the machine could become an artist in its own right. In Enrico Prampolini's *Futurist Scenography* (1915) manifesto, the machine (in the form of luminous entities) replaced the human actor: 'Vibrations, luminous forms (produced by electric currents and colored gases) will wriggle and writhe dynamically, and these authentic actor-gases of an unknown theatre will have to replace living actors' (Dixon, 2007: 54).

The futurists' legacy was marred by their totalitarian ideology and nihilistic bravado fuelled by their passion and enthusiasm for mechanical machines. In *The Futurist Manifesto* (1909), Futurist founder Marinetti (in Apollonio, 2009: 23) envisioned a society that embraced the machine's potential of renewal through destruction: 'Art, in fact, can be nothing but violence, cruelty, and injustice.' Yet this was not the de facto position of other avant-garde art movements at the time. Deleuze and Guattari (in Raunig, 2007: 22) contrast the futurists' penchant for a fascist desiring-machine with the humanist anti-machine of Surrealism, where desire was assembled against a totalitarian form of alienation by turning against the industrial machine. Despite their differences, both movements had a common trait: they highlighted the role of performance as a collective event that unfolds through a process of distributed agency against the logic of art as a form of representation and an autonomous domain disconnected from everyday life. This was a stance shared by other avant-garde art movements at the time that confronted the nineteenth-century model of artistic autonomy, as Gerald Raunig (2007: 150) points out:

> Along with the biting criticism of bourgeois cultural enterprises, Futurism, Dadaism and Productivism strove for performative, provocative and subversive strategies to thwart the logic of representation both in the aesthetic and in the political sense. In this way they also carried out a tendential turn from the 19th century model of artistic autonomy toward an avant-gardist collective and self-determined heteronomy.

Among the emerging avant-garde movements of this period, Raunig (2007: 23) suggests that a more balanced approach that neither glorifies nor vilifies the art machine – and that recognises the machine as one component in a machinic assemblage of distributed agency – can be found in Russian Futurism, Constructivism and Productivism. According to Raunig (2007: 23), these movements 'address[ed] the conditions of production and envision[ed] the machine in the context of new production conditions determined by collective appropriation'.

Raunig (2007: 23) places particular emphasis on the Agit-Theatre of Attractions as an example of a movement that 'investigated new links of human-machine, technical machines and social machines'. The Agit-Theatre of Attractions was part of the Soviet avant-garde art movements of the early twentieth century, which sought to involve the audience in the narrative, and attempted to mould it according to a specific set of post-revolutionary political ideologies. Rather than foregrounding the machine as a superior form (as in Futurism), it sought to assemble – rather than oppose – human actants and technical apparatus, as Raunig (2010: 43) points out: 'The machine material of the post-revolutionary Soviet theater encompassed the bodies of the actors, the construction, the audience: it anticipated the concatenation of human organs, technical apparatuses and social machines that constitute the machine for Deleuze and Guattari.'

This assemblage was most prominent during Theater October's re-staging of the storming of the Winter Palace during the October Revolution, which involved 100,000 participants and took place across the city of Petrograd, transforming it into a larger-than-life stage (Raunig, 2007: 152). However, for Raunig it was during the smaller (but no less revolutionary) performances of the Agit-Theatre of Attractions that the dissolution of aesthetic representation was most effective. As he points out, these performances enabled 'the complete elimination of the stage, tearing down the boundary between viewer and actor, between theater and everyday life, between reality in life and reality in art' (2007: 154). This involved strategies of 'calculated agitation of the audience in the theater' (Raunig, 2007: 154), such as in Eisenstein and Tretyakov's collaboration in the play *Protivogazy* (Gas Masks) in 1924. This play was enacted in 'the gigantic hall of the Moscow gas works at the Kursk train station [to] the workers in this plant' (Raunig, 2007: 154). Such an audience, as Raunig (2007: 155) points out, 'was not intended or willing to correspond to abstract notions of the dissolution of art and life'. The actors performed 'alongside the gigantic apparatuses of the plant on the scaffolding of the stage in workers' uniforms' (Raunig, 2007: 155). Raunig notes that the play wasn't successful with the audience (who asked them to leave after the fourth performance), but it was nonetheless successful in dissolving aesthetic representation into everyday life (2007: 155).

The techniques of the Agit-Theatre of Attractions were carefully constructed through an assemblage of 'events and of actors, things, sounds and viewers' (Raunig, 2007: 157). As in *A Machine To See*

With, the assemblage was composed of actants that were seemingly unrelated, but that were assembled together in unexpected ways: the infrastructure of the plant became the stage, and the actors assumed the guise of the intended spectators, as they donned their uniforms. The apparent failure of the performance to engage the audience is also an unexpected outcome of this unusual machinic assemblage and is in direct contrast with the ideology and clearly defined purpose of political propaganda attached to the Russian avant-garde art movements that emerged in this particular political context.

As Eisenstein stated in his 1923 manifesto *The Montage of Attractions*, these performances sought to '[mould] the audience in a desired direction (or mood) [as] the task of every utilitarian theatre' (in Bordwell, 1993: 115). Nevertheless, the aim in these performances to incorporate machinist techniques with specific participatory outcomes in mind precedes contemporary digitally mediated performance art. According to Eisenstein, the spectacle 'subjects the audience to emotional or psychological influence, verified by experience and mathematically calculated to produce specific emotional shocks in the spectator' (in Bordwell, 1993: 116). This is achieved by resorting to attractions, described as techniques 'to stimulate strong perceptual and emotional reactions' that are arranged in specific patterns through montage (Bordwell, 1993: 120).

The technique of montage, in particular, demonstrated how such machinist techniques – despite their stated intention of producing precise emotional outcomes – could enable alternative forms of meaning that were not prescriptive. This becomes evident in Eisenstein's translation of the technique of the montage from the Agit-Theatre of Attractions to film production. In film, montage equates to the juxtaposition of two unrelated single shots to achieve a third meaning. According to Bordwell (1993: 121), it was Kuleshov who gave montage particular significance in Soviet cinema by conducting informal experiments to show that 'editing could create emotions and ideas not present in either of the single shots'. The technique of montage, despite its precise editing technique (where the two unrelated shots have a clear beginning and end), demonstrates its potential as a machinic assemblage that is open to interpretation.

Deleuze emphasises the indeterminacy of the effect of montage –
despite it constituting a whole – and the importance of the relation
between what he defines as movement-images towards its overall
effect:

> Montage is the determination of the whole ... by means of conti-
> nuities, cutting and false continuities [...] Montage is the operation
> which bears on the movement-images to release the whole from
> them, that is the image *of* time. It is a necessarily indirect image,
> since it is deducted from movement-images and their relationships.
> Montage does not come afterwards, for all that. (Deleuze, 2005: 30;
> original emphasis)

Deleuze points out that montage is a whole, but not a totality that
can be deduced at the end, as every time there is movement (or
translation in space) there is a 'qualitative change in the whole'
(Deleuze, 2005: 8). Therefore, the montage's outcome cannot be
prescriptive: its meaning emerges at the moment the spectator
encounters the montage. The production of meaning is shaped by
the spectator's previous experience and understanding of the different components present in each single shot and their interpretation
of these components as the shots collide in the montage. Deleuze
(2005: 5, 6) argues that Eisenstein '[extracts] from movements or
developments certain moments of crisis, [picking] out peaks and
shouts, [pushing] scenes to their climax and [bringing] them into
collision'. In other words, the construction of a situation through
the use of montage – involving the collision of unrelated situations,
forms or actants – is always emergent and undefined. Deleuze
(2005: 7) refers to this potential as the any-instant-whatever, where
such forms respond to 'accidents of the environment'.

While Eisenstein's technique suggests a posed and measured
elaboration of movement through montage, Deleuze (2005: 6)
argues that this does not pre-empt the any-instant-whatever.
Eisenstein's assemblage of montage through moments of crisis that
are forcefully brought together through shock and collision enables
a dialectic that is open to interpretation and that enables multiple
third meanings, rather than a single, prescriptive one. In the case
of performance art events, the production of the third meaning
emerges from the ability of the narrative to assemble situations

through the collision of events – rather than images – in urban space as it activates multiple collectives of urban actants. Therefore, the production of meaning emerges through a machinic assemblage of actants where narrative, technology, urban space and participation collide.

Cinematic machines

One of the most relevant films that illustrated the concept and potential of montage as a machinic assemblage was Dziga Vertov's *Man With a Movie Camera* (1929), where his conceptualisation of the *kino-eye* (or cine-eye) foresaw the potential of a hybrid human-machine towards reconfiguring public space through performance. The conceptual device of the *kino-eye* performed as an autonomous and mobile human/mechanical eye. Through its cognitive power and technical prowess, it assembled an imaginary city from unrelated images shot across the cities of Moscow, Kiev and Odessa. In this process it disassembled and reassembled the city and its technical apparatus through a performative process. It revealed, as Vertov (in Roberts, 2011: 19) states, a unique (and emergent) world that was stitched together through the superhuman prowess of the *kino-eye*: 'I am the Cine-Eye. I am a mechanical eye. I, a machine, show you the world only as I can see it. Now and forever I free myself from human immobility. I am in constant motion.' The *kino-eye* leads the viewer through a non-linear narrative of the city and is conceptualised as a machinic assemblage of the (previously human) roles of camera operator, director and editor with the machine apparatus of cinema, as Vertov (in Dixon, 2007: 66) describes: 'I take the most agile hands of one, the fastest and most graceful legs of another, from a third person I take the handsomest and most expressive head, and by editing I create an entirely new perfect man. I am eye. I am mechanical eye.'

As Dixon (2007: 66) notes, *Man With a Movie Camera* 'parallels the visual compositing functions of computer systems', predating the transformation of the visual language of cinema through digital technology. Yet it is also representative of the process of fragmentation and reassembling of the city by media forms. Deleuze

(2005: 40) points out that Vertov positions all actants – machines, landscapes, buildings and human beings – in a 'material system in perpetual interaction' that is non-hierarchical in nature. The *kino-eye* operates as a machinic assemblage that is universal, unbounded and unmeasurable. Deleuze (2005: 41) emphasises that montage in *Man With a Movie Camera* occurs at various levels and times: the intervals occupied by the camera-eye, in the editing room, and also 'in the audience, who compare life in the film as it is'. The same is true of *A Machine To See With*, where a form of montage emerges as a distributed process that involves the artistic narrative, the technological apparatus (computer servers, automated call systems and mobile phones), public space and the subjective interpretation of participants.

In Chapter 2 I described how *A Machine To See With* emerged from a locative cinema commission, and how Blast Theory realised at an early stage that the cinematic experience that the commission sought could be achieved without a screen. This in turn enabled participants to perform the role of the cinematographer and the editor, filming with their own eyes while simultaneously interpreting the narrative and the surrounding urban environment as they participated in the event. As in Vertov's device of the *kino-eye* in *Man With a Movie Camera*, the human-machine hybrid in *A Machine To See With* is mediated by the artistic narrative as it reconstitutes the fragmented space of the city. All the machines (including the human-machine) that constitute this hybrid form are situated in a flat topology, where, as Deleuze (2005: 40) argues (by referring to Vertov's work), any actant is capable of receiving and re-emitting movements, and in doing so 'making matter evolve towards less "probable" states'.

The narrative of *A Machine To See With* makes several direct references to a fictional surveillance machine that is supposedly tracking the participant's every movement while stating to them that 'everything around you is just pretend' (Blast Theory, 2011a). This heightens the expectations of participants, whose interpretation of the narrative is influenced by their previous cinematic experiences. I argue that the sensorial experience of the participant can be analysed according to a typology of three shots commonly used in film production: wide angle (used for landscape shots that are used to establish the overall environment); close-up shots (used to frame a particular person or object in dramatic detail with limited background context); and dolly shots (where the camera moves along a path following the action and defining a moving frame).

The participant's experience of shooting and editing their own 'movie' in *A Machine To See With* through their 'camera-eyes' involves a combination of these shots. Some of these shots are explicitly prompted by the narrative, while others emerge through the participant's own interpretation of the events (regardless if they were triggered or not by the narrative). For example, the following prompt from the narrative's script asks the participant to frame a close-up shot of a banal feature of the urban landscape for no apparent reason: 'On the right, you pass the boarded-up side entrance to the theatre. On your left, through the green painted bars, is the leafy yard of solicitors' offices' (Blast Theory, 2011a).

An example of a close-up shot emerging from the participant's own interpretation of events was participant Dany's encounter with the chatty bystander (described previously in Chapter 2), which prompted her to scrutinise a beer mat through a close-up shot due to her suspicion that the phone number on the back of it had something to do with the performance. Each participant stitches (or edits) together these different shots to compose their own performative experience (or film edit), which is unique and unpredictable. The spatial effect of the cinematic machine is to temporarily interpellate participants to frame (as in framing a film shot) spaces that would usually go unnoticed in the everyday experience of navigating Brighton's streets.

These spaces – activated by the relationship between the participant and the performance – become temporary relationship-specific spaces (Massumi, 2003: 7). While the character of such spaces is preserved, they temporarily assume another role as they become the focal attention of the participant. This temporary role is assembled through a combination of the usual associations connected to each of these spaces and the associations suggested by the narrative. For example, the section of the narrative that is played out in a public toilet cubicle builds upon the reputation of this type of space as a place for transgressive acts, as it asks participants to stash away all their money under their clothes. The claustrophobic and intense experience of being in such a confined space also benefits from the same association present in close-up shots, which are used to generate tension and unease in the viewer. Such a spatial experience is conducive to the development of paranoia, which is activated by the assemblage of the narrative and this particular type of space.

Some participants – such as Danny and Paul – noticed actions taking part just outside their cubicles, which they thought were related to the narrative. Danny (in Dias, 2011) stated that: 'There were a couple of people screaming outside the cubicle', while Paul's (in Dias, 2011) attention was drawn to a cleaner outside his cubicle: 'I can see mop strings whipping in and out at the bottom of it.' The bystanders screaming desperately in need of a toilet cubicle and the cleaner handling the mop had nothing to do with the performance, yet briefly became actant-mediators during Danny and Paul's participation. For Danny, the screaming incident was the standout moment of his performance, while for Paul the mop incident triggered a comical train of thought: 'I'm thinking: "Do I pretend to be having a piss?" You know, it's kind of: "Do I just … What do I do? How do I deal with this? Do I go out and wash [my] hands, at least give the impression? Am I gonna get invited for the shag around bike?"' (in Dias, 2011).

This reveals the potential of the narrative to reshape a functional space of the city into a scene of imaginative potential and dramatic action. As Danny's and Paul's accounts reveal, this potential is driven by cinematic and cultural references, but also by the expectation – triggered by the narrative at the very beginning – that participation in the performance will involve illicit and dangerous acts. As in Vertov's *Man With a Movie Camera*, *A Machine To See With* demands active interpretation of the artistic montage. However, in the latter this montage is assembled dynamically as the participant progresses through the performance. This experience draws from a lineage of post-1960s avant-garde art movements associated with the performative turn.

The post-1960s performative turn

The term performative turn is associated with the emergence of art practices that foregrounded participation from the 1960s onwards, although some of these practices were already emerging in the 1950s. Fischer-Lichte (2008: 22) argues that the performative turn equates to the 'dissolution of boundaries in the arts', where '[t]he pivotal point ... is no longer the work of art [...] Instead, we are dealing with an event, set in motion and terminated by the actions of all the subjects involved – artists and spectators.' The performative turn consolidated the dissolution of aesthetic representation initiated by the earlier avant-garde art movements of the twentieth century, while also consolidating the dissolution of the barrier between stage and audience through performances in everyday urban spaces. The avant-garde art movements that emerged through the post-1960s performative turn generated sensorial and spatial experiences that explored embodied encounters (Neo-Concretism), playfully engaged with the city (Situationism) and experimented with randomness and ambiguous narratives (Fluxus and Happenings).

Despite its relatively low-key presence in historical accounts of avant-garde movements, I argue that the Brazilian Neo-Concretist movement is of key importance to the performative turn. It emerged out of the *Manifesto Neoconcreto* (1959), defending 'freedom of experimentation, return to expressive intentions and the restoration of subjectivity' (Enciclopédia Itaú Cultural, 2013; my translation). It sought the 'recovery of the creative potential of the artist – no longer considered an inventor of industrial prototypes – and the effective incorporation of the spectator – who, by touching and manipulating the works, becomes an integral part of them' (Enciclopédia Itaú Cultural, 2013; my translation). Hélio Oiticica and Lygia Clark were key artists associated with the Neo-Concretist movement, fusing avant-garde art and popular forms of expression. Osthoff (1997: 280) points out that the Neo-Concretists sought to question representation in art by moving away from visuality and foregrounding the body, 'exploring haptic space through tactile, auditory, olfactory and kinetic propositions'. They 'created unique universal interactive vocabularies' through their work with 'manipulable objects, immersive environments and experiential propositions based on wearable works' (Osthoff, 1997: 280).

These vocabularies are being reclaimed through the rapid rise of digitally mediated wearable technologies that reconfigure embodied encounters in public space. For example, Clark's *Dialogue* (1968) – consisting of two pairs of goggles connected by a retractable side frame that was meant to be used by two participants – is reminiscent of contemporary augmented reality (AR) and virtual reality (VR) headsets, through their shared aim of focusing the user's vision for a specific task. In the case of *Dialogue*, the focus was the participants' eyes, as it 'restrict[ed] the visual field of the two participants to an eye-to-eye exchange [towards the aim of] merging interactivity and dialogism' (Osthoff, 1997: 283).

Oiticica developed wearable creations such as the *Parangolés*, which consisted of wearable colourful draped fabrics of variable shapes that were meant to be worn by the participants in any way that they wished. They were conceived as 'proposals for behavior' and 'sensuality tests' and were meant to emphasise 'the fluidity of life in opposition to any attempts to fix and systematize the world' (Osthoff, 1997: 284). The Neo-Concretists attempted to demystify the concept of participation in art. In a letter to Lygia Clark, Hélio Oiticica (in Bishop, 2006: 111) foregrounds the role of relation and the lived experience towards reconfiguring participation:

> What I think is that the formal aspect of this issue [participation] was overcome some time ago, by the 'relation in itself', its dynamic, by the incorporation of all the lived experiences of precariousness, by the non-formulated; and sometimes what appears to be participation is a mere detail of it, because the artist cannot in fact measure this participation, since each person experiences it differently.

As Bishop (2006: 110) notes, the key term for both artists (Clark and Oiticica) was *vivência* (which translates as lived experience), defined as 'the body's heightened sensory presence as authentic, immediate, and resistant to ideological capture'. Oiticica (in Bishop, 2006: 111) states that participation is not quantifiable due to *vivência*.

While the Neo-Concretists constructed situations through embodied practices and wearables, the Situationists (in the 1950s) constructed situations through interventions in the space of the city. Founding member Guy Debord (1995: 135; original emphasis) states the movement's intention to dissolve any form of aesthetic representation: 'This is an art that is necessarily *avant-garde*; and it is an art that *is not*. Its vanguard is its own disappearance.' This initially involved tactics to provoke the audience that were similar to those employed by the Futurist and Soviet avant-garde theatre, as illustrated by Debord's 1952 screening of his first film, *Hurlements en Faveur de Sade*. It had no images and only a few text fragments interspersed with long black and soundless sequences. The audience rebelled and the film was stopped. This fulfilled Debord's (in McDonough, 2002: 47) ambition of 'provoking [the spectators'] capacities to revolutionize [their] own life'. As Debord's work moved towards the space of the city, he became preoccupied with the '*construction* of situations [as] the continuous realization of a great game' (Raunig, 2007: 172: original emphasis).

The Situationists sought to foreground the role of the city streets as sites of social encounters through urban interventions – or situations – that were intended to 'alert people to their imprisonment by urban routine' (McQuire, 2008: 144). This is illustrated by the Situationists' influential theoretical framework, including Debord's (1995) critique of contemporary society in *The Society of Spectacle*. Sadler (1999: 105) points out that the 'situationists' ultimate goal was to reconstruct the entire city.' The Situationist Ivan Chtcheglov argued for the need to '*play* with architecture, with time and space' (Raunig, 2007: 173; original emphasis). However, as Raunig (2007: 173) points out, there is 'little to be found in the extensive texts of the bulletin of the Situationist International … about the way in which the construction of situations and the constructed situation itself may actually have occurred'.

Their ideas where mostly expressed through temporary interventions in the city that 'sought to find – or rather *invent* – disruptions of the familiar' (Raunig, 2007: 173; original emphasis). One of their techniques of intervention was the *dérive* – translated as drift – a critique of functional living. In the *dérive* 'the main occupation was unproductive of anything except encounters with other people and with places, and of ideas about enhancing those encounters' (Sadler, 1999: 93, 94). They were also expressed through unconventional techniques of mapping, such as Paul-Henri Chombart-de-Lauwe's mapping of the movements of a female student living in Paris, which intended to evoke the standardised and meaningless life of the everyday citizen – described by Debord (in Sadler, 1999: 94) as evidence of 'the narrowness of the real Paris in which the individual lives'.

As Raunig points out, the Situationists foregrounded the potential of aesthetic intervention in the city as a form of experience and as a form of resistance against capitalism's performance: 'The potential of experiencing the city is developed as the production of desire and the possibility of directly, "situatively" resisting the objectively posed "situations" of capitalist societization' (Raunig, 2007: 174). The Situationists' term *viveurs* (similar to the Neo-Concretists' *vivência*, or living) represented their desire to question and reinterpret the everyday routine of urban life mediated by the capitalist machine (Raunig, 2007: 175). Contemporary performance art shares with the Situationist movement the ability of displacing everyday life through temporary situations that are assembled as open-ended narratives.

This element of openness was also a defining factor of Happenings and Fluxus, two important movements associated with the performative turn emerging in New York from the 1950s onwards. Happenings emerged as a 'late-fifties art form in which all manner of materials, colors, sounds, odors, and common objects and events were orchestrated in ways that approximated the spectacle of modern everyday life' (Kelley in Kaprow, 1993: xii). The term happening was defined by Alan Kaprow, the key figure of the movement. Participation was the essence of Happenings, as Kelley (in Kaprow, 1993: xviii) states: 'To Kaprow, participation is whole: it engages both our minds and bodies in actions that transform art into experience and esthetics into meaning. Our experience as participants is one of meaningful transformation.'

Kaprow (1993: 7, 9) states that Happenings would tap into the material world of everyday life and reveal its hidden potential:

> Objects of every sort are materials for the new art: paint, chairs, food, electric and neon lights, smoke, water, old socks, a dog, movies, a thousand other things that will be discovered by the present generation of artists. Not only will these bold creators show us, as if for the first time, the world we have always had about us but ignored, but they will disclose entirely unheard-of happenings and events.

As Judith Rodenbeck (2011: 5) notes, happenings are part of the 1950s renewal of the New York art scene that 'had begun to produce event-structures, performances with one foot in the theater and the other in collage tradition'. According to Rodenbeck (2011: 9), Kaprow chose the term happening to 'avoid associations ... with the theater and to conjure more popular kinds of events – sporting events, for example, or rallies'. Happenings' performances unfolded through events that were not bounded by traditional narrative scripts, fixed roles or stages. Instead, they were bounded by randomness, as Rodenbeck (2011: 30) points out: 'The happenings that would emerge presented an aleatoric performance paradigm structured by a score, with varied options for roles, site, and props. Action was task-driven and discrete ... the scores often resembling charts and musical scores more than they did traditional theatrical scripts.'

John Cage's experimental scores underlined Happenings' foregrounding of the element of chance and indeterminacy and of the individuality of each performance despite the suggestive determinacy of the score, as he points out: 'An indeterminate piece ... even though it might sound like a totally determined one, is made essentially without intention so that, in opposition to music of results, two performances of it will be different' (John Cage in Goldberg, 1996: 124). This is best illustrated by Cage's silent musical piece *4'33"* (1952), where he sat at a piano and turned over the sheet music pages for the duration of the score without playing the piano. In doing so, John Cage 'removed expressivity from duration, harmony, and touch, relying on the auditory capacities of his audience to "play" the piece' (Rodenbeck, 2011: 250). According to Rodenbeck (2011: 250; original emphasis): 'Cage contended that his composition produced an *active* kind of listening [that renounced] interpretive closure.'

As in Neo-Concretism, there was a strong emphasis on embodied interaction. For Kaprow's first happening – *18 Happenings in 6 Parts* (1959) – performed in the Reuben Gallery in New York, he issued invitations stating that: 'You will become a part of the happenings; you will simultaneously experience them' (Kaprow in Goldberg, 1996: 128). It consisted of a sequence of events spread across three different rooms. The events had no discernible connection between them, as Goldberg describes:

> In the three rooms thus created, chairs were arranged in circles and rectangles forcing the visitors to face in different directions. Coloured

lights were strung through the subdivided space; a slatted construction in the third room concealed the 'control room' from which
performers would enter and exit. Full-length mirrors in the first
and second rooms reflected the complex environment. Each visitor
was presented with a programme and three small cards stapled
together ... Spectators were warned to follow instructions carefully.
(Goldberg, 1996: 128)

The performance was defined by the ambiguity of the purpose of the
props and room arrangements and also of the narrative. It also challenged the audience to actively partake in and reflect upon the performance, as Rodenbeck (2011: 250; original emphasis) points out:
'It activated the audience in several ways: by breaking the crowd up
into clusters and moving those clusters around in response to audio
cues, by allowing for an inordinate amount of "free" time for the
audience to mill between parts, and by *not* providing a coherent
whole view or narrative.'

Happenings also incorporated critiques of contemporary society
practices. Kaprow's *Bon Marché* (1963) consisted of a surreal participatory performance that took part as a journey inside a Parisian
department store outside of working hours. Featuring a critique of
processes of 'labor, circulation, the gendering of consumption [and]
the circulation of "bread"' (as symbolic of money), the performance
triggered interaction between strangers through a set of instructions (Rodenbeck, 2011: 63). One reviewer (Sheffy in Rodenbeck,
2011: 63) described the oddity of the narrative prompts of the
performance:

> We were handed packages ... containing stones, and told to ask our
> neighbors 'Have you got the bread?' (i.e. money). We were also given
> explicit instructions to ignore the blaring loudspeaker giving weather
> reports, the odd, half-naked man slithering through the aisles, and the
> girls standing on counters and being wound and unwound in ropes.

Fluxus emerged from a group of artists that were previously
involved in Happenings, and also employed indeterminacy in narratives with socially constructive objectives that were open to the performative interpretation of participants. They organised ensemble
events that were monomorphic, structured on puns, and that followed a model of 'low theater, cheap entertainment [and] carnival

fare' (Rodenbeck, 2011: 251). For example, George Brecht's (in Sell, 2008: 140; original emphasis) *Tea Event* (1961) employed a minimalist, haiku-like score suggestive of Japanese traditional tea ceremonies that – despite its clear instructions and outcomes – was open to individual interpretation and performance by participants:

Tea Event
Preparing
Empty Vessel

Rodenbeck (2011: 251) argues that 'both happenings and Fluxus events were devised as critiques of the dealer-gallery-museum system and of notions of the art experience as grounded in anything but the everyday'. The grounding of these events in everyday life enabled them to counter systematisation and categorisation despite their use of scripts, score sheets and instructions.

The movements associated with the post-1960s performative turn share with contemporary performance art the features of indeterminacy, embodied interaction and the prompt for participants to interpret the artistic narrative through their own subjectivity. The somewhat radical and at times surreal outcomes of performance art events of the post-1960s movements are not completely absent from contemporary performance art events. On some occasions, these outcomes emerged through unexpected intervention from unsuspecting bystanders, such as in the example of Dany's conversation with a stranger over a beer mat (as described in Chapter 2) in *A Machine To See With*. On other occasions, it emerged from radical and non-conformist interpretations of the narrative by participants as they actively interfered with the artistic narrative, leading to situations that were completely out of the control of the artists. This is illustrated by an incident during the Sundance Film Festival premiere of *A Machine To See With*, where participants who had previously taken part in the performance hijacked another participant. As Blast Theory artist Nick (in Dias, 2012a) describes:

We had one instance of people who'd done the project and, knowing where one of the start positions were, they were driving past in a van and saw someone waiting to start. They pulled up, they opened the side of the van and they said: 'Get inside!' And they then drove that person, I think, all the way to the end, all the way to the bank and then dropped them off and said: 'This is where you are going', and then left them there. And I think they also took this circuitous route round town.

In this incident, not only was the unsuspecting participant hijacked, but the artistic narrative itself was also hijacked, as it became hostage to an unexpected and highly disruptive intervention that rendered it unsustainable. The hijacked participant ended up partaking in an alternative performance that was not under the scrutiny of the artists anymore, but of participants. This was an extreme example that is reminiscent of Blast Theory's *Kidnap* (1998), which I described in Chapter 1. While these examples are at the more transgressive end of the performative scale, they are not representative of the majority of contemporary performance art events, and in particular those that involve the use of digital media technologies emerging from the 1990s onwards. The latter draw from a lineage of participatory art performances and installations employing computers, electronic devices and sensor technologies that can be traced back to the 1960s, and that involve an assemblage of art and science.

Aesthetic machines and the digital paradigm

Early aesthetic experiments with electronic and digital technologies emerged in parallel with the avant-garde art movements of the 1960s performative turn, and sometimes (as was the case with Fluxus) emerged from within these movements. These experiments did not share the futurists' extrovert bravado and glorification of the machine, but rather revealed the potential of assembling art with electronics, computers and the emerging discipline of cybernetics. In doing so, they paved the way for contemporary digitally mediated performance art events. Artist Nam June Paik, who was involved in the Fluxus movement, deconstructed media apparatuses and enabled participants to manipulate electronic signals in his interactive installations. In *Participation TV* (1963), 'visitors spoke into a microphone to visually mutate abstract electronic images on a video monitor' (Dixon, 2007: 93). And in *Random Access* (1963), 'strips of audio tape were hung on a wall for spectators to play by running them over the playback head of a magnetic tape player' (Dixon, 2007: 109). Paik's aesthetic machines deconstructed the procedural logic of electronic media devices, enabling participants to distort electronic signals through an open-ended form of participation.

A key event of the conflation of art and computers was the Cybernetic Serendipity exhibition that took place in the Institute of Contemporary Arts (ICA) in London in 1968. It showcased a collection of innovative interactive installations enabled by a collaboration between 'artists, engineers, and computer systems designers' (Dixon, 2007: 101). The exhibition drew an eclectic crowd together, as a review of the exhibition in the *Evening Standard* newspaper (in Dixon, 2007: 102) at the time suggested: 'Where in London could you take a hippy, a computer programmer, and a ten-year-old schoolboy and guarantee that each would be perfectly happy for an hour without you having to lift a finger to entertain them?'

The artworks displayed in the Cybernetic Serendipity exhibition foregrounded the artistic potential of the computer's procedural logic as a non-human actant. Yet the potential of the exhibition was defined by assemblages of human and machine agency, and therefore it stands in contrast to the futurists' bravado of the superiority of the machine half a century earlier. Margaret Masterman's *Computerized Haiku* (1968) – one of the most popular installations of the exhibition – was influenced by traditional Japanese haiku poetry. It combined human and machine input, as Dixon (2007: 101) describes:

> The computer was equipped with a thesaurus and programmed with semantic directives and an algorithm using a haiku-frame corresponding to the pattern of the Japanese poem: three lines of 5, 7, and 5 syllables. Users chose a number of single words from different menus corresponding to different frames, and the computer filled in the gaps using its thesaurus to produce a completed haiku.

While the computer system was being controlled by the procedural logic of an algorithm, it enabled, as Dixon (2007: 101) argues, a 'creative partnership and cybernetic feedback relationship between human and machine'. Masterman (in Dixon, 2007: 101) provides an example of one of the completed haikus:

ALL BLACK IN THE MIST,
I TRACE THIN BIRDS IN THE DAWN.
WHIRR! THE CRANE HAS PASSED.
ALL GREEN IN THE BUDS,
I FLASH SNOW PEAKS IN THE SPRING.
BANG! THE SUN HAS FOGGED

While Masterman's *Computerized Haiku* and Paik's *Random Access* shared the ability to assemble human and machine agency, they differed in how they dealt with the machine agency. *Computerized Haiku* demanded human input in the form of precise informational signs (words) that were processed through algorithms. This is indicative of a stable feedback loop in cybernetic terms, where the computer is merely an input/output device waiting for input from the participant and following procedural rules to provide a reasonably predictable outcome. In contrast, Paik's *Random Access* was defined by a dynamic feedback loop between human and machine. The audiotape's procedural logic (consisting of information orderly recorded in a linear format on a magnetic tape) was disrupted by Paik's action of pulling it apart and reassembling it on a wall in a disorderly fashion. The end result – in the shape of an emerging audio piece – was dependent on the participant's performative subjectivity as they ran the playback head of the magnetic tape player on the tape displayed on the wall. The participant's performance displaced the procedural logic of the magnetic tape, rather than following a prescriptive mode of engagement with technology (as was the case with *Computerized Haiku*).

As in Brecht's *Tea Event*, which also employed a haiku-type structure, Paik's *Random Access* enabled open-ended participation. Brecht's and Paik's events are examples of the performative disassembling and reassembling of language structure and media forms governed by strict rules and procedural logic. In this process, the outcome is dynamically reshaped by an embodied process that is largely absent from *Computerized Haiku*, where the mode of interaction is pre-empted. While the narrative of *A Machine To See With* is mediated by the procedural logic of computer servers and an automated call centre system, it is embedded with intentional ambiguity and uncertainty, which is a prevailing feature in Happenings and Fluxus events. The unpredictable assemblage of computer code and an ambiguous narrative is further displaced by the participant's encounter with the unruly actants of the mediated city, whose environment is also embedded with computer code.

As Bolter and Grusin (2000: 13) remind us, digitally mediated technologies are remediations of older media forms, and therefore are not necessarily revolutionary: 'Digital visual media can best be understood through the ways in which they honor, rival, and revise linear-perspective painting, photography, film, television, and print.' However, they argue that there is a double logic in the process of normalisation of digital media forms: while they strive for transparency, hiding away their inner workings, they also multiply the media inputs of information. In this process, according to them, 'the excess of media becomes an authentic experience' (Bolter and Grusin in Dixon, 2007: 136). The double logic of remediation that Bolter and Grusin refer to is reflective of our inability to fully comprehend the inner workings and the impact in our lives of digital media ecologies where 'software and the spatiality of everyday life become mutually constituted' (Kitchin and Dodge, 2011: 16).

The digital paradigm that emerges from this mutual constitution (the assemblage of computer code and urban space) has three important outcomes: first, it reconfigures trust. As we become involved in 'a state of continuous electronic engagement with [our] surroundings', as Mitchell (2003: 2) states, we become increasingly reliant on machine intelligence in everyday interactions and the systems of trust that emerge from them. Second, it reconfigures access. These systems are inherently fragmented, difficult to interpret and governed by what Mitchell defines as logic prisons that replace traditional urban barriers: 'Logic prisons define zones of inclusion and exclusion in both cyberspace and physical space. They are built not from stones and bars, but from access management lists, software, and electronic gadgets ranging from RFID tags and GPS anklets to card-key access locks' (Mitchell, 2003: 201). Third, it reconfigures how we participate in the city as it increasingly becomes the domain of machines that not only respond to human input, but also sense and interpret the reality of everyday life autonomously.

The machine as artist

One of the outcomes of the reconfiguration of participation in the city through machine sentience is the potential for machines mediated through computer code and artificial intelligence to replace – or to collaborate with – human beings as artists. As Steyerl (2017: 47) points out, 'contemporary perception is machinic to a large degree'. One of the premises of producing art is to be influenced by and conceptualise what surrounds us. Machine-artists achieve this by sifting through large quantities of data, finding patterns among noise and filtering information through algorithms that have their features defined by programmers. Therefore, as Steyerl (2017: 161) states: 'correlation of pattern is the new model, and similarity or likeness replaces cause and effect'. Google's *Deepdream* is an example of a machine-artist that operates through this new model. It works through what Google describes as 'noise "inceptionism" or "deep dreaming"': *Deepdream* operates by '"recognizing" things and patterns that were not given [and] identifying a new totality of aesthetic and social relations' (Steyerl, 2017: 56, 57). Google's *Deepdream* consists of an artificial intelligence-enabled network of computers that is fed millions of pictures and is subsequently programmed to interpret specific objects as other structures, such as, for example, interpreting a tree as a building (Russon, 2015). The end result is the generation of 'artworks' that are unusual, unsettling and disturbing, such as a plate of spaghetti with meatballs in the shape of dogs' faces and eyes.

As machines become autonomous artists and mediators of everyday life, we partake in an inverted model of the Turing test, which states that machines can think if they can 'pass as a human being' while answering questions. We must now prove to machines that we are human beings through the 'most mechanical and mindless activity, namely reading and copying a string of symbols' (Steyerl, 2017: 159). Steyerl is referring to CAPTCHA, a user identification technology widely used for security in websites, which ask us to identify features in images to prove that we are not robots prior to accessing specific content. As our own nature is translated by machines as a string of correlated patterns, Steyerl

(2017: 160) ponders if 'mathematics thus finally [became a] being'. Statistical modelling, pattern recognition and algorithmic scoring have transformed art into a game, where art is categorised, scored and commoditised, and where the most 'original' abstract patterns are derived from the same set of data with slight algorithmic variations, a process defined by Jerry Saltz (in Steyerl, 2017: 167) as 'crapstraction'.

This process foregrounds the increasing role of artificial intelligence in assemblages of the aesthetic machine and the digital paradigm that is algorithmic in essence. This is illustrated by the new standard for art curation based on gamification, scores and ranking, as Steyerl (2017: 164) points out: 'For artists, this is a daily reality. Various algorithmic scores, such as those computed (or conjectured) by companies like Artfacts or Art Rank, reflect different interpretations and quantification of past and future measures of success.' It is worth reflecting on this outcome by referring to Guattari's (1995: 107) argument that the creativity of the aesthetic paradigm is assembled with the creativity of technoscience, but only if we 'shed our mechanist visions of the machine'. If the procedurality of the computer becomes the main register for art projects, their ability to enable reflection is lost in the quest for quantifying and commoditising art, where the benefits of hybrid human-machines are replaced by an overwhelming focus on the prowess of future technical machines.

The translation of this mechanistic model from the art world – based on 'crapstraction' and art curation through pattern recognition, quantification and gamification – to the machinic city, is a process that demands reflection on its future consequences. One of the most compelling examples of algorithmic gamified control in urban space is China's Social Credit System, an ongoing program aimed at creating a countrywide social scoring system for the stated purpose of encouraging trustworthiness among citizens (Kobie, 2019). By combining public and private database records – including social media data – with mass surveillance through facial recognition cameras (moderated by artificial intelligence), China aims to give each citizen a 'unified social credit code' (Kobie, 2019). By identifying social credit offences – 'from not paying individual taxes or fines to spreading false information and taking drugs [and also] more minor violations [including] using expired tickets, smoking on a train or not walking a dog on a leash' – the Chinese government aims to separate trustworthy from non-trustworthy citizens (Kuo, 2019). As Kuo states: 'according to a government document about the system … the aim is to "allow the trustworthy to roam everywhere under heaven while making it hard for the discredited to take a single step"' (Kuo, 2019).

In Chapter 6, where I discuss future machines, I will reflect on the implications of the increasingly machine-driven nature of both aesthetic and urban machines and its implications for matters of trust, access and participation. Prior to that, in the following chapter I focus on the element of participation in digital mediated performance art by focusing on the role of the participant as translator of the artistic narrative and also on the importance of dissensus in the machinic city. To illustrate this, I provide examples of performance art projects that operate in different urban contexts and analyse their ability to produce multiple, unexpected and meaningful patterns of participation.

5

Participation in the machinic city

Participation in digitally mediated environments

In order to analyse how participation unfolds through digitally mediated performance art events, I turn back to Dixon's argument (discussed in Chapter 1) about the introversion of the computer paradigm. In his comparison of the Futurist movement and contemporary digital performance, Dixon (2007: 64) highlights the futurists' extreme enthusiasm for the technologies that were emerging at the time. As he points out, the futurists appropriated them in expressive performances, as they singled out machines – 'film, automobiles, airplanes, and ... electricity' – as actants that not only superseded human actants but also replaced them. In contrast, he argues that contemporary digital performance is marked by 'the introversion of the computer paradigm' and the absence of any manifestos (in comparison to the plethora of Futurist manifestos). To a certain extent, this reflects the nature of contemporary technical machines. While the machines of the early twentieth century were 'all out there' (in the physical sense) as they revolutionised transportation and communication exchanges in the city, contemporary digital technologies – despite radically reshaping (once more) social and spatial exchanges – did so through a more inward trajectory.

This is illustrated by the diversity of digitally mediated communication forms emerging in the last few decades – cable TV, the World Wide Web, large urban digital screens, smart phones – that operate by directing our gaze towards screens. But it would be too simplistic to label these as inward and introverted communication technologies.

It is more productive to analyse how the impact of these technologies is felt when they assemble with other actants towards producing unique forms of social interaction, and to reflect on their effect beyond their immediate presence in the shape of screens. To achieve this, we must account for their inner workings and their innovative actant-components as mediators of agency. These include the seamless integration of computers into the real world in the shape of ubiquitous computing (Weiser, 1991), the widespread use of artificial intelligence and the increasing influence of remote computing processes on urban interaction through online cloud computing, video conferencing and real-time online collaboration. All of these factors facilitate new modes of participation.

Performance art events provide a way of analysing the effect of such technologies on contemporary urban living without pre-empting their participatory outcome. They reveal multiple modes of participation that are influenced by the translation of the artistic narrative by the participant, but also by the emerging assemblage of expected and unexpected actants. These do not necessarily fit in with the digital introversion paradigm. To observe how these patterns emerge, it is necessary to combine multiple methods of investigation (interviews, recordings, observations, participation) across different venues, assembling what Marcus (1998) refers to as a multi-sited ethnographic study, enabling a discourse that '[refocuses] ethnography from structure to voice/discourse', and where multiple perspectives – or voices – are assembled together (Marcus, 1998: 66). Another research framework that is quite fitting for the purpose of tracing the multiple actants involved in performance art events in urban space is mobile methods research, described by Büscher, Urry and Witchger (2011: 4) as a 'project of establishing a "movement-driven" social science' where movement is 'constitutive of economic, social and political relations'. This involves a series of techniques that I employed in my research on participation in *A Machine To See With*: observing and following people and objects, '"participating" in patterns of movement while simultaneously conducting research', making recordings on the move (through audio, photos and videos), getting participants to record their own activities and reflexively thinking about one's own trajectory while researching on the move (Büscher, Urry and

Witchger, 2011: 7–9). As I dealt with the unpredictable mobility of actants, I became aware that I was performing research on performance: I had to track participants as they moved briskly through the streets of Brighton while engaging with (and being engaged by) other actants along the way, such as busy traffic, 'fake' participants (the bystander I accidentally tracked down thinking she was a participant) and changes in weather.

Through my observations on *A Machine To See With*, I identified three distinct modes of participation that are not mutually exclusive: play (defined by game-like, immersive and task-oriented participation; exploration (defined by reflective and emotional engagement with the city through the narrative); and critique (defined by the desire to understand the mechanics of the narrative). These patterns did not refer to the level of introversion or extroversion of the participant, but to different modes of translating the artistic narrative and of engaging with the performance. For example, participant Tim engaged with the performance in a playful mode. Tim (in Dias, 2011) stated that he wanted to completely immerse himself in the performance, and described his participation as a fun, exciting and adrenalin-laden experience. And despite his playful engagement with the performance, Tim described one of the highlights of his participation as a reflective and emotional engagement, which is more suggestive of the exploration mode that I defined above. This in turn illustrates how the three modes of participation that I identified – play, exploration and critique – can overlap during any performance of the event.

Tim's highlight was triggered by the narrative's prompt to say goodbye to a pub staff member after listening to the section of the narrative that is played out in a public toilet cubicle (in this case, the pub's toilet) (see Figure 5.1): 'I think the only real social interaction I had was with the woman in the pub when I left [and I was told] to say goodbye. She was busy serving someone, so she couldn't see me say goodbye, so I had to kind of wait and then she looked at me and then I kind of said goodbye and she thought: "What the hell is going on?"' (Tim in Dias, 2011). For Tim, the narrative's prompt was an excuse to engage in an interaction that challenged his normal mode of engagement with public space and bystanders.

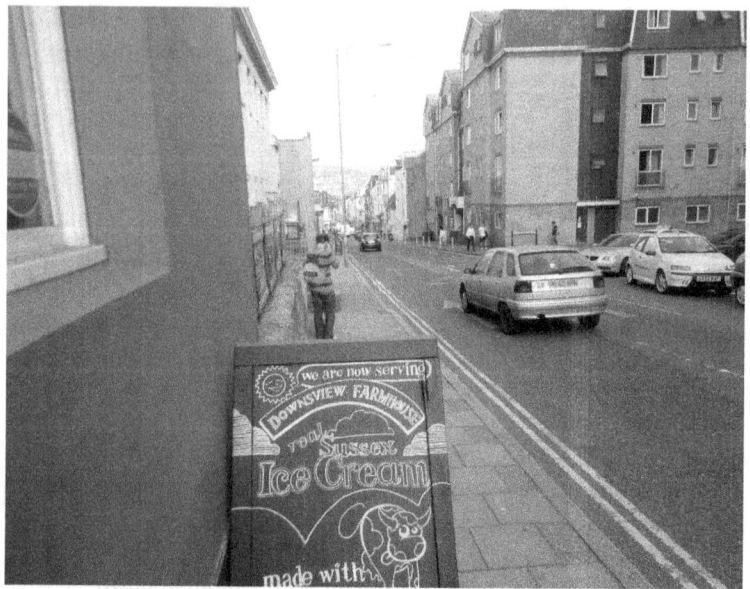

Figure 5.1 *A Machine To See With* – participant Tim outside the
Jolly Butchers pub

The exploration mode of participation involves participatory
nuances that only emerged through my interviews with participants,
such as the serendipitous opportunities for interaction with both
non-human actants (Paul's encounter with the impostor car park
described in Chapter 3) and human actants (Nicholas' encounter with the mother and child in the leisure arcade described in
Chapter 2). Finally, the critique mode of participation is defined
by a reflective and detached engagement, where participants were
preoccupied with trying to understand the mechanics of the performance. However, participants in this category were also exposed to
unexpected and puzzling interventions, such as Dany's encounter
with the beer mat guy (also described in Chapter 2). Regardless
of their mode of participation in the event, participants also demonstrated different modes of interpretation of particular artistic
strategies. For example, the intended film noir effect of the voice
of the narrative (Adams in Dias and Adams, 2013) was interpreted
in many different ways by the participants (in Dias, 2011): Hazel

described it as a 'black and white exchange'; Alex described it as having 'a good sort of tone'; and Dany described it as having 'a kind of poetic element to it'.

These accounts and many others that emerged through my observations of participation, interviews and my own participation in *A Machine To See With* are indicative of the need for a nuanced analysis of participation in performance art events in urban space. Such an analysis must consider not only unpredictable failures, detours and unexpected participatory encounters, but also the many ways in which participants sought to translate and adapt the artistic narrative to their own needs, interests and desires. The same can be said of participation in the machinic city, as our participation in everyday urban life is subject to inefficiencies of technical machines, serendipitous encounters and unexpected interactions with both human and non-human urban actants.

Participation, failure and adaptation

I will refer to some of Rafael Lozano-Hemmer's large-scale performance art projects to illustrate the unpredictability of performance art. Some of Lozano-Hemmer's projects involve custom-made interactive installations in public spaces in major cities across the world that enable participants to engage with large light projections onto buildings, custom-made props and the sky. In a similar way to Graffiti Research Lab's *Laser Bombing*, these projects empowered participants to create and transform large-scale light inscriptions onto public spaces. One of these projects – *Solar Equation* – was part of Melbourne's 2010 annual Light in Winter Festival and was installed in Federation Square, one of the city's prime public squares (see Figure 5.2). It consisted of a visual animated simulation of the Sun's surface activity projected onto a large-scale spherical balloon suspended above the square. The animations were produced through mathematical equations that simulated the Sun's turbulence, flares and sunspots.

During his speech on the launch day, I was present at the performance as Lozano-Hemmer introduced a free app for Apple iPhone, iPod touch and iPad devices that enabled participants equipped

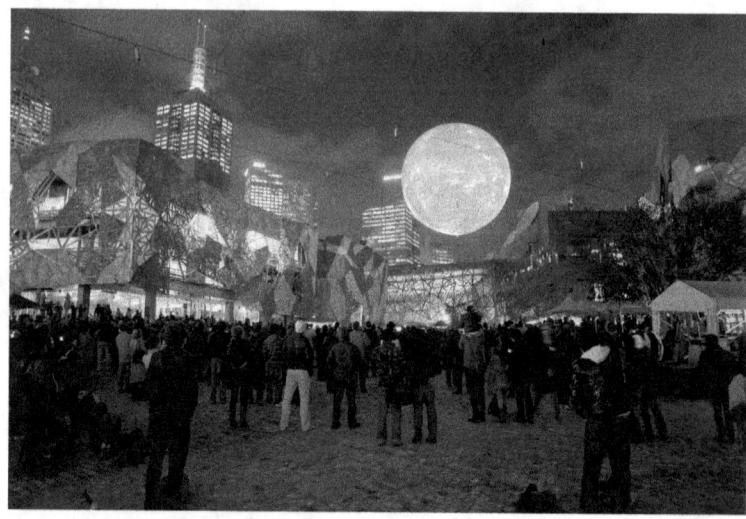

Figure 5.2 Lozano-Hemmer – *Solar Equation*, Relational Architecture
16, 2010. Federation Square, The Light in Winter Festival,
Melbourne, Australia

with these devices to alter the patterns projected onto the balloon. However, the application wasn't yet available on Apple's online App Store due to Apple's extended review process that each app has to undertake prior to being published. It wasn't available on alternative app platforms either (such as Google's Android system). Therefore, participants were unable to download the application prior to and during the launch event. As a contingency measure, an iPad was made available for members of the public to interact with the installation during its premiere. A queue suddenly formed with people eager to interact with the performance through the iPad provided. This triggered a participatory chasm: while anyone present in the square could appreciate the installation's visual impact, only those queuing up could temporarily interact with the installation and reconfigure the patterns projected onto the balloon.

Another large-scale project by Lozano-Hemmer – *Vectorial Elevation* (1999) – had a striking presence in public space and augmented participants' agency through an online website, as described by McQuire (2008: 150): '*Vectorial Elevation* consisted of eighteen powerful searchlights mounted around the plaza, with the alignment of the individual lights remotely controlled by an internet interface. Internet users could log on to the site and design a lighting configuration to be displayed in public. The light patterns changed every 6 seconds.' McQuire (2008: 152) points out that *Vectorial Elevation* reinterpreted the spectacle of large-scale light displays: 'Lozano-Hemmer ... explicitly evoked Albert Speer's notorious "light dome" created for a Nazi Party rally.' Lozano-Hemmer's approach differed from Speer's as he 'aimed to use media networks to redistribute social agency in public space' rather than seeking to convey power through spectacle (as in Speer's approach) (McQuire, 2008: 152). However, as McQuire (2008: 152) points out, the spectator at street level had a very different experience, which is comparable to the experience of the spectators that didn't have access to the iPad in *Solar Equation*: 'While user-configuration of the searchlights via the web created a more varied and whimsical light show than an "official" choreography would have, at street level *Vectorial Elevation* was still primarily experienced as spectacle.'

In *Body Movies* (2001) (see Figure 5.3), Lozano-Hemmer combined projectors and powerful light sources to create a performance accessible to any member of the public. It involved robotically controlled projectors pointed towards a large-scale public facade to project one thousand portraits of citizens taken from the cities where the project was being showcased. However, powerful lights situated at street level and directed at the facade intentionally obscured the portraits. Members of the public could block the light sources by standing in front of them, and in turn enabling the images beamed by the projectors to become visible. Once all the images had been revealed, a video surveillance system triggered a new set of images to be displayed (McQuire, 2008: 153). *Body Movies* generated an unexpected mode of participation, as bystanders unknown to each other engaged in improvised theatrical performances, as McQuire (2008: 153) describes: 'Perhaps the most striking aspect of *Body Movies* was the playful engagement it sustained among groups of erstwhile strangers who came together in public space and discovered that, by enacting a collective choreography, they could affect the visual ambiance of that space.'

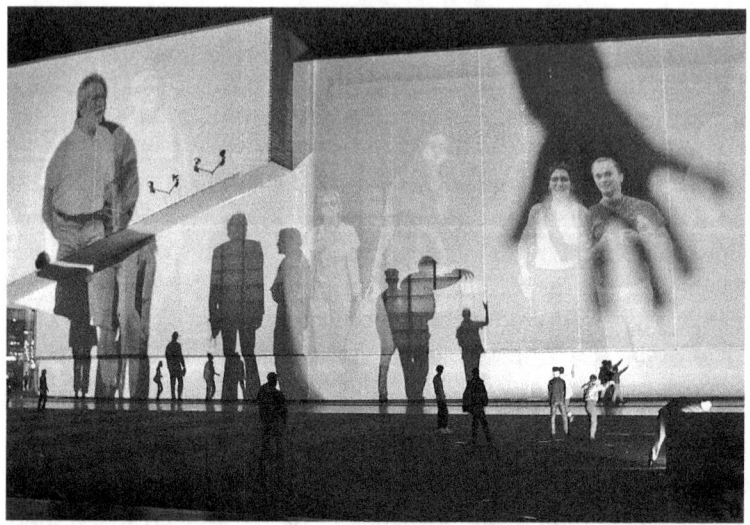

Figure 5.3 Lozano-Hemmer – *Body Movies*, Relational Architecture 6, 2001. Schouwburgplein, V2 Cultural Capital of Europe, Rotterdam, The Netherlands

McQuire (2008: 153) emphasises the role of embodied participation 'in limiting the work's appropriation as abstract spectacle [and] creating a ludic public space'. He argues that *Body Movies* differs from 'more manufactured "media events"', where media is portrayed as being spontaneous while revealing at a closer inspection a more formulaic approach 'to minimize the risk of "nothing happening"' (McQuire, 2008: 154). Instead, he argues, *Body Movies* provides a less machine-oriented and more reflexive experience: 'Rather than adhering to the cybernetic goal of informational speed and transparency, media technology in *Body Movies* becomes the basis for affective experience capable of sustaining *reflexive* public interactions' (2008: 154: original emphasis).

The projects by Lozano-Hemmer that I described above demonstrate how different participatory modes can emerge through different levels of access to the performance and technological failure, but also through serendipitous opportunities for transgressive acts, such as the improvised theatrical performances in *Body Movies*. They also demonstrate how participatory intervention is assembled through a collective of actants. In this distributed process, events such as the spontaneous interaction between bystanders described above and transgressive forms of participation – such as the hijacking event in the Sundance Film Festival premiere of *A Machine To See With* described in Chapter 4 – are testament to the ability of the participant (or participants) to translate the artistic narrative of performance art events in ways that the artist could never have envisioned.

A critique of the emancipated spectator

Contemporary performance art events dissolve the perceived barrier between stage and audience and between actor and spectator, foregrounding the paradigm of the spectator-turned-participant. There is an assumption that contemporary performance art events – which go through denominations such as locative media, atmospheric art, installation art and interactive art – turn the spectator into an active participant. This in turn would entail that there is also the category of passive participation. Yet, assuming we can make such a distinction, how do we know if and when the participant is actively participating in a performance?

The perceived active/passive dualism of participation assumes that the participant needs to be liberated – or emancipated – from their condition of passive imprisonment. In his book *Theatre of the Oppressed*, Augusto Boal (2000: 155) states that: 'The spectator is less than a man and it is necessary to humanize him, to restore to him his capacity of action in all its fullness [...] All these experiments of a people's theater have the same objective – the liberation of the spectator, on whom the theater has imposed finished visions of the world.' Boal suggests a renewal of the figure of the spectator by coining the term spect-actor. According to him, the spect-actor is a spectator that 'is transformed into a protagonist in the action' (Boal, 2002: 141). I argue that two issues emerge from the oversimplification of the concept of the spectator-participant (or spect-actor in Boal's words). First, it directly associates the generation of meaning in participatory art with so-called active participation against a perceived machinisation and stereotyping of participation. Second, it might imply that the aim of participatory performances is to enable a consensual and predefined outcome, in the shape of a desired effect of the artistic narrative. However, as we have seen through the accounts of performance art projects that I have described so far, participants interact with each other and on their own according to their own needs, desires and translation of the narrative of each performance. In this process, artists and participants share intensities and sensations without necessarily achieving consensus.

Rancière (2009a) critiques the ideal of the emancipated spectator in need of enlightenment and the assumption that the production of meaning is exclusively mediated by the narrative of performance art. Rancière's critique is directed towards the interpretation of the spectator as a passive individual that is isolated from both the process of production of the performance (concealing its reality) and the action unfolding on the stage of a traditional theatre setting:

> There is no theatre without a spectator ... But according to the accusers, being a spectator is a bad thing for two reasons. First, viewing is the opposite of knowing: the spectator is held before an appearance in a state of ignorance about the process of production of this appearance and about the reality it conceals. Second, it is the opposite of acting: the spectator remains immobile in her seat, passive. To be a spectator is to be separated from both the capacity to know and the power to act. (Rancière, 2009a: 2)

According to Rancière (2009a: 2, 3), the critic's diagnostic unfolds through two theoretical moves: first, by equating theatre with a 'scene of illusion and passivity that must be abolished in favour of ... knowledge and action'. Second, by arguing that theatre in its traditional form cannot overcome the figure of the spectator. Rancière (2009a: 3) argues that the critic's solution to the perceived need to emancipate the spectator is to abolish the role of spectating and the association of theatre with illusion (or simulacra) through mobilisation of the body.

Rancière argues that there are two formulations that attempt to address the need for a theatre without spectators: either identifying spectators with the characters on stage through empathy or abolishing the distance between spectators and actors. He associates these with, respectively, Brecht's epic theatre and Artaud's theatre of cruelty. In the Brechtian paradigm, 'theatrical mediation makes [the spectators] conscious of the social situation that gives rise to it and desirous of acting in order to transform it' (Rancière, 2009a: 4). As Bishop (2006: 11) states, Walter Benjamin 'explains [how] Brechtian theatre abandons long complex plots in favour of "situations" that interrupt the narrative through a disruptive element' towards the aim of enabling reflection. In contrast, Artaud's theatre of cruelty draws the spectator into the middle of the action: '[It] makes [the spectators] abandon their position ... they are surrounded by the performance, drawn into the circle of action that restores their collective energy' (Rancière, 2009a: 8).

Through either reflection (epic theatre) or immersion (theatre of cruelty), the elimination of the figure of the spectator is accomplished to satisfy its critics. Dismissing the claim of the 'death of the spectator', Rancière (2009a: 14) argues that a certain distance must remain between the artist and the spectator; yet this does not imply that the artist alienates the spectator. Instead, he states that the artist seeks to generate an intensity of feeling that is activated through performance: 'It will be said that, for their part, artists do not wish to instruct the spectator. Today, they deny using the stage to dictate a lesson or convey a message. They simply wish to produce a form of consciousness, an intensity of feeling, an energy for action' (Rancière, 2009a: 14).

Rancière states that we are always already spectators. Faced with the increasingly complex and hybrid set of theatrical techniques that defines contemporary performance art, he argues that there are three paths that artists might follow. First, a path that ascribes to the 'total artwork', where art becomes life and any distance between them is eliminated. He equates this to 'outsize artistic egos or a form of consumerist hyper-activism' (Rancière (2009a: 21). Second, a postmodern approach where there are no fixed roles or identities (such as between artist and spectator, or spectator and actor), or separation between the virtual and the real. Rancière argues that this approach leads to stultification as it 'enhance[s] the effect of the performance without questioning its principles' (2009a: 21). And finally, the vision that Rancière supports: one that foregoes the desire to 'transform representation into presence and passivity into

activity', but instead restores performative theatre with 'the telling
of a story, the reading of a book, or the gaze focused on an image';
Rancière emphasises that this involves 'linking what one knows with
what one does not know; being at once a performer deploying her
skills and a spectator observing what these skills might produce in a
new context among other spectators' (2009a: 22).

The spectator as translator of artistic narrative

Rancière's argument is constructed on the assumption that the artist
narrates, and the spectator translates. And while collaboration
might occur between artist and spectator in performance art events,
it is not a prerequisite for the generation of meaning. In this process
of narration and translation, the artist does not relinquish their role
as an author, nor does the spectator need to accept the artist's vision
at face value. To illustrate this, Rancière (2009a: 22) uses the metaphor of the idiom to describe the artist's vision and its subsequent
reinterpretation, which is yet to be realised:

> Artists construct the stages where the manifestation and effect of
> their skills are exhibited, rendered uncertain in the terms of the new
> idiom that conveys a new intellectual adventure. The effect of the
> idiom cannot be anticipated. It requires spectators who play the role
> of active interpreters, who develop their own translation in order to
> appropriate the 'story' and make it their own story. An emancipated
> community is a community of narrators and translators.

Rancière's argument draws from Umberto Eco's (1989) earlier
conceptualisation of the open work, published in his book *The
Open Work* at the dawn of the 1960s performative turn. While
Eco argues that a work of art is a 'complete and closed form in its
uniqueness as a balanced organic whole', he states that it remains
'an open product on account of its susceptibility to countless different interpretations' (Eco, 1989: 4). Therefore, as he states: 'every
work of art is an interpretation and a performance of it' (Eco,
1989: 4). It is worth noting that Eco referred mostly to literary
works, music and visual arts, yet his argument applies equally to
performance art events. His definition of the open work denies the

foreclosing of the meaning of performance art events or their strict categorisation through a single theme or definition, such as political, tactical, social, playful, and so on. For example, as I discussed earlier, participants in *A Machine To See With* engaged with the narrative in many different ways, by playing it as a game, emotionally engaging with its narrative or simply through a more critical and detached form of participation while trying to understand the mechanics and objectives of the performance. Regardless of Blast Theory's aim to generate reflection on the main themes behind *A Machine To See With* (tyranny of consumption, financial crisis and cinema), the level of participant awareness of these themes varied significantly, due to either their inability to spot some of these themes in the narrative or their own decision to ignore them.

Performance art, dissensus and contemporary urban living

The process of narration and translation that occurs between the artist and the spectator-participant implies that there is no process of consensual generation of meaning or fixed participatory outcomes. Instead, there is an expectation that every actant involved in the performance – artists, participants, bystanders, communication technologies, urban landscape, and so on – will participate in this process through a relational distribution of agency. Rancière defines this as a process of weaving together a 'sensory fabric', which is initiated by the artist:

> What the artist does is to weave together a new sensory fabric by wresting percepts and affects from the perceptions and affections that make up the fabric of ordinary experience [...] Human beings are tied together by a certain sensory fabric, a certain distribution of the sensible, which defines their way of being together; and politics is about the transformation of the sensory fabric of 'being together'. (Rancière, 2009a: 56)

In this sensory fabric, dissensus emerges as an outcome of the distribution of the sensible against the assumption that there is 'a reality concealed behind appearances [or] a single regime of presentation and interpretation of the given imposing obviousness on all'

(Rancière, 2009a: 48, 49). Dissensus enables 'both the obviousness of what can be perceived, thought and done, and the distribution of those who are capable of perceiving, thinking and altering the coordinates of the shared world' (Rancière, 2009a: 49). This provides an alternative against the analysis of performance art (or art in general) as enabler of consensus, where meaning is pre-empted in favour of a common interpretation of the artistic narrative. Rancière (2009b: 115) argues that consensus is only achieved by denying the political role of dissensus: 'Consensus ... defines a mode of symbolic structuration of the community that evacuates the political core constituting it, namely dissensus.'

Rancière's analysis of dissensus in participation uncovers the role that art might play in reinterpreting cosmopolitanism. According to Papastergiadis (2012: 81), aesthetic cosmopolitanism reflects a process of world-making that is undergone through cosmopolitan imaginary rather than a simple quest for openness or a utopian quest for universal equality. In Rancière's terms, according to Papastergiadis (2012: 97), the critical stance of art is not to confront power or to claim its independence from it, but rather to find 'ways to rework the meaning and form of power through collaborating with the public'. This ties in with Stengers' (2005: 995) conceptualisation of cosmopolitics as a combination of the articulations of multiple and divergent worlds (the meaning of cosmos) and a 'space for hesitation' (the task of politics). Therefore, art foregrounds its potential to promote a form of cosmopolitanism – or cosmopolitics – that accommodates dissensus (or difference) and generates liminal spaces that are not tied to prescriptive outcomes, empty claims of autonomy or universal interpretations.

A participatory account of *Ciudades Paralelas*

To illustrate this process in more detail, I will provide a participatory account of a project that has generated performative interventions in functional urban spaces. In June 2012 I travelled to Cork in Ireland to participate in a series of performance art events of the project *Ciudades Paralelas* (Parallel Cities) curated by Lola Arias and Rimini Protokoll artist Stefan Kaegi during the Cork

Midsummer Festival. Lola Arias is an Argentine writer, theatre and film director and performer and has worked with documentary theatre since 2007. In 2010 she curated *Ciudades Paralelas* with Kaegi, described in her website as a 'festival of urban interventions' (Arias, 2019). Stefan Kaegi is one of three artists of Rimini Protokoll (along with Helgard Haug and Daniel Wetzel), described as a 'team of author-directors' working since 2000 'in the realm of theater, sound and radio plays, film and installation' (Rimini Protokoll, 2019). Working individually or in groups of two or three and writing collectively under the Rimini Protokoll label, they define the 'focus of their work [as] the continuous development of the tools of the theater to allow unusual perspectives on our reality' (Rimini Protokoll, 2019). Their work is described as 'a theatre that is documentary ... relating directly to the world as we experience it' (Dreysse and Malzacher, 2008: 9).

A key aspect of their work is the lack of professional actors; instead, they employ 'non-professional performers as experts of their own life [who] create the performances through their stories, their professional or private knowledge and lack of knowledge, through their experiences and personalities' (Dreysse and Malzacher, 2008: 8, 9). The concept of the expert is 'consciously opposed [to] amateur theatre', as Malzacher points out, adding that 'the real motivation to participate as an expert in a Rimini production ... is not a particular interest in new, contemporary forms of theatre; not an interest in art, but rather in being able to tell your story' (in Dreysse and Malzacher, 2008: 23, 27). The possibility of performative mistakes or failures in Rimini Protokoll's performances due to the limited ability of most of their experts to act in a fluid and predictable way is not only acceptable but desirable as representative of the ephemeral and elusive character of theatre as its essence (Malzacher in Dreysse and Malzacher, 2008: 28).

Some of Rimini Protokoll's performances take place in traditional theatre settings, with seated audiences and a fixed stage, such as *100% Berlin*, a project that 'cast 100 Berliners to play the parts of 100 different percentiles making up a statistical cross-section of the city' (Fordyce in Dreysse and Malzacher, 2008: 170). This project illustrates well Rancière's (2009a) concept of the distribution of the sensible, where the relations between the different

participants – including their similarities, incongruities, disagree-
ments and particular traits – are assembled through a narrative that
foregrounds these differences as they turn into a performative story
of dissensus in the city. Displayed along the edge of a revolving
green circular stage (representative of a statistical chart), the participants had to improvise as they introduced themselves to the audience and responded in their limited time slot (Fordyce in Dreysse
and Malzacher, 2008: 173). As Fordyce (in Dreysse and Malzacher,
2008: 176) points out, the audience 'has the impression of watching democracy in action – a bit messy, unsynchronized, variable
[and] sees neither an overall faceless statistic, nor a series of abso-
lute individuals'. Fordyce (in Dreysse and Malzacher, 2008: 173)
emphasises the character of *100% Berlin* as a form of performance
art (rather than documentary theatre) as 'it tends to take place in a
version of "real time" rather than "dramatic time"'; where real time
is representative of the emerging nature of a performance where
the narrative provides a series of guidelines that must be further
interpreted by the experts on stage.

I was able to see an adapted version of that specific performance –
entitled *100% Zurich* – during the reART:theURBAN conference in
Zurich in October 2012. The most striking aspect of the performance for me was how I felt connected to the 'experts' on stage.
It is as if they had just been pulled out of the audience and thrown
into an unpredictable performance that celebrated the diversity of
Zurich's urban population (they were selected based on statistical
criteria). By giving a voice to each of those 'experts', it enabled them
to express their expertise as a citizen without being constrained by
a specific narrative. The overall impression conveyed to me by the
performance was in clear contrast with my own interpretation of
the urban space of Zurich; as I walked through its orderly streets
as a regular visitor, it gave me the impression of a very organised
and formal place with a cold, detached character. Yet *100% Zurich*
provided me with a completely different perspective of the city as its
embodied actants took centre stage, revealing a diversity of personalities, opinions and facts that made me reflect on my preconception
of the city.

While *100% Berlin* and *100% Zurich* told the story of the inhabitants of the cities of Berlin and Zurich through a stage/audience

format, *Ciudades Paralelas* intervened directly in the fabric of the city through a series of performances taking place in functional and everyday spaces of the city, reconfiguring them temporarily through interventions that included the performance of both experts (in Rimini Protokoll's terms) and participants. Lola Arias and Stefan Kaegi invited several artists to choose a location with a defined type in the city and develop a performative intervention in that location. The chosen types included: an apartment block, a factory, a library reading room, a court building, a railway station, a shopping mall, a hotel and the roof of a building. The project aimed to change people's perception of these spaces through performative events where the performer/experts included singers, writers, residents, passers-by and participants. The official description of the performance stated that: 'The projects make theatre out of public spaces used every day, and seduce the viewers into staying long enough for their perception to change. They invite you to subjectively experience places built for anonymous crowds' (*Ciudades Paralelas*, 2019a). The interventions are described as a form of 'mobile research laboratory … building up an archive of guerrilla tactics for appropriating cities' (*Ciudades Paralelas*, 2019a).

During my visit to the Cork Midsummer Festival I participated in four of the eight interventions: *Hotel: Hotel Maids* (by Lola Arias), *Station: Sometimes I Think, I Can See You* (by Mariano Pensotti), *House: Prime Time* (by Dominic Huber from blendwerk) and *Shopping Centre: The First International of Shopping Malls* (by LIGNA). In *Hotel* (see Figure 5.4), Lola Arias addressed the gap between the lack of acknowledgement of the crucial role of cleaning staff in hotels. Describing the environment of the hotel as a uniform, functional space that we inhabit temporarily and where we avoid the responsibility of cleaning up after ourselves, Arias (in *Ciudades Paralelas*, 2019b) attempted to foreground and give a voice to the 'anonymous beings [that] make our beds, clean our baths, change our sheets'. Pointing out that most of them are non-locals (as are most of the guests), Arias (in *Ciudades Paralelas*, 2019b) questions who they are, where they are coming from and what they do:

Who are these ghosts who come into our room when we're not there? Where do they come from? A war zone, an economic crisis, a suburb?

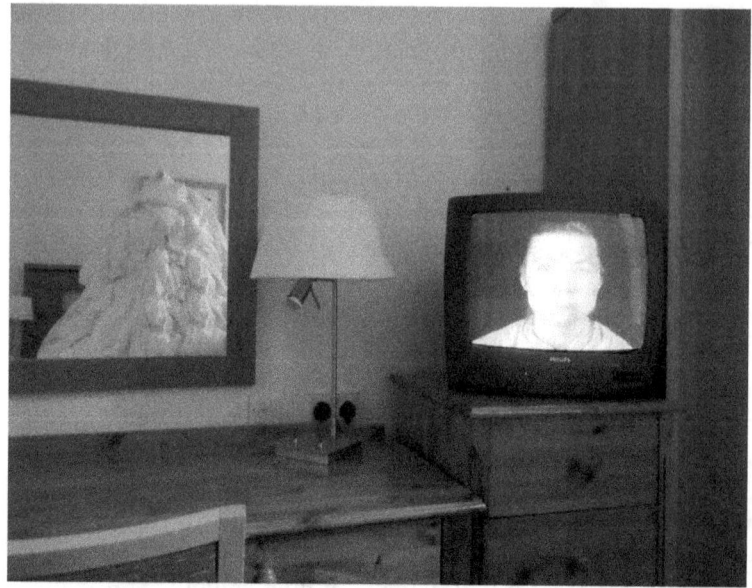

Figure 5.4 *Ciudades Paralelas – Hotel: Hotel Maids*

What have they experienced, what do they know about other people's lives? How many naked bodies, flooded bathrooms, dishevelled beds, sleeping people, strange clothes and smells do they encounter in the course of one day?

Participants are invited to adopt 'the role of a room cleaner responsible for five rooms per hour' (Arias in *Ciudades Paralelas*, 2019b). However, instead of taking over the cleaning duties, participants spend the hour exploring the five rooms and discovering 'portraits of the cleaning staff: films, original voice recordings and photographs that bring to light something of the invisible spirits who clean up after others' (Arias in *Ciudades Paralelas*, 2019b). In the following section, I describe my participatory experience published in my blog at the time, while commenting on my description.

I arrived in the Maldron hotel and was given five key cards for five different rooms. I was told to enter them in a specific order and to exit them as soon as I heard the phone ringing. A festival volunteer guided me to the first room and … I was then left on my own.

I apprehensively entered the first room and was directed to some notes left on the desk and some photos inside a pillowcase. They told the story of one of the [room cleaners] that worked in the hotel. I spent some time looking for other clues. The phone rang. I made my way to the second room. On entering, I was surprised to see a massive pile of sheets and towels on top of the bed that nearly reached the ceiling. It was rock solid. I sat on the bed, leaning against the pile. On the TV set in front of me, the static image of a [room cleaner] [not the one in the photos] suddenly started talking to me, knocking on the TV screen (as if she was trapped inside the TV) to get my attention. While it was a recording, it was quite engaging. She [sounded] quite confident, and eager to tell me about the hard work she undertakes on a daily basis, making me [feel] slightly guilty of all those hotel rooms where I stayed before ('I clean 20 rooms per day, that's 600 rooms per month'). Her image freezes, the phone rings, and I am off to the third room. (Dias, 2012b)

While the experience of the first room was a sort of tame introduction, the surreal experience of the second room contextualised the hardship of the room cleaner's work, with the pile of sheets forming a solid cone-shaped structure as representative of the amount of work and weight handled by each of them on a daily basis. The room cleaner on the TV screen sounded like she was interpellating me in a slightly angry tone (although it was a recording).

The third room seemed to have been customised by a [room cleaner] from Ghana, including photos of her daily routine ... and several references to her home country: colourful bed sheets, sculptures from Africa, a Ghana flag hanging over the window. In one of the photos, she is portrayed praying. The writing accompanying the photo states that she attends [an] Adventist church. There was an MP3 player hanging over the door. I picked it up, and as I walked around the bedroom looking at the photos and reading their descriptions, I was also listening to the [room cleaner's] voice describing her daily routine. She was studying hospitality at a university in Cork and working part-time in the hotel. So far, the three different stories, despite pointing to different origins and countries, all depicted stories of humble origins, hard work, and determination to persevere. (Dias, 2012b)

There was an interesting pace provided by the narrative during my visit to the first three rooms in the performance: the first room provided a gentle introduction to the performance's structure, while in the second room the narrative became more dramatic and I felt immersed in the story of the harsh reality of the room cleaner's work duties. The third room slowed down the pace of the narrative once more and it became more introspective, as I was invited to engage with the everyday life story of one of the room cleaners through props, images and audio. The MP3 player audio recording of the room cleaner's voice telling her story helped me to engage with it.

> The fourth room was the most amazing! [As I opened] the door I couldn't believe my ... eyes when I encountered a real 'forest'! This was quite a surreal and unexpected experience. Pine trees, an overpowering smell from the [layer of] earth covering the carpet, loudspeakers playing forest sounds, carps swimming in the bathtub, and a soundtrack with a voice-over of a male [room cleaner] from Poland. Also, a meter-high sculpture of Jesus on the windowsill and a bible over the sink. The Polish [room cleaner's] voice spoke of his strong opinions: he thinks that the recent death of the Polish president in a plane accident was a conspiracy, and he said he had proof of that. He ... said he wrote edited content for a Polish radio programme that attempted to provide an alternative political discourse. He also spoke of his religious beliefs. (Dias, 2012b)

The fourth room was an overwhelming and surreal experience, and it took a while for me to actually re-engage with the narrative as I explored the room and the bathroom enjoying its surreal embodied experience, which consisted of a natural environment recreated inside the sterile, controlled and functional environment of a hotel room. This part of the performance involved the senses of sight, sound, smell and touch, providing a unique experience. I re-engaged with the narrative through the voice-over that described the personal story of the Polish room cleaner in his own words. I wonder if he got to see the room in its customised state (I would assume that it would be an empowering experience for him). The forest theme was inspired by one of the most cherished experiences of the room cleaner back in Poland: walking through his native forest.

> After the intense experience of the forest, on entering the fifth bedroom I was invited to lie down on the bed and watch a video projected onto the ceiling. The image was [beamed] from a small

projector located under the bed [onto the ceiling] through the use of a mirror. It portrayed an Irish cleaner that worked [occasionally] as [a cleaning] supervisor. She said she hated the hoovering but didn't mind cleaning the toilet. The video displayed her skilfully making the beds and pillows ... she worked really fast and with perfection. She said that every time she entered a room she feared the worst, such as rooms that were destroyed by hen parties. But the worst was when she encountered a dead lady in one of the rooms, after being asked to check [the room] because the lady had the 'do not disturb' sign up for days. Apparently, the lady had overdosed on drugs. Worst of all, the cleaner had to keep working on that day. (Dias, 2012b)

The fifth bedroom tuned down the intensity of the narrative while triggering reflection on another room cleaner's experience of the challenges involved in the cleaning process. The invite to lie down on the bed to watch the video was a relaxing experience akin to the feeling of just having arrived in a hotel room and having a quick rest. It also provided a sense of closure, suggesting that the narrative was about to end. However, this ended up being the prologue to the sixth component of the narrative, which took me by surprise:

The five stories together provided an amazing journey through the lives of these 'invisible workers', with a crescendo of emotions and experiences that brought [me] right into their lives. But that wasn't the end. After hearing the customary phone call to exit the room, I was surprised to open the door and encounter the [room cleaner] from Ghana! This was a slightly [uncanny] experience: meeting a stranger after her daily life was described in reasonable detail in room three. It felt like meeting a character from a book in person. She introduced herself and took me on a quick tour of the hotel, showing the room where her boss worked, where they kept the cleaning equipment and sheets and towels and asking if I had any questions. I nearly felt I should offer the same question, wondering if she [was] curious about her guests. But instead I was just happy to listen to her. Strangely, it felt like she was performing yet another daily chore, but she seemed to be interested enough [in my attempt at conversation] as I asked her about her studies. (Dias, 2012b)

All of the stories were very engaging, and the blurring of the functional space of the hotel room, the narratives of the hotel workers and the physical objects [in] the room triggered in me awareness, curiosity and surprise. Rather than simply trying to make [me] feel guilty listening to [accounts of] the hardship of the hotel workers ('hen parties are the worse, the stains from fake tan are hard to clean'), the narrative brought [me] quite close to their personal worlds, [enhanced] through the [unusual] room furniture and decoration, and the [inclusion] of audio and video [resources] in different ways. I said goodbye to the [room cleaner], and as I walked through the hotel lobby, I felt like I was crossing a line back into the mundane [and] banal … everyday life of being a hotel guest. (Dias, 2012b)

The performance of *Hotel* was my first experience of *Ciudades Paralelas* and the most memorable, due to the personal and embodied experience and the element of surprise combined with a narrative that triggered reflection (on the stories of the room cleaners), guilt (on my experience as a hotel guest throughout the years) and empathy (for the room cleaners). The performance fits in with Rimini Protokoll's artistic strategies to employ experts (the room cleaners) and to create experiences that unfold through real time as defined above.

On that same day, I attended two other performances: *Station: Sometimes I Think, I Can See You* (by Mariano Pensotti) and *House: Prime Time* (by Dominic Huber from blendwerk). *Station* involved passers-by as the main protagonists of the performance, as they were interpellated by messages typed on display screens installed above the main hall of the train station for the purpose of the performance. The written content of each screen was typed up by four authors, who wrote messages from their laptops and mobile phones with the specific aim of interpellating passers-by: 'Over the space and the time they share with the authors, the viewers are able to influence the fictionalization, and become part of a collective story' (*Ciudades Paralelas*, 2019c). As in *Hotel*, the performance unfolded in real time, as the interpellations were fully dependent on opportunistic moments and accurate timing: 'Passers-by reacted with surprise when they noticed that the screen was addressing them … Some people laughed, others just carried on with their lives … a child with her mother spent about five minutes looking at the screen, clapping and dancing after being prompted [to do so]' (Dias, 2012c). In this performance, the experts (the interpellated passers-by) and the audience (other passers-by) were assembled dynamically. *Station* is reminiscent of the score-based structure present in Fluxus performances, such as George Brecht's *Tea Event* (1961); however, in *Station* the score was written on the spot and influenced by chance encounters and the keen observations of the writers.

In *House: Prime Time* (Ciudades Paralelas, 2019d), the stage was the facade of a residential apartment block in the centre of Cork and the residents took on the role of the experts. On the project's website the biography of Dominic Huber, the artist from blendwerk who developed *House*, states that he 'is interested in expanding, manipulating and altering physical spaces, situations and realities by means of precise artistic interventions, inventing new ways of interpreting the world that surrounds us' (Ciudades Paralelas, 2019d). *House* is at the same time an exploration of the social relations in the confined environment of an apartment block, but also a speculative project that seeks to explore new connections between the inhabitants of each apartment and between them and the participants. Each participant is given a pair of headphones connected to a radio transmitter, which enables them to listen to the residents' stories as they engage (or pretend to engage) in their daily activities.

As the performance progresses, the activities become more coordinated, as the project's webpage describes: 'The separate activities are more closely connected than it seems at first – as links, reflections and duplications unfold, the residents' evening rituals begin to look like they are coordinated, almost as if the after-work activities are part of a large-scale conspiratorial choreography' (Ciudades Paralelas, 2019d). As in *100% Berlin*, *House* succeeded in revealing how citizens inhabiting the same urban space (whether an entire city, a neighbourhood or an apartment block) are able to live side by side despite having distinct cultures, ways of living, interests and origins. The performance of *House* in Cork included: 'an Indian couple with two daughters that were [sewing] clothes, a lone engineering student with his turtle tank and guitar, a gay couple who were into music producing and partying, a German girl [who] liked to play darts [and] a Hungarian florist ... Some of the neighbours seemed to know each other, but most of them had nothing in common' (Dias, 2012c).

House unfolded as a crossover of cinematic urban space and theatre play, as each window became a frame for a particular performance as a microcosm of the bigger frame (the facade of the apartment block). One of the most interesting outcomes of this particular performance was the inversion of the gaze at the end: 'At the very end ... the audience/stage relationship had been inverted: it ended with participants looking at us through their binoculars ... The whole experience felt slightly voyeuristic, with the inversion of the gaze at the end providing a slightly uncanny experience: are they really pointing those binoculars at me out of curiosity, or it this part of the narrative?' (Dias, 2012c).

The following day I took part in *Shopping Centre: The First International of Shopping Malls*, developed by LIGNA. This was by far the most demanding performance from my point of view as a participant. It involved active participation inside a shopping mall on the outskirts of Cork prompted by instructions delivered by portable radio transmitters given to each participant. These transmitters were tuned into a portable radio station carried inside a backpack by one of the project's facilitators. As in *A Machine To See With*, the narrative addresses the capitalist machine and consumerism. The project's webpage describes the shopping mall as 'a utopian place' and acknowledges the role of the shopping mall and the products as non-human actants: 'Architecture and merchandise alike seem mute. And yet, they do possess a voice' (*Ciudades Paralelas*, 2019e). Describing the type of projects previously undertaken by LIGNA, the webpage states that they enable 'audiences [to] almost unconsciously turn into subversive crowds' (*Ciudades Paralelas*, 2019e). In the following section, I describe my participatory experience of *Shopping Centre* as it was published on my blog at the time with comments on my description (Dias, 2012d):

> We met at the Cork bus station at 3pm, where a double-decker bus was waiting to bring us to the venue, an undisclosed suburban shopping mall [...] There were between forty and fifty people taking part. On entering the bus we were given a radio transmitter with headphones. They asked us for some 'collateral' as a deposit, I gave them my student card.

I didn't interact with other participants in the bus, but it was obvious to me that some of them knew each other. The slightly transgressive nature of the performance became evident when – in a similar way to the initial narrative prompts in *A Machine To See With* – participants were warned about what to do if they were confronted by security guards:

> [We were told that] if we were confronted by security, we should just pretend that we were listening to music on our transmitters; if – in the worst-case scenario – we were asked to leave the shopping mall, we should obey. However, according to them there shouldn't be any reason for that, as the performance was designed to avoid breaking any 'rules of common behaviour' in shopping malls (is there such [a] thing?). (Dias, 2012d)

We were told to enter the shopping mall and to walk in any direction we wished. The narrative generated a sense of anticipation, as we waited for the radio transmission to commence. It was somewhat reassuring to know that we were part of a semi-organised crowd, and that would provide some damage limitation to our reputation if we were asked to do something out of the ordinary. As the narrative began, it brought the non-human actants – the shopping mall's physical space and its products – to life:

> The narrative initially takes you on a psychological journey exploration of [the] non-human actants [of the shopping mall] and the objectives of the First International of Shopping Malls. It suggests [the process of] 'altering the space in a subliminal way', comparing the mall to a prison and the commodities on sale to hieroglyphs of society, waiting to be deciphered. It argues that the mall is a place where commodities are venerated and where 'visitors are meant to lose sight of any objectives'. It asked the following question: 'When does a collective movement become a demonstration?'. (Dias, 2012d)

As this section of the narrative played out on my headphones, I was browsing some products in a shop, and tried to visualise them as having agency and rights. This was followed by a call for action, in the form of multiple interventions that reminded me of the structure of flash mobs.

> As part of our membership of the First International of Shopping Malls, it suggested that we carry out a number of 'tests' [that] consisted of slightly transgressive acts: giving secret directional signals to fellow participants [...] walking backwards; walking at different paces for different effects ('Walk fast until the façades

become a blur'); [discreetly] exchanging pieces of paper with other participants – where you had written an alternative function for the space of the shopping mall; clapping, joining and rejoining other participants in random walks; and at the very end, [jumping] up and down to the sound of music. I found myself a bit embarrassed to carry out some of the demands [and] noticed the same of other participants. But … it was amusing to see the reaction of unsuspecting security and passers-by. (Dias, 2012d)

The performance certainly caused confusion among security guards and shoppers; some of the latter attempted to join in on the action, which illustrates the multiple ways in which participants and bystanders could interpret the narrative:

I witnessed one of the participants bouncing [around] and dancing at the end, in a sort of uncontrolled fashion; an individual form of expression triggered by the narrative. In comparison, I felt that I was doing too little to justify my membership of the First International of Shopping Malls, but nevertheless it was thoroughly enjoyable to be part of a slightly surreal moment in a place where [people] perform very similar, established routines (browse, buy, eat, repeat). (Dias, 2012d)

The radio transmission was subject to a lot of interference, but this technical failure did not have any significant impact on participation.

The *Ciudades Paralelas* events that I described above intervened in many different ways in the fabric of the city and triggered different patterns of participation. *House* unfolded through an unusual reinterpretation of traditional theatre, where the stage was the apartment block and the audience was located on the street. In *Shopping Centre* and *Station*, the performance demanded the active engagement of participants (in the former) and passers-by-turned-participants (in the latter). In *Hotel*, the experts (room cleaners) mediated the performance through their stories told through different media forms and props, while at the end they directly interpellated participants to get involved in the narrative. The three modes of participation that I described earlier – play, exploration and critique – are all present in *Ciudades Paralelas,* and they were facilitated by different narrative prompts. These include (among many others): the playful prompts in *Shopping Centre*, the exploration prompts in *Hotel* (prompting reflective and emotional engagement with the room cleaners' stories) and the ambiguous event in *House* that triggered critical engagement with the narrative (such as when the experts looked towards participants through binoculars).

While these modes of participation are useful towards understanding the process of artistic narration and participant translation, they are only indicative of the many ways in which participation unfolded during these performances, and the multiple emotional responses triggered in participants. Despite the different modes of participation and emotional engagement, the four events of *Ciudades Paralelas* described above share in common the ability to provide a temporary alternative reality for the functional purposes of urban spaces and buildings while enabling unusual ways of participating in the city. To that extent, they share with previous avant-garde art movements, which I have described in Chapter 4, the ability to play with, reflect upon and reconfigure everyday urban life.

Throughout this chapter, I have argued that performance art enables multiple modes of participation; these modes emerge as an assemblage of the translation process of artistic narrative by the participant with the agency of expected and unexpected human and non-human actants. In this process, performative failure is not necessarily a negative outcome, but rather an indication of the openness of performance art and its potential to generate liminal spaces through cosmopolitics (Stengers, 2005) as it accommodates multiple worlds (cosmos) and multiple points of view (politics), while assembling them with the imaginative and reflective potential of performative narratives. In the following chapter, I discuss the potential of performance art to help us reflect on future assemblages of media, performance and participation in the machinic city, as it assembles with emerging technologies while at the same time probing the social output of these technologies.

6

Future machines

Probing the future

In the *Cyberpunk* documentary by Marianne Trench, William Gibson (in Leonard, 2015) reflects on the concept of the posthuman, as he describes how the condition is attached to the unequal distribution of the future in time and space. Comparing the condition of a millionaire in Beverly Hills who can 'buy himself a new set of organs' and a 'man starving in the streets in Bangladesh', Gibson (in Leonard, 2015) argues that 'the future has already happened' for the millionaire – who he describes as a posthuman being – but not so much for the man in Bangladesh. Gibson's argument suggests that we should consider how certain practices, territorial arrangements, technologies, biotechnological developments, visionary concepts and alternative modes of living can provide us with a fragmented vision of the future and unequal access to its potential benefits.

Many of the performance art projects that I have analysed so far reflect on how digital communication technologies are reconfiguring current modes of social engagement with the machinic city. However, an important role that performance art can fulfil is to probe future patterns of the assemblage of technology, participation and urban space by speculating on the future of urban living, as we negotiate the tension between emerging technologies – sensor technologies, artificial intelligence, nanotechnology and biotechnology – and the desires, needs, rights and ethical concerns of citizens. This is not an easy task, due to the fast pace of social and cultural transformations imposed by digitally mediated communication technologies in the last decades. When speculating about future scenarios in urban space, performance art projects have to avoid futuristic clichés, technologically deterministic narratives and prescriptive outcomes. They must also take into account all the machines that, assembled together, define the current urban landscape but also hint at how this landscape might evolve in the future.

The aesthetic machine of performance art is particularly efficient as a testbed for forthcoming technological assemblages and to speculate on their future agency, foregrounding technical issues and their participatory outcomes. For example, after Blast Theory encountered issues using GPS as a positioning system in *Can You See Me Now?* (2001), they decided to ask street participants in *Uncle Roy All Around You* (2003), to self-report their location through the handheld computers given to them. As I described in Chapter 1, some of the participants sought to take advantage of this technological constraint by reporting their location ahead of their arrival, enabling them to 'get information in advance' from the online players (Benford et al., 2004).

Nine years later in 2011 – at a time when locative media-enabled mobile phones were already widespread – I asked Blast Theory artists Matt Adams and Nick Tandavanitj if they would make any changes to *A Machine To See With* after observing participants taking part in it. Nick (in Dias, 2012a) jokingly replied: 'Hack it as a mobile phone app?' A few years later, Blast Theory started developing performance art projects that used apps as a media form. *Karen* is an app-based project that addresses the 'science of psychological profiling' and that unfolds as a one-to-one experience between the participant and Karen, described as a 'a life coach [who is] happy to help you work through a few things in your life' (Blast Theory, 2015). Blast Theory stated that when they developed *Karen* in 2015, they 'were keen to create a personal and intimate experience for smartphones in which you interact directly with the lead character' (Blast Theory, 2015). *Karen* addresses our dependence on our mobile phones and also how we increasingly interact (at an intimate level) through apps with both people we know and strangers. Another project that deals with similar issues but through a live performance is Dante or Die's *User Not Found* (2018). While *Karen* engages the participant through a standard app, *User Not*

Found takes place in an actual café (that fulfils the role of stage and audience) and is narrated by an actor. Both the actor and participants share the same screen through mobile phones with a custom interface developed for the performance and provided by Dante or Die to each participant. It unfolds as a critique and reflection on our social media legacy, which uses social media as its main media form to relay the narrative.

Karen and *User Not Found* demonstrate performance art's ability to develop innovative narratives that both reflect on and employ cutting edge technologies as media forms as they probe their future social impact. This process involves a renewal of the aesthetic paradigm, which Guattari (1995: 134) associates with creative uncertainty and the process of building new 'existential territories' as opposed to mechanistic certainty:

> Promoting a new aesthetic paradigm involves overthrowing current forms of art as much as those of social life! I hold out my hand to the future. My approach will be marked by mechanical confidence or creative uncertainty, according to whether I consider everything to be worked out in advance or everything to be there for the taking – that the world can be rebuilt from other Universes of value and that other existential Territories should be constructed towards this end.

Through a process of traversing and building relations with emerging 'Universes of value', the aesthetic machine can probe the future, but not predict it or pre-empt it. The twentieth century avant-garde art movements, events and groups that I have previously analysed – Futurism, Neo-Concretism, Happenings, Fluxus, Cybernetic Serendipity and Archigram – have probed future social machines while developing referential concepts and artistic strategies that are still highly influential. If, as Guattari suggests, they resorted exclusively to mechanical (or technological) confidence, they would have repressed their aesthetic potential or ability to trigger desire, which they share with contemporary performance art.

While the future of the city is a source of intense speculation, more often it is outlined through a technocentric narrative, from which social outcomes are drawn out as secondary motifs or materialise as overarching utopian or dystopian statements, with little or no consideration for the relations between actants across the technological, social and spatial spectrums. In the following sections I will explore performance art's potential to investigate and speculate on future machines through two main themes: first, the future outcomes of existing and emerging technologies, through future projections of current patterns of use, social outputs and trends. Towards this aim, I will present an account of my own participation in Dante or Die's *User Not Found*, which was conceived as a reflection on the afterlife of a deceased person's social media output.

Second, the future of cities as complex machinic assemblages where issues of trust, human redundancy, machinist agency, global resources depletion, overcrowding, surveillance by code and cosmopolitanism are analysed through a narrative that artist Liam Young (in Griffiths, 2015) describes as an 'exaggerated present'. I will refer to several projects by Young that address his description, while also discussing another project by Blast Theory – *2097: We Made Ourselves Over* (2017) – which combined live performance and film through a collaboration between artists, citizens and experts to discuss the future of the city at the end of the twenty-first century.

A participatory account of *User Not Found*

Dante or Die is composed of artistic directors Daphna Attias and Terry O'Donovan, who met while studying theatre practice and shared an interest in 'physical theatre and site [and] in manipulating and choreographing an audience' (O'Donovan in Murphy, 2014). Terry states their interest in being close to the audience and how this enables unscripted interactivity: 'I love the immediacy of this sort of theatre and being that close to the audience; you can't sit back and not be part of it' (O'Donovan in Murphy, 2014). Like Blast Theory and Rimini Protokoll, Dante or Die also produce site-specific performances for unusual places, such as department stores, car parks, ski lifts, leisure centres, hotel rooms and cafés. They collaborate with academics researching different subjects (such as social medicine, immersive performance and gender issues), and also with writers, designers and developers (Dante or Die, 2019).

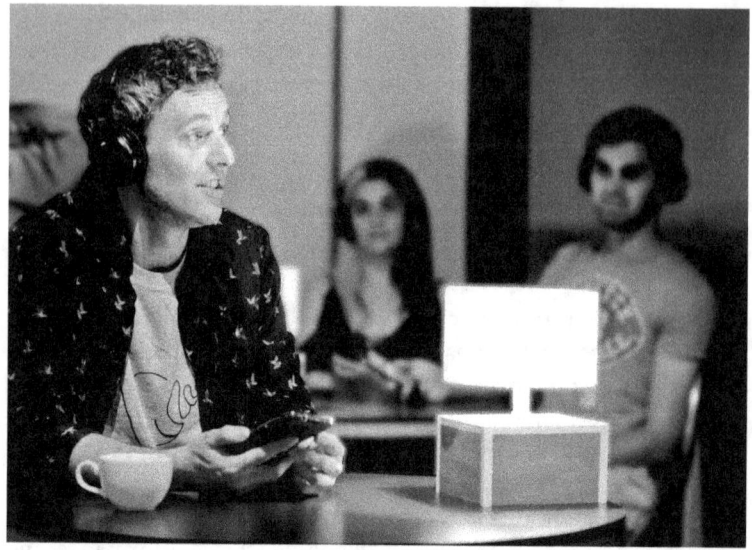

Figure 6.1 Terry acting in *User Not Found* (by Dante or Die)

In *User Not Found* (2018) (see Figure 6.1), they collaborated with academics researching social media (Lib Taylor) and death studies (John Troyer) and also with a cardiologist (for a specific section of the narrative that refers to Broken Heart Syndrome). They also collaborated with writer Chris Goode, who wrote the original script for *User Not Found*. Describing *User Not Found*, Goode (in Dante or Die, 2018a) states that: 'We are ... thinking about how the digital and in particular the devices that we carry with us change our experience of the world and of ourselves and of our relations with other people.'

User Not Found consists of a performance about digital afterlife that was part of the Cork Midsummer Festival 2019 programme. It took place inside the café in Kino, an arts venue located near Cork's city centre, through a combination of live performance (with a single actor – Terry from Dante or Die in his role as Terry), smart phones, audio, video and lighting. The inspiration for *User Not Found* came from an article published by Caroline Twigg (2015) about her husband's sudden death and how she dealt with the issue of what to do with his online legacy. Terry and Daphna realised that this was a topic that wasn't discussed enough, despite the important issues that it raises in relation to 'growing concerns about privacy, data and what remains about us in the ether' (in Stewart, 2018).

They also wanted to address our dependence on social media apps and mobile phones and our 'emotional connection ... with these devices that have become like another limb to us' (in Stewart, 2018). As Daphna (in Stewart, 2018) points out, one of the difficulties encountered was the need to coordinate the production of the project and its narrative with the development of the custom phone interface by their creative partners (the digital creative agency Marmelo): 'It takes so much longer to build an app or change a page of screen information than we're used to ... Terry and I had to learn how to write in great detail what needs to be on each screen so that they could then build it – it took a while to figure out the best way to collaborate.'

During my participation in the performance, I was particularly impressed with how the digital (or virtual) world of the app seamlessly integrated with the physical environment of the café (transformed by the sound and lighting control and production) and Terry's performance.

The narrative unfolds through a fictional story based on a digital media dilemma that the protagonist needs to deal with: Terry's former partner Luka, who died recently, decides to assign Terry as his digital executor. Terry is contacted by the company managing Luka's data (Fidelis) and has to decide what to do with Luka's digital assets, spread out across several social media websites, apps, email and video repositories. Having broken up with Luka months before his death, Terry has to deal with both his grief and the responsibility bestowed on him. The performance lasted for approximately ninety minutes. Participants were seated in the café that had been transformed into a participatory stage and were given an Android mobile phone with a fully customised interface and a pair of wireless headphones connected to the phone. There was no separation between stage and audience. In the following sections I will present my participatory account of the event (in the present tense) while reflecting on the narrative, the technologies employed, the stage and the participatory outcomes.

This is the last of three performances of *User Not Found* during the Cork Midsummer Festival 2019, and the café is full. As the performance begins, the focus shifts to Terry seated at one of the tables as he begins to tell his story. The screen of the phone provided to me started flashing and a message reminds me to put on the wireless headphones (also provided by the artists). From this moment onwards, I can hear everything that Terry is saying while every swipe and click by him on his phone interface is mirrored onto mine. The screen displays a combination of social media apps, other types of apps (such as a 'music for mood' app), full screen videos, emails and memes. Terry occasionally points at participants (including myself) as he tells his story and also sits on chairs next to them, but he is never too intrusive. Apart from these mild forms of interpellation, the performance unfolds through Terry's description of the memories of his ex-partner Luka and the difficult decision that he needs to make.

The age range of participants is quite broad, varying from twenties to sixties; I am sitting at a table with theatre practitioners in their thirties and forties. Most people seem to be seated with other people known to them. A young couple sits across from my table. A guy in his forties in a suit and tie is concentrating hard on the screen of the mobile phone provided. During the performance, my focus of attention shifts: I find myself looking at the screen of the customised phone, at Terry (as he walks around the room) and at other peoples' reactions. I notice that participants interact with the mobile phones provided in many different ways. The participant sitting next to me props the mobile phone onto an object on the table and occasionally picks it up. The guy in the suit and tie looks at the screen regularly. I have a strategic point of view as I am seated near one of the corners looking towards the middle of the room. Some participants are facing the walls and have to turn around awkwardly to see Terry's performance. There is a lot of attention to detail in the production. The audio, lighting and the several screen interfaces of the mobile phone work in sync with Terry's performance, with a clever use of memes and glitch design towards the end that added a comic touch to the performance. The focal point of the narrative shifts between Terry's live performance, the content displayed on the screen of the mobile phone (social media apps, videos, images), an immersive soundtrack and the stage lighting, where lamps on the tables and lighting located underneath them are controlled remotely.

The performance unfolds through nine scenes. The first scene introduces the audience to Terry as he reflects on the space of the café as a place where we 'come to be alone together': 'We're all in the café. The café that doubles as a metaphor. For … Life or something. Here we are. That's all. That's what we do. We come here. To be together. Alone together' (Dante or Die, 2018b: 21). Terry describes a series of archetypal café frequenters while directing his attention to specific participants, as he pretends they fit his descriptions (even if that isn't the case). As Terry mentions a subject called Giancarlo, a 'pansexual flirt [that has never] had to pay for a shot of syrup in his life', he points in my direction. I chuckle awkwardly as I realise that I am the focus of attention for a couple of seconds. An older couple sits on the opposite side of the room and are amused at being interpellated by Terry as he carries on talking: 'The retired couple, Dennis and Barbara. Sit in comfortable silence with two teas and two flapjacks. Maybe it isn't comfortable. Maybe they're screaming inside' (Dante or Die, 2018b: 19).

Terry selects the (fictitious) Relaxing Sounds app on his phone, and all participants see the same app on their phones as it plays the sound of a waterfall. Suddenly the phone shows a screensaver displaying the time and date as it shifts backwards six weeks. The background image morphs from the picture of a sunrise to the shadow of a man. Terry starts getting a barrage of social media and text messages that suggest that something serious has just happened, but he is not aware at this stage of Luka's death (and the messages do not explicitly mention it). As the sound of the waterfall gets louder, the phone shows an incoming call from Luka's mother Maria, implying that she is going to deliver the bad news to Terry. In an emotional crescendo, the scene finishes with a full screen video of a burning object that looks like multiple sheets of paper with gaping holes and warm colours.

The second scene exposes Terry's difficulty in dealing with his memories of Luka. The mobile phone shows blurred pictures of his time with Luka as a form of illustrating Terry's inability to deal with his favourite memories of his partner. As the photos change on screen, Terry describes them in detail while stating that he has no recollection of them – 'I can't picture it […] I don't know what that looked like […] Nope. Not a clue' (Dante or Die, 2018b: 36–8). During this scene, the screen interface acts as a supporting visual guide for the narrative and is not focused on a particular app or phone function. Towards the end of this scene, the photos slowly come into focus and we see a close-up photo of Luka in bed lying down and smiling while staring directly at the screen.

The third scene opens with a comic critique of the assemblage of art and educational practices: Terry receives a condolence email with a video attachment from a friend called Tim, described as a performance artist who 'teaches, mostly, to pay the rent' (Dante or Die, 2018b: 44). Tim is forced to teach his performance module under the new title of Digital and Pervasive Media Arts, despite being described by Terry as someone 'who can hardly even work a toaster' (Dante or Die, 2018b: 44). A video plays on the mobile phones showing Tim doing a performative exercise with his students where they are all holding hands as he states: 'digital means we use whatever digits we have in order to touch each other' (Dante or Die, 2018b: 44). This is followed by an email sent to Terry by Fidelis, the company in charge of Luka's digital legacy. Terry clicks on the video link in the email and it shows an introductory corporate video about the company and the steps necessary to connect to Luka's assets. Terry slowly comes to terms with the fact that he had agreed to be Luka's digital executor in a distracted moment of their relationship: 'He says will I be his digital executor? I say yeah. I take another bite of nectarine. And then I say: Baby you're going to live forever' (Dante or Die, 2018b: 48). This scene ends with the 'I'm Gonna Live Forever' song from *Fame* showing up on the mobile phone screens in a music player interface while Terry does a slow dance around the café with exaggerated body expressions as he lip-synchs to the song.

The fourth scene deals with technological failure and how this affects the transmission of messages: Terry calls Luka's mother Maria and – greeted by the voicemail prompt – starts leaving a lengthy voicemail that is part apology and part reflection on how he regretted being designated Luka's digital executor. He gets agitated and starts swearing while still recording the voicemail. This is followed by him regretting his action as he starts apologising to

Maria, until he hears a beep and a message telling him that Maria's mailbox is full. The voicemail emerges as an inadequate media form to transmit the message between Terry and Maria, and the limitations of the technology (the full mailbox) become exposed. The scene ends with the screen interface of the mobile phone showing a dysfunctional keypad (where the keys are in the wrong place) while Terry is prompted to choose an option from a menu after his failed voicemail. I don't notice that the keypad buttons are in the wrong place, as I am focused on Terry's acting as he struggles to convey his message through a technology that proves untrustworthy.

The fifth scene opens with Terry ordering a cookie from the bartender in the café, who is at the same time a real bartender (she served the coffee that I am sipping as I enjoy the performance), temporary actress and also participant. This sequence blurs the functionality of the café with Terry's narrative prompts and actions, the screen interface of the mobile phone and an elaborate (yet discreet) audio and lighting design. The focal point of attention of the narrative is constantly shifting, as it moves between the phone, Terry's acting, participants (interpellated by Terry) and the ambience of the café as it is transformed by the lighting design. The narrative suddenly takes a surreal turn as Terry mentions a lioness 'coming in through the door of the café' (Dante or Die, 2018b: 55), which is accompanied by a loud roaring sound.

Terry reflects on the immateriality of digital media: 'Here's a strange idea. Someone told me that the whole internet, all the electrons that are in motion at any time that between them constitute the entire internet, together weigh about as much as a strawberry' (Dante or Die, 2018b: 56). Terry opens the Fidelis app and starts scrolling through Luka's digital assets. He selects Facebook and focuses on a photo of Luka having a good time with unknown people and holding a balloon. The balloon becomes a prompt for him to reflect on why Luka left him: 'I never saw him hold a balloon ... what was it that I actively did, that made him feel unable to hold a balloon around me? To express his true balloon-holding self. Is that why he left me? So he could feel that string in his hand' (Dante or Die, 2018b: 59). This section of the narrative foregrounds our obsessive scrutinising of social media and the meaning and symbolic value of its visual props: photos, icons and emojis. It also deals with the difficulty of interpreting the meaning of these visual props, and also our obsession with the process of reflecting on past events as we scrutinise our digital selves stored – with or without our consent – in online clouds of information.

In the sixth scene, the narrative explores Terry's dilemma to decide about the destiny of Luka's digital legacy by posing the same dilemma to all participants, as Terry asks us: 'Listen, what would you do? ... I mean what would you do with all your online stuff after you die?' (Dante or Die, 2018b: 62). Terry's question explores our ability to reflect if our digital selves are actually a true representation of our embodied beings, and if we are willing to let our digital selves die or carry on living as a non-human entity:

> It can all disappear with your final breath. Or it can outlive you. It can remain, to say who you were. *If* that's who you were. So that as long as the digital cosmos survives, you survive, and you'll never be forgiven – Forgotten. Did I say forgiven? I mean forgotten. Forgotten. So. Do you? Reach out and push the button? [to delete your entire digital self]'. (Dante or Die, 2018b: 62, 63; original emphasis)

Terry turns on the Relaxing Sounds app again and, as the sound of the waterfall gets louder, the ambience of the café is flooded with blue light from a light source concealed under each table. The sound and lighting combine to create a dreamy atmosphere similar to the experience of being immersed in a quiet swimming pool in the darkness, as Terry 'slides underneath the table and through people's chairs and tables, floating through the café. Terry's voice [a recording] gets muffled as if he is underwater' (Dante or Die, 2018b: 66). The narrative suggests that Terry is 'drowning in data': 'this body of water / depthless / not really water / but data / and I'm swimming and sinking at the same time / I'm resisting and I'm letting it take me / I'm falling through ... endless edgeless code' (Dante or Die, 2018b: 67). The scene ends with the screen interface of the phone showing the screensaver with the date and time displayed as if a week had gone past (Dante or Die, 2018b: 68). Due to the immersive experience of the room flooded in blue light and enhanced by the audio soundtrack, I didn't spot the difference in date and time.

The seventh scene once more deals with our obsession of scrutinising our lives and other people's lives by trawling through the databases of social media apps. Prompted by the Fidelis account manager, Terry starts trawling through Luka's Twitter account, composed of thousands of messages. Luka immediately starts searching for 'how [their] first night together shows up in his time-line' (Dante or Die, 2018b: 70). He finds a tweet with a link to a fictional French pop star called Laurent Mercier whose love ballad video clip starts playing on the mobile phone's screen. The message written on the tweet by Luka suggests that they both got along very well when they first met: 'Good morning! Waking up into a new world' (Dante or Die, 2018b: 71). For Terry, that social media post represents Luka's love for him: 'I look at the timestamp. Yeah, I'm pretty sure he tweeted this while I was in the shower. That was real. That was a real thing that happened' (Dante or Die, 2018b: 73).

As he keeps trawling through Luka's Twitter account, he reminisces about his memories with Luka through an emotional journey that is intensified by the background music of Mercier's love ballad: 'and on and on goes this ballad / and he's so incredibly untouchably alive / and I realise I'm crying / I'm crying my eyes out here / because suddenly Laurent Mercier / is singing his song to me / and it's about me' (Dante or Die, 2018b: 75). This scene alludes to the potential of social media databases as raw material to construct emotional and personal narratives through the curation of its content by the user. This is similar to the process of montage in film, except in this case the montage consists of social media posts that, depending on the way in which they are put together, might trigger multiple interpretative patterns.

The eighth scene returns to surreal and comic territory: Terry is at home, getting drunk while trying to sleep. He switches off his phone and he starts to dream about a singer that 'looks like Sheryl Crow, but [he knows] she's Norah Jones' (Dante or Die, 2018b: 80). The mutant singer character appears on our mobile phones as a glitch video, and as Terry initiates a conversation with her, the singer's replies and body gestures are glitchy and out of synch. It gets even stranger as the singer opens her hand to reveal a snail that looks like it is made out of soft material with an oversized mouth full of teeth.

Terry suddenly wakes up and realises he was dreaming and decides to go for a walk to a place where he used to go to with

Luka. As he sits on a bench on the top of a hill, the mobile phone's screen displays the image of a cityscape with trees and buildings as the sun rises behind them. In a nod to Simmel's ([1903] 1950) argument that dissociation is a key factor in social interaction in metropolitan life, Terry discusses the city as a place where – as he stated previously in relation to the café – one can be 'alone with everybody': 'I sit on Doreen's bench [name on the bench's plaque] and I look at the city waking up and it's not about me. It's not really about any of us. I mean I know we're all just waking up, that's all a city is really, a bunch of vulnerable people strewn across a map made out of litter and roadworks, but I love the distance that everyone's at, that means I can't see them. I can only see the lights they switch on' (Dante or Die, 2018b: 83).

This is followed by a scene in which Terry visits Maria as she is in a hospital bed being treated for Broken Heart Syndrome, a temporary heart condition that is triggered by stressful situations and intense emotions. As he sits beside Maria, Terry reflects on the relation between different types of machines as non-human actants, as the 'heartbeat' of one of the machines inside the hospital room reminds him of the unstoppable pace of information conveyed through electronic means: 'There are many machines. I don't like them but I'm glad they're there. She should have all the machines. One of them, I don't know which one, is going ping with the exact ping my emails used to make on my old laptop. She's just lying there sleeping and I'm hearing: "You've got mail. You've got mail. You've got mail"' (Dante or Die, 2018b: 90). The scene proceeds with a reference to fingers, as representative of digits transmitting information through embodied touch: 'She can't reach very far. But far enough. I reach out too and my fingers touch her fingers. Mine underneath hers. It's very gentle, and it makes no sound. But information is rushing through my body into hers, and coursing through hers into mine. Gigabytes and gigabytes of data' (Dante or Die, 2018b: 90, 92).

In the end after returning home, Terry decides to flip the switch and delete all of Luka's files, the equivalent of a digital death. This was a slightly frustrating moment, as I did expect a more nuanced resolution for this key moment, or perhaps a decision by Terry to curate the deletion phase. But this radical decision is a powerful representative of the nearly unimaginable possibility of a digital reboot of our lives. To be faced with an empty email inbox or a social media app with no reminders might be seen in this day and age as an achievement. There is a feeling of weightlessness and freedom associated with this possibility, although it is implausible and unnerving at the same time. These contradictions reveal the impact of digital media on our material world, and on our physical and mental wellbeing. They also reveal how the digital becomes metaphorically heavy, making us feel its omnipresence and inescapability.

The ninth and final scene brings us back to the reality of the café, through Terry's invitation to all of us to let go of the digital apparatus moderating our participation in the performance to be able to have an intimate chat: 'I wonder, shall we just ... Can we just talk? Do you want to take these off?' (Dante or Die, 2018b: 98). As I take off the headphones that we have all been wearing for the last hour and a half, it feels great to hear Terry's unmediated voice: 'Hi. It's only me. I don't know what to say, really. I just wanted to say it to you. I wanted the words to travel through the air' (Dante or Die, 2018b: 98). Terry briefly refers back to some of the fictional characters in the café for a last time (Giancarlo, Barbara, Maria) followed by a challenging and slightly uncanny prompt to the whole audience:

> It's not what you keep that defines who you are. It's the things that you let go. So listen: you don't have to do this. This is just, I don't know, just an invitation. If you're sitting close enough to someone else that you can do this, would you just maybe put your fingers on their fingers. Just gently. Just your fingers touching. You don't have to. But if you'd like to make the offer to someone near you. Just touch. Digits, right. Just let that be what we do for a moment. I'm going to go now. I'll let you decide. When you're ready to stop touching, you can stop. And when you stop, that'll be the end of the story. Take as long as you like. Thanks for being here. Safe home. (Dante or Die, 2018b: 99)

This is one of those moments where you are made to feel slightly uncomfortable, but at the same time feel challenged to try something unusual and to reach out to a stranger. It reminds me of the prompt in *A Machine To See With* to give money to a stranger (and

which only one of the participants I observed was able to achieve).
I tentatively touch the fingers of the participant sitting next to me.
The participant on my other side is too far away to reach without
being awkward, so we mutually refrain. As I look around the room,
it seems that most participants have followed Terry's prompt. Terry
leaves the café, the main lights of the café are switched on, and participants start applauding (including myself).

This has been an intriguing journey into our relationship with
our digital selves and the hard decisions that we might need to make
one day in relation to the fragmented assemblage of digital data that
acts as the virtual reflection of ourselves. The participant to my right
(one of the theatre practitioners) expresses her disappointment with
the sudden deletion of Luka's digital legacy, but also states that the
narrative was very good and that she enjoyed the performance. The
way in which the narrative is structured into scenes (or acts) is reminiscent of traditional theatre, and Terry's interpellations (comparing
the characters in the narrative to participants), weren't blatant or
forceful; he never demanded or expected an answer back.

As the performance unfolded by critically analysing our digitally mediated lives through the very own digital media forms that
intermediate this process, it revealed its potential as an aesthetic
machine that traverses the multiple domains – or 'Universes of
value' in Guattari's (1995) terms – that are part of everyday life in
the machinic city, while revealing the potential of performance art
to temporarily reconfigure these domains. Despite the temporary
duration of the performance, the narrative encourages us to translate Terry's dilemma into our own lives. One of the most significant
aspects of *User Not Found* is how it illustrates the influence of 'the
logic of [the] computer … on the traditional cultural logic of media'
(Manovich, 2001: 46). This is carried out by the assemblage of the
narrative and the technological apparatus of the performance, as
they both highlight our level of dependence on the screen interface
of the mobile phone and its associated data streams. At the same
time, the procedurality of the technological apparatus is assembled
with Terry's engaging performance, and therefore the former does
not have a dominant or privileged status.

The aesthetic treatment of the mobile phone's screen interface
also illustrates the influence of the procedurality of the computer on

contemporary culture. This is illustrated by the use of glitch design in the eighth scene in the video of the mutant singer and the digital collage of the snail and relates to the emergence of the New Aesthetic as a visual trend (rather than an art or design movement) that is representative of 'the increasing proliferation of visual languages dependent on self-generative computational structures rather than on natural language' (Contreras-Koterbay and Mirocha, 2016: 9). The New Aesthetic is a form of post-digital aesthetics (or aesthetic machine), where 'art becomes programmable, and design becomes a function of computation [and] the historical distinction between the digital and the non-digital becomes increasingly blurred' (Berry and Dieter, 2015: 2). As Berry and Dieter (2015: 5) state, the post-digital is also representative of the 'issues attached to the entanglements of media life after the digital', in particular what they define as the shift from 'an almost obsessive fascination and enthusiasm with new media to a broader set of affectations that now includes unease, fatigue, boredom and disillusionment'. These issues emerge in the narrative of *User Not Found*, through Terry's frustration as he tries to decode the meaning of Luka's digital legacy, and as the thought of managing it becomes overwhelming. In the end, Terry's decision to delete Luka's digital legacy and his prompt to participants to connect through an embodied gesture symbolises the opportunity to reflect on the overwhelming influence of digital media in our lives.

Collaborative future machines

Other performance art projects explore how future cities might be conceptualised to probe the wider impacts of digital media. Such performances may combine several media forms and modes of engagement. In *2097: We Made Ourselves Over* (Blast Theory, 2017a) (see Figure 6.2), Blast Theory combined live performance with film and an app to create a collaborative platform for discussing the future of cities that was performed in two cities: Hull (in the United Kingdom) and Aarhus (in Denmark) (Blast Theory, 2017a). Blast Theory (2017b) describe it as: 'a science fiction project that took audiences on a journey into an imagined future'. They worked

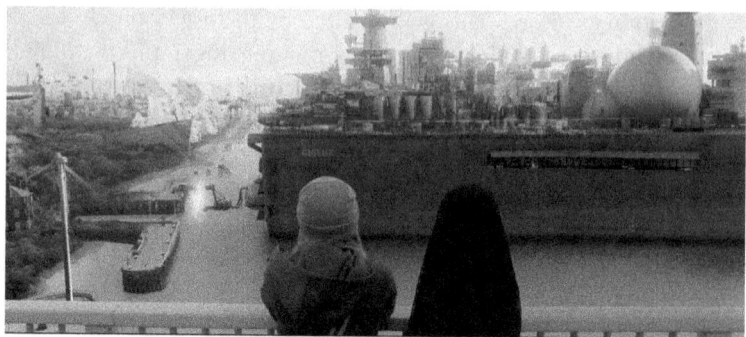

Figure 6.2 Blast Theory – *2097: We Made Ourselves Over*

collaboratively with the communities in both cities 'to develop a speculative vision of the world in 2097' (Blast Theory, 2017b). They included feedback from both residents and experts in several areas of knowledge pertaining to the future, including 'futurologists, technologists and climate scientists' (Blast Theory, 2017b). Feedback from the experts was used to define the overall narrative of the project:

> Three young girls must make a decision which will affect their entire city, as well as members of their own families. The future of the city relies on their ability to embrace the unknown, face the future and act. *2097: We Made Ourselves Over* takes you on a journey to the cusp of the next century. Come into a world where consciousness is transferred from the dead to the living. See molecular harvesters destroy cities and rebuild them. (Blast Theory, 2017b)

In Hull, the performance included two phases. In the first phase, residents queued up outside phone boxes to answer a call from the fictitious character Hessa – 'one of the three rulers of the future city' – as she asked for help. The participants' ideas for the future of the city were recorded during the conversation with Hessa (Blast Theory, 2017b). In the second phase, over the course of five weekends, Blast Theory hosted pop-up film screenings of the films recorded for the project across several neighbourhoods of Hull. Concurrently, a fleet of electric cars picked up participants and took them on a journey with an actor in the role of one of the characters from the narrative of *2097: We Made Ourselves Over* inviting them 'to reflect on the changes they want to take place in the decades to come' (Blast Theory, 2017b).

In Aarhus, the performance unfolded in a derelict velodrome that was repurposed for the performance. Participants where driven by a fleet of electric cars to the velodrome. During the journey, 'a young woman's voice [began] speaking as ... she count[ed] the years ticking by, recounting each decade of the 21st century as it was and how it came to shape the city' (Blast Theory, 2017b). Arriving at a deserted car park, participants were asked to put on a pair of headphones and walk past an illuminated entrance towards a tunnel. At the end of the tunnel, a flood of light blinded participants temporarily, and as their eyes adjusted, they found themselves in the centre of the velodrome, where 'a field marked out with a grid of light [came] into focus' (Blast Theory, 2017b). As the participants explored the field, they were able to 'unearth recordings from the three girls who have now come to rule over the city' (Blast Theory, 2017b). Afterwards, participants were taken to a place in the velodrome where they had a panoramic view of Aarhus and were interviewed about their vision of the future (Blast Theory, 2017b).

The embodied interaction of *2097: We Made Ourselves Over* is accompanied by standalone films and a downloadable app that involves participants in a process of speculation and reflection about the future of our cities. The films are available to watch on YouTube and make heavy use of visual effects, showcasing a speculative future that is dystopian as much as it is hopeful. They highlight the impact that each individual citizen will have in a future where resources must be managed very carefully.

The app adds an element of interactivity to the narrative and enables the performance to be accessible to a wider audience. Hessa, the main protagonist, appears in short video snippets engaging in a conversation with the app users as they are guided by a branching interactive narrative structure where the user's choices have implications for the final outcome. Hessa is featured facing the user in a close-up shot as she poses challenging questions about survival, death, relationships and the value of our personal belongings. Sometimes the app switches to Hessa's point of view, as she looks around her room and also the landscape outside as she makes her way to the new city.

The project's website includes several interviews with the experts consulted, including a tarot reader, a human geography lecturer, a community activist, an urban planner, a smart city researcher, a food consultant, a designer and a professor of cognitive science (Blast Theory, 2017c). Their feedback on future speculations about the city has been incorporated into the fictional films, which address the effect of climate change on seashore communities, food scarcity (addressed by fake meat and insect diets), the transmission of knowledge and consciousness from dying to living people, how life-changing political decisions will be made in the future and planning for future cities.

2097: We Made Ourselves Over is an intricate project that combines many points of view, performances and media forms into a speculative vision of future cities that is slightly dystopian: in one of the films an entire city is razed to the ground by a giant machine (a molecular harvester) in a process that symbolises urban renewal. Yet, it also provides a human perspective to a theme usually discussed in infrastructural terms and through the potential of future technological advances. The narratives are driven by citizen empowerment and collaboration, where the human figure is not lost inside the machine apparatus. As in *Karen*, the app in *2097: We Made Ourselves Over* attempts to generate empathy by making the protagonist face the participant directly as the former asks questions that are answered through a branching interactive narrative (where the participant chooses a predefined answer out of a list of options). This helps towards drawing participants into the narrative and interpellates them to reflect on its outcomes.

Speculative architecture

While *User Not Found* and *2097: We Made Ourselves Over* put the user and social issues at centre stage, other performance art projects focus on the infrastructure of future cities instead, reflecting on the ways in which architecture is combined with emerging technologies to speculate on future social interaction. Some of these depictions of future urban living demonstrate technologies that are already impacting on our urban lives, such as assemblages of artificial intelligence with the surveillance apparatus of sensor technologies, automated cameras, GPS, Wi-Fi, Bluetooth and laser distance measuring technology (LIDAR). Australian born Liam Young is one of the most distinguished architects exploring visions of future urban living. His body of work includes installations, films and performance art, and he collaborates with scientists, science fiction writers, musicians and artists. Young 'operates in the spaces between design, fiction and futures [and is the] founder of the think tank *Tomorrow's Thoughts Today*, a group whose work explores the possibilities of fantastic, speculative and imaginary urbanisms' (SCI-Arc, 2019). Young describes himself as a speculative architect '[constructing] alternative worlds as a means to understand our own world in new ways' (in Griffiths, 2015). His films merge fiction and reality, and past and present to inform a future vision of urban landscapes dominated by biotechnology, surveillance and autonomous machines.

In his *New City* (2014) project, Young created animations of futuristic cities displayed in a large-scale format in a gallery, which are composed of a collage of 'merged photographs taken on expeditions around the world [by Young] with images sourced online to produce a vision of what he described as an "exaggerated present"' (Griffiths, 2015). The cities look strikingly familiar (as they are composed from photos of existing cityscapes), yet uncanny at the same time. In this project he collaborated with science fiction writers, who wrote short fictional stories to accompany each piece of the project: *Samsung City, Edgelands* and *The City in the Sea.* The pieces also have a soundscape created by electronic musicians, Coldcut, which is intended to reinforce the immersive character of each piece. According to Griffiths (2015), the panoramic point of view offers a vantage point that 'give[s] the animations a sense of scope and realism.'

Samsung City is a critique of the influence of corporations on city developments promoted as smart cities, where branding extends from the electronic goods inside each residential dwelling to entire buildings and neighbourhoods, such as the Songdo City project in South Korea. Songdo was built as a smart city from scratch on land reclaimed from the Yellow Sea. Songdo highlights both the conveniences and the annoyances (including surveillance concerns and intrusive media) of living in a city saturated by ubiquitous technologies controlled by an '"Integrated Operations Centre" – a Big Brother control room where reams of data are funnelled in real time from thousands of sensors across the city' (Wainwright, 2019). In Songdo 'your apartment block knows to send the elevator down to greet you when it detects the arrival of your car [and] sensors in every street track traffic flow and send alerts to your phone when it's going to snow'. The convenience of this totalitarian machinist assemblage has its pitfalls, as Wainwright (2019) points out in his description of one of the dwellings:

> At 8.30 every morning, an announcement is piped though a speaker in the ceiling of Kim Jong-won's apartment, barking the daily bulletin in a high-pitched voice. The disembodied broadcaster details new parking measures, issues with the pneumatic waste disposal chute and various building maintenance jobs to be carried out that day. 'There's no way of turning it off,' sighs Kim's wife, Jung-sim, as she prepares breakfast. 'I hate technology but my husband is an early adopter. He has to have everything first.'

The futuristic vision outlined by Liam Young in *Samsung City* mirrors the reality of Songdo, presenting similar technological issues and annoyances. The accompanying text written by science fiction writer Tim Maughan – entitled *Keeping Up Appearances* – describes a couple (Sang and Duri) living in an apartment building that is entirely branded by Samsung, from the mobile phone charger to the surveillance system installed in the access corridors that can be viewed by all its inhabitants on their Samsung-branded wristwatches. Duri arrives home and notices that Sang is (proudly) installing a non-Samsung-branded TV system 'the width of the room'. Duri's response reflects her concern that their tenancy might be affected by what the neighbours and the building committee might see as treason: 'I just hope nobody from the building standards committee is back from work yet [...] Are you trying to get us thrown out? Our lease is up for review in three months and you brought an LG TV into a Samsung housing block? What the hell will the neighbours say?' (Young, 2014). Maughan's text is a comic take on the concept of digital brandscaping extending from the cityscape (depicted through Young's animation) to single urban dwellings; a totalitarian assemblage of architecture and technology to transform the city into an efficient machine that is reminiscent of modernist urban planning's similar ambitions. However, *Samsung City* is modelled on both existing urban streetscapes and on technological concepts that have a strong grounding in built urban spaces (such as Songdo) rather than simply speculative plans (such as modernist urban plans).

Future machinic cities

The conceptual idea of the exaggerated present as a form of speculative urbanism is also developed in *Future Perfect*, a project curated by Liam Young for the Lisbon Architecture Triennale in 2013. It centres on a fictional future city 'developed with a think tank of scientists, technologists, futurists, illustrators and science fiction authors' (Young, 2013: 9). The exhibition consists of a series of 'large-scale districts of the future city [in the shape of] movie miniature models, illustrations, installations, props and performances' (Young, 2013: 9). *The Garment District*, a performance art installation by Bart Hess that was part of the *Future Perfect* exhibition, addresses the transformation and augmentation of the body through technology. During the performance 'people [were] dunked in a pool of wax to create sculptural dresses' (Frearson, 2013a). They were strapped to a robotic harness and lowered into a pool of hot water and wax, which bonded to the skin creating an organically shaped garment. Hess wanted to 'explore ways in which humans can augment and extend the shapes of their bodies, creating a kind of prosthetic that is unique each time' (Frearson, 2013a). The exhibition organisers describe how the project is inspired by emerging technologies and the glitches of digital media forms (as a manifestation of the New Aesthetic):

> From this context of surveillance, facial recognition, avatars and virtual ghosts, we imagine a near future where digital static, distortions and glitches become a new form of ornament. For the youth tribes of Future Perfect the body is a site for adaption, augmentation and experimentation. [...] It is a physical glitch, a manifestation of corrupt data in motion, a digital artefact. (Frearson, 2013a)

Chupan Chupai, a teaser movie commissioned for the *Future Perfect* exhibition and developed by Factory Fifteen, depicts a 'future city controlled by a supercomputer, where architectural structures can be hacked and insect-like drones police the streets' (Frearson, 2013b). In this dystopian city, a 'group of children [is] playing hide and seek around the city' and discover how to hack the urban fabric (Frearson, 2013b): 'One child uses gestures to create a staircase by extruding a wall, while another is able [to] manipulate surroundings to find camouflage' (Frearson, 2013b). The movie combines footage filmed 'on location in India using a group of local children as actors, then used animation to exaggerate and manipulate the imagery' (Frearson, 2013b). In *Chupan Chupai* the experience of being in the city is mediated by both physical embodiment and virtual gestures and props, and the space of the city is at the same time highly controlled (through insect drones) and deeply disorienting (through the loss of stable referential markers).

Future Perfect was accompanied by an e-book entitled *Brave New Now* (Young, 2013), consisting of 'specially commissioned short stories set in a fictional future city [where] authors have been invited to inhabit the city, to breathe life into its characters and cultures and give form to its streets and spaces through narrative' (Young, 2013: 4) In the foreword for the book, Young states that 'nothing dates like images of the future' (Young, 2013: 5). To emphasise the idea of the future as an exaggerated present, most of the illustrations in the book are photographs of actual urban and non-urban landscapes, data centres and robots that provide a dystopian background to the stories and support Gibson's (in Leonard, 2015) proposition that 'the future has already happened'.

Young describes the effect of speculative visions of the future city as a form of offering a 'critical view back on the present cities we currently inhabit' (Young, 2013: 7). He argues that the role of the speculative architect is to instigate debate: 'Cast as a provocateur and storyteller, the speculative architect instigates debate, raises questions and enables the public as active agents in the future of their cities' (Young, 2013: 8). *Brave New Now* provides speculative insights into how embodied practices might develop in the future city, and how our own bodies might merge with the city and its biotechnological systems. In the short story *Foam* by Warren Ellis, the rebel protagonist Nisha is portrayed escaping from a surveillant security hoverfly in a totalitarian city where citizens have given away their privacy in order to be able to access the city's services. As the hoverfly gets closer, a house made out of foam starts forming around her, as she tries to escape by running up the staircase as it is forming. Eventually, she jumps onto the barely gelatinated roof of the next house and gets stuck. As a defence agent kills her, Nisha's body dissolves into foam and is drained away by the City's digestive system (Young, 2013: 12–17). *Foam* fulfils Mitchell's (2003: 19) statement that '[our] biological body meshes with the city' through an extreme dystopian vision where surveillance and totalitarian control leave no space for spontaneous agency or dissensus.

In *Up and Coming* by Tim Maughan, a young couple is guided by an estate agent (Faruq) through a residential property that is in a derelict state, yet – viewed through augmented reality specs (donned by both the couple and the estate agent) – appears as a comfortable and trendy place to live in (Young, 2013: 18–29). Faruq, the estate agent, is wearing a cheap purple suit where 'the enzymes [as a component of the suit] are inferior quality, unable to deal with the body's humidity' (Young, 2013: 18). Faruq 'sells potential' (Young, 2013: 19). As he accompanies the couple on a walk through the property, Faruq makes slight adjustments to the virtual furniture according to the couple's reaction to what they see. As Faruq prepares to close the deal, the couple looks down towards the atrium of the building from a walkway and a child riding a skateboard crashes into the woman, causing her to lose her augmented reality specs (Young, 2013: 26–7). Faruq tries to give her back the specs, but the woman refuses and also takes off her partner's specs. They are immediately exposed to the stark reality of the building that they are in, an old marketplace in a derelict state, where children play 'soccer with a clattering tin can ... as the adults quietly huddle around the filthy, worn, UN issue refugee tents' (Young, 2013: 28).

The fictional stories *Foam* and *Up and Coming* depict future urban environments that are prone to surveillance in very oppressive and tangible ways, but at the same time are highly unstable and shapeless (foaming walls, walls morphing into staircases) while appearing to have more virtual than physical potential (such as in the virtual experience disguising the stark reality of the derelict building in *Up and Coming*). The idea of hacking physical space is a common theme across these stories (and also in *Chupan Chupai*), where the built urban environment is not only a media form but also – as Easterling (2016: 80) states, a 'set of instructions for an interplay between variables [where] design acquires some of the power and currency of software'. *Future Perfect* not only suggests this translation of the urban environment into software (and vice-versa) but also implies that we are either on the good side of the city-as-software paradigm – for example, by wearing our augmented reality specs and accepting the illusion of the virtual as real – or on the bad side of it, trying to hack into the software of the city to find escape routes from its totalitarian space. The stories described above suggest scenarios where surveillance and control are deeply embedded in the urban fabric, and where the city is not only reconfigurable and hackable, but also capable of literally assembling with our own bodies.

Another piece directed by Liam Young and written by author Tim Maughan that discusses the concept of hacking the city is the film *Where the City Can't See* (see Figure 6.3), part of the project of the same name that was launched in 2015 and that includes 'live performances, installations and [the] film' (Abandon Normal Devices, 2017). It is described as 'the first fiction film shot entirely through

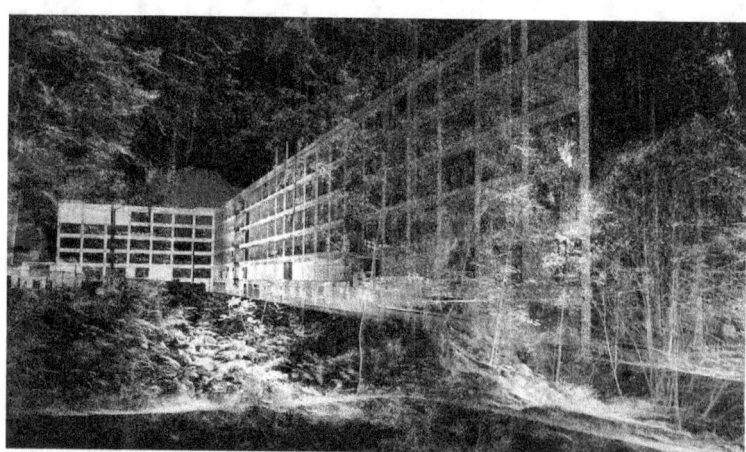

Figure 6.3 Liam Young – *Where the City Can't See*

laser scanning technology [LIDAR]' (Abandon Normal Devices, 2017). This gives the piece a unique aesthetic quality, where pixelated and slightly glitchy images emerge through the analysis of the surrounding environment by machine vision. Set in a fictional future where China owns the Detroit Economic Zone (DEZ), a reference to existing free trade zones around the world, it depicts an urban landscape 'where Google maps, urban management systems and CCTV surveillance are not only mapping our cities but ruling them' (Abandon Normal Devices, 2017). It describes a group of young factory workers that work on a production line during the day and at night 'adorn themselves in machine vision camouflage and the tribal masks of anti-facial recognition, enacting their escapist fantasies in the hidden spaces of the city' (Abandon Normal Devices, 2017). They hack a driverless taxi and make their way through the city 'searching for a place they know exists, but that the map doesn't show' (Abandon Normal Devices, 2017).

In *I Spy with my Machine Eye*, a visual performance by Liam Young, the protagonist is a drone that tells its story, narrated by Young on stage against a large screen displaying drone footage from around the world. The drone renews the conceptual device of Vertov's *kino-eye* (machinic vision), with the added capabilities of artificial intelligence and enhanced mobility, as it states: 'I am your remote eyes free from the tyranny of fixed location. I have been tasked to survey a new landscape and I haven't seen the world like this before' (Young, 2017). The performance makes reference to other projects by Liam Young, including *In the Robot Skies* (2016), a short film entirely shot with pre-programmed camera drones.

Where the City Can't See, *I Spy with my Machine Eye* and *In the Robot Skies* foreground the sentience of the city as an actant-mediator, as Willis (2017) points out: 'this sensing city … suggests another form of intelligence as much as it does a new aesthetic of the city, and it is this shift, from the city as backdrop to the city as participatory agent enabled by new technologies and networked infrastructures, that interests architect Liam Young'. Describing *Where the City Can't See*, Liam Young (in Willis, 2017) states: 'The idea of using the Lidar scanner was to depict and describe the city entirely through the machines that now manage it, in order to explore the subject positions that are emerging.' Young emphasises his aim to give agency to the city as a protagonist rather than as a simple backdrop for both human and non-human agents: 'What does it mean to occupy and navigate those cities when the city itself is a character that can think, can talk back and can interact in ways they never have before?' (in Willis, 2017).

Revisiting the machine-city

It is worth revisiting Simmel's ([1903] 1950) argument – formulated at the dawn of the twentieth century – that the machinist efficiency of metropolitan life translated into a machinised citizen with a calculating mind. Simmel argued that the calculating mind was a strategic way of coping with the overwhelming impact of new modes of living in the city. Yet it also highlights the inevitability of the hybrid human-machine as a defining feature of contemporary urban living. The issue of overstimulation identified by Simmel is also a contemporary matter, yet this overstimulation has become more individualised – for example through our use of social media to interact with the city – and the machines have become more diversified and more pervasive, as machine-driven rhythms permeate most social practices.

Young's extensive body of work speculating on future urban living highlights the unresolved tension between machine agency and human agency in the city. The many scenarios that he explores expose the pitfalls of totalitarian surveillance, where machines control and mediate most of the spatial exchanges and where unhindered human agency is only possible through the practice of hacking the technologies controlling urban space. The extreme interpretation of this paradigm involves machines that have acquired the ability to recreate the city on their own terms through autonomous machine-building capacity (such as in Warren Ellis's *Foam*), multiplying themselves without any human assistance. Despite this, in Young's projects there is still room for human expression and agency through unplanned and transgressive interventions in the techno-urban fabric, such as when the children in *Chupan Chupai* hack the augmented space of the city and when the line workers in *Where the City Can't See* hack a driverless taxi to look out for hidden raves. These fleeting moments symbolise the resilience and solidarity of human beings in a machinised and totalitarian environment composed of oppressive infrastructure, ubiquitous communication technologies and centralised surveillance.

As I mentioned previously, the most compelling contemporary example of the blurring of human and machine agency towards a model of universal control is China's ongoing Social Credit System project, and its ambition to impose social control over the whole country through a centralised system combining mass surveillance, artificial intelligence and data-mining to identify and punish any actions considered non-trustworthy. This is taking place through distributed 'performances' that are at times so incredulous (for outsiders) that they might be mistaken for being performance art. For example, public toilets in Beijing have been installed with automatic facial recognition toilet paper dispensers to stop people from stealing toilet paper, as Haas (2017) describes:

> Those in need of paper must stand in front of a high-definition camera for three seconds, after removing hats and glasses, before a 60cm ration is released. Those who come too often will be denied, and everyone must wait nine minutes before they can use the machine again. But there have already been reports of software malfunctions, forcing users to wait over a minute [for the toilet paper to be dispensed] in some cases, a difficult situation for those in desperate need of a toilet.

One can imagine the performative potential of assembling an artistic narrative with this technocentric contraption. Yet, while this is one of the more visible manifestations of control through machine agency in the urban fabric, the forms of control embedded in the machinic city are largely governed by machines whose boundaries are less defined, more malleable and more resilient, some of which I have outlined previously, such as: the capitalist machine, ensuring that patterns of consumption remain stable; the media machine, ensuring that citizens are amenable to the social and spatial controls encountered in urban space; and electromechanical machines of all types and sizes – such as wearable fitness trackers – constantly reminding us to maintain an adequate balance of work, sleep and leisure.

Future urban living

The examples described above are permeated by the predicaments of the machine-city, and its desire for social obedience through a combination of built environment, social relations and machine-driven artefacts of control. The utopian and dystopian urban environments described by these projects provide a sense of emptiness – regardless of their urban density – and loss of grounding, as the future urban machine presents itself as a shapeless, volatile and unstable environment largely devoid of meaningful social relations and increasingly controlled and mediated by machine agency. Citizens become trapped by the infrastructure of the city (*Chupan Chupai* and *Foam*), have to watch hopelessly as their cities are forcefully renewed through a destructive process (*2097: We Made Ourselves Over*), and are deceived by virtual representations that disguise and embellish the actual city (*Up and Coming*).

While we cannot predict the social and spatial outcomes of future urban living, we will need to generate sustainable and adequate solutions to address increasingly crowded urban areas: '55 % of the world's population [was] residing in urban areas in 2018 ... and by 2050, 68 % of the world's population is projected to be urban' (United Nations, 2018). As the potential for tension, chaos and conflict in urban areas is intensified, the United Nations (2018) emphasised the need for sustainable urbanisation and 'management of urban growth, especially in low-income and lower middle-income countries where the most rapid urbanisation is expected between now and 2050'.

The machine-city narrative is present in the current trend to build cities from scratch to address world urban growth and to further the financial interests of countries, in particular in Asia and Africa, where 90 per cent of the world's urban population growth is predicted to happen between 2018 and 2050 (United Nations, 2018). A combination of real estate and tech companies have explored this huge market, as new cities are built on reclaimed land or empty landscapes, mostly 'in places where rapid urbanisation and population growth have overwhelmed existing cities' (Voce and Mead, 2019).

The aim to build new cities from scratch is sometimes connected to political aims and marketed through the media machine, as Moser (in Voce and Mead, 2019) points out: 'It's easy for leaders to whip up some nationalist frenzy and sell the new city as a source of national pride. The computer-generated models look beautiful too – all the old city problems are just gone – and it looks magically real. It's compelling for people who live in overcrowded and polluted places.' These include cities such as Songdo (discussed above) in South Korea and Putrajaya in Malaysia, built to become the country's new administrative capital as an alternative to the 'congested, overcrowded Kuala Lumpur' (Voce and Mead, 2019).

The social effects of the marketing of the machine-city model are addressed in Liam Young's *Samsung City*, and Tim Maughan's short stories *Keeping Up Appearances* and *Up and Coming*. These narratives sometimes simply confirm patterns of urban living that are already emerging in the so-called smart cities across the world, as I described above in my account of Songdo. And while these patterns usually present themselves through dystopian accounts, they are subject to individual translation by each citizen.

For example, a study of China's Social Credit System potential as a '"state surveillance infrastructure" and as a tool for social management', shows strong support from citizens, in particular those that 'are more likely to be older, have a higher income, male, more highly educated, and live in urban areas' (Kostka, 2019: 1588). As Kostka (2019: 1588) points out, citizens that support the implementation of the Social Credit System perceive it 'not as an instrument of surveillance, but as an instrument to improve [their] quality of life ... leading to more honest and law-abiding behavior in society'. Therefore, patterns of participation in the machinic city that is subject to tight political control are conditional on how citizens translate its totalitarian narrative through their own desires and needs. What is important (and missing) in this case is a reflection on the ethical and wider social consequences of the unconditional acceptance of social control from digital media technologies, and also the unequal distribution of the benefits associated with these technologies. Performance art is capable of probing these incongruities and contradictions (such as freedom associated with

control), while generating reflection on them and suggesting potential alternative approaches.

Liam Young's exploration of the concept of the 'exaggerated
present' in his projects as he discusses current and future urban
issues (drones, ubiquitous surveillance, machine agency, urban
hacking), Blast Theory's collaborative exploration of social relations in a distant future in *2097: We Made Ourselves Over* and
Dante or Die's exploration of our current engagement with mediated urban space in *User Not Found* are examples of performance
art reimagining, reconfiguring and speculating about the machinic
city. While these projects acknowledge the importance of non-
human actants as mediators of agency, they also eschew a technocentric narrative where passive human beings are at the mercy of
artificial intelligence agents, pervasive surveillance and an oppressive urban infrastructure. By probing the complex assemblages of
current and future urban machines, performance art highlights the
issues associated with contemporary urban living while also speculating on how these issues might be reflected upon and addressed.
Yet this process, as Guattari (1995: 134) reminds us, must always
be carried out through an aesthetic paradigm that aligns itself with
creative uncertainty (including the creativity of technical machines)
rather than mechanistic certainty.

Conclusion

This book began with a simple proposition: take a walk through your city. As you walk, you are subject to an embodied experience that is increasingly mediated by machine agency and subjectivity. Many of these exchanges are mediated by informational urban interfaces that perform as functional actants (as long as they don't fail) and symbolise the ideal of the machine-city as an efficient and predictable assemblage. But when you encounter performative urban actants that don't have a clear role, or perform in an unusual way, it makes you reflect on their meaning, and how they assemble with other machine-actants, steering the narrative of everyday life towards unpredictable outcomes. These performative machinic assemblages are representative of the potential of performance art to probe, reconfigure and enable reflection on the social and spatial exchanges in the machinic city.

No matter how controlled (or not) your experience of the city turns out to be, your mode of engagement with it is a unique performance and an interpretation of it. This performance consists of an assemblage where agency is distributed across its components. The assemblage of human agency, technology and urban space – mediated through performance art – is always open, a rhizomatic structure subject to mutations and unexpected connections. As a form of aesthetic machine, performance art inflicts tension, uncertainty and unpredictability in the unattainable ideal of the machine-city and its orderly structure championed by the logic of the capitalist and cybernetic machines. Yet it does so without any holistic ambitions to confront these machines or to claim the status of an autonomous revolutionary tool emancipating citizens from oppressive machines. Instead, performance art probes, disassembles and reassembles the machines that constitute the city while demanding active interpretation.

In this reflective journey through performance, unforeseen assemblages emerge between incongruous actants, which in turn generate narratives that are much richer than any forms of technocentric narratives. Some of these narratives extend beyond the performance itself, and into quotidian urban life: a beer mat becomes a prop for an intense conversation between a participant and a bystander; a bystander prompted by a display screen in a train station improvises a dance routine; an improvised performance by an atmospheric actant becomes a meaningful experience for a participant; and a bystander improvises an ad hoc performance with a stranger that unfolds through a gigantic game of shadows. These might be fleeting moments, but they are symbolic of the infinite potential of the assemblage of the aesthetic, performative and urban machines for the renewal of social and spatial practices.

The case studies of performance art that I have analysed illustrate this by simultaneously employing and critiquing digital media technologies that mediate urban life. Through ambiguous, challenging and reflective narratives, they operate as machinic probes in the urban fabric, exploring the unpredictability of urban space as both 'stage' and as a loose collective of actants. Combined with technological failures, serendipitous moments and meaningful encounters, these artistic narratives are reconfigured and generate individual patterns of meaning for each participant. The case studies I have analysed illustrate not only the importance of acknowledging the process of artistic narration and participant translation, but also remind us that the translation process is not human-centric, but also influenced by various machine-actants.

The best way to understand how this process of translation unfolds is by participating in these performance art projects and getting acquainted with the unexpected machinic interactions that they generate. As I took part in *A Machine To See With*, my own translation of the narrative was reconfigured by unexpected participatory outcomes that were not scripted by the performance. I was also subject to the pitfalls of technological failure, such as when

I ran out of mobile phone credit and was unable to listen to the final narrative prompts of the performance.

While *A Machine To See With* was heavily influenced by the embodied experience of the city, the influence of media also played a key role towards defining its overall experience. The narrative played a part in this process, by referencing cinematic language and reconceptualising the city as an assemblage of performative actants repurposed from functional buildings, spaces and urban furniture. The use of cinematic language illustrates performance art's ability to repurpose other media forms and their associated narratives, leaving the participant to translate these forms through their own cultural references.

My analysis of the machine-city – machinist and pre-empted in nature – and the machinic assemblages that intervene in the urban fabric reveals the ongoing tension between efficient and not-so-efficient machines, or between machines modelled on prescriptive outcomes (where desire has been stultified) and machines modelled on rhizomatic structures where relations are always emergent (and where desire is always present). However, I argue that this tension is not resolved by pitting these machines against each other, but by investigating the potential to assemble them.

My own analysis of these machines is limited to an assemblage that I have deemed important for the purpose of this book. However, there are many other machines that constitute the machinic city that I haven't analysed in depth, and that deserve to be probed further (through the assemblages that they generate), such as: political, social, authoritarian, ecological, global, tactical, among many others. The detailed breakdown of actants and their relations in my analysis of *A Machine To See With* enabled me to trace the relations emerging from these actants and their social and spatial outcomes.

This provides a framework that can be applied towards analysing future performance art projects and other aesthetic machines, but also towards analysing particular aspects of the machinic city and of future patterns of urban living. These machinic assemblages unfold through the process of coupling and decoupling machines as they become actants and mediators of agency and as they reveal their abstract potential. This framework provides an alternative to accounts that either prioritise the technical capabilities of the machine or that fail to consider the many ways in which urban citizens translate, adapt and reimagine the narratives emerging from these machinic assemblages. It also acknowledges the potential of assemblages of efficient and not-so-efficient machines, as the latter materialise through many different forms: technical failures, ambiguous artistic narratives, unanticipated modes of participation and unexpected actants.

Performance art provides a platform for these emerging assemblages, through narratives that both involve the machines through which contemporary urban life is mediated while also enabling reflection on them. It can also help us to re-evaluate and reflect on our role in the machinic city, as machines acquire new modes of agency through the ability to sense and interpret the world (within the limitations of machine thinking), producing innovative human-machine hybrids and non-human hybrids.

The machinic city that I conceptualise is not simply a fictional alternative to the machine-city. Instead, it is the de facto model of contemporary urban living, with all its complexities and relational assemblages that cannot be reduced to stultified models of urban living. The machine-city remains as the utopian model that is desperately sought after by proponents of a totalitarian model of urbanism where technology is the main driving force, and where human participation can be scripted and controlled to maximum effect. The model of the machine-city emerges through fictional narratives – from More's ([1516] 2016) account of living in the island of Utopia to Liam Young and Tim Maughan's conceptualisation of *Samsung City* – that demand reflection. But it also emerges as an influential model for built urban space: through some of the greatest achievements of modernist urban planning, such as the city of Brasilia; the new cities that are being branded as smart and eco-cities; and ultimately, through the assumption that citizens' needs and desires are best left to be mediated and controlled by major corporations and governments (such as in China's Social Credit System).

Faced with all these variations of the machine-city model and the rapid evolution of digitally mediated technologies of control, we need to pay close attention to machinist agency and how it attempts to control performance in urban space. Yet the machine itself is not the enemy. By reconceptualising the machine as a device with abstract potential and by analysing the ability of the aesthetic machine to probe and traverse other 'Universes of value' (or other machines), I have focused on the potential of digitally mediated performance art to probe the virtues, pitfalls and outcomes of the assemblage of digital media, performance and participation in urban space.

The projects that I have analysed draw from several avant-garde art movements of the twentieth century (such as Futurism and Neo-Concretism) and from the performative turn of the 1960s, yet they also differ significantly from these due to the unhindered potential of innovative and emerging media technologies in the last three decades: the World Wide Web, artificial intelligence, digital video and audio editing, sensor technologies, virtual reality, augmented reality, robotic technologies, Internet-enabled mobile phones, social media apps and cameras with laser scanning technology (LIDAR).

The future machines conceptualised by performance art assemble these technologies with cultural references and speculative scenarios to imagine the future of urban living. These future machines – speculative and intangible as they may be – are important probes to think about the ethical, social and spatial consequences of emerging technologies. Online virtual worlds, social media and data-mining coupled with vast databases have transformed the ways in which we inhabit, navigate and socialise in urban space. Yet we certainly haven't felt the full brunt of the effect of this assemblage yet. As our world becomes more sentient, machine-like and automated, and as both physical and virtual space get more crowded and quantified, the full effect of assemblages of media and urban machines is yet to materialise and will depend on the limits that we impose (or not) on these technologies. Prior to the advent of the World Wide Web, no one would have imagined that 'Big Brother' would arrive in a distributed and discreet fashion – a network of sentient machines – rather than as an all-encompassing behemoth. Yet by conceptualising the machinic city, we can eschew technocentric narratives by reminding ourselves that the human-machine will always find ways to break and bend technology, to reshape it to its own needs, to put a personal touch on it, or to refuse technology if it adds no value to its desires and needs.

The relational nature of the machinic city foregrounds the nuances of participation and provides a counterpoint to the more dystopian narratives of technology applied to urban living that suggest the need to emancipate citizens. This is not to say that we must understate the potential of digital media technologies, but simply to confirm that they are only conferred agency when combined with other actants: political, corporate, spatial, legislative, and so on. Likewise, the potential of performance art as an aesthetic machine only materialises as it encounters and traverses other 'Universes of value' and triggers – in Neo-Concretist terms – *vivência*, the lived experience that is not quantifiable.

References

Abandon Normal Devices (2017) *Where the City Can't See*. Available: www.andfestival.org.uk/events/where-the-city-cant-see-liam-young/ [accessed 5 July 2019].

Apollonio, U. (2009) *Futurist Manifestos*. London: Tate Publishing.

Apprich, C. (2017) *Technotopia: A Media Genealogy of Network Cultures*. London: Rowman and Littlefield.

Arias, L. (2019) 'Lola Arias'. Available: http://lolaarias.com/bio/ [accessed 9 July 2019].

Barad, K. (2003) 'Posthumanist Performativity: Toward an Understanding of How Matter Comes to Matter', *Signs: Journal of Women in Culture and Society*, 28(3), pp. 801–31.

Benford, S. and Giannachi, G. (2011) *Performing Mixed Reality*. Cambridge, MA: The MIT Press.

Benford, S., Drozd, A., Rowland, D., et al. (2004) 'Uncle Roy All Around You: Implicating the City in a Location-based Performance', *Proceedings of the International Conference on Advances in Computer Entertainment Technology 2004 (ACE 04)*. Singapore, 3–5 June.

Berry, D. and Dieter, M. (eds) (2015) *Postdigital Aesthetics: Art, Computation and Design*. New York: Palgrave Macmillan.

Bishop, C. (ed.) (2006) *Participation*. London: Whitechapel.

Blast Theory (2019) 'Who We Are'. Available: www.blasttheory.co.uk/about-us/ [accessed 1 October 2019].

Blast Theory (2017a) 'Welcome to 2097'. Available: http://wemadeourselvesover.com [accessed 1 June 2020].

Blast Theory (2017b) *2097: We Made Ourselves Over*. Available: www.blasttheory.co.uk/projects/we-made-ourselves-over/ [accessed 1 June 2020].

Blast Theory (2017c) 'Interviews'. Available: http://wemadeourselvesover.com/find-out-more/#find-out-more [accessed 1 June 2020].

Blast Theory (2015) *Karen*. Available: www.blasttheory.co.uk/projects/karen/ [accessed 4 July 2019].

Blast Theory (2011a) 'Script for the Brighton Performance of *A Machine To See With*', unpublished.

Blast Theory (2011b) 'AMTSW Technical Manual', unpublished.

Blast Theory (2010) *A Machine To See With*. Available: www.blasttheory. co.uk/projects/a-machine-to-see-with/ [accessed 23 August 2014].

Blast Theory (2009) *Ulrike and Eamon Compliant*. Available: www. blasttheory.co.uk/projects/ulrike-and-eamon-compliant/ [accessed 30 October 2020].

Blast Theory (2003) *Uncle Roy All Around You*. Available: www.blast theory.co.uk/bt/work_uncleroy.html [accessed 12 February 2012].

Blast Theory (2001) *Can You See Me Now?*. Available: www.blasttheory. co.uk/bt/work_cysmn.html [accessed 27 September 2019].

Blast Theory (1999) *Desert Rain*. Available: www.blasttheory.co.uk/pro jects/desert-rain/ [accessed 30 October 2020].

Blast Theory (1998) *Kidnap*. Available: www.blasttheory.co.uk/projects/ kidnap/ [accessed 30 October 2020].

Boal, A. (2002) *Games for Actors and Non-actors*. London: Routledge.

Boal, A. (2000) *Theater of the Oppressed*. London: Pluto Press.

Bogost, I. (2007) *Persuasive Games: The Expressive Power of Videogames*. Cambridge, MA: The MIT Press.

Boltanski, L. and Chiapello, È. (2005) *The New Spirit of Capitalism*. London: Verso.

Bolter, J. D. and Grusin, R. (2000) *Remediation: Understanding New Media*. Cambridge, MA: The MIT Press.

Bordwell, D. (1993) *The Cinema of Eisenstein*. Cambridge, MA: Harvard University Press.

Büscher, M., Urry, J. and Witchger, K. (eds) (2011) *Mobile Methods*. London: Routledge.

Butler, J. (1997) *Excitable Speech: A Politics of the Performative*. New York: Routledge.

Castells, M. (1996) *The Rise of The Network Society*. Cambridge: Blackwell Publishers.

Ciudades Paralelas (2019a) 'Concept'. Available: www.ciudadesparalelas. org/conceptoing.html [accessed 10 July 2019].

Ciudades Paralelas (2019b) 'Hotel: Chambermaids – Lola Arias'. Available: www.ciudadesparalelas.org/hoteldan.html [accessed 10 July 2019].

Ciudades Paralelas (2019c) 'Station: Sometimes I Think, I Can See You – Mariano Pensotti'. Available: www.ciudadesparalelas.org/estacioning. html [accessed 10 July 2019].

Ciudades Paralelas (2019d) 'House: Prime Time – Dominic Huber / blendwerk'. Available: www.ciudadesparalelas.org/edificioing.html [accessed 10 July 2019].

Ciudades Paralelas (2019e) 'Shopping Centre: The First International of Shopping Malls – Ligna'. Available: www.ciudadesparalelas.org/shop pinging.html [accessed 10 July 2019].

Contreras-Koterbay, S. and Mirocha, L. (2016) *The New Aesthetic and Art: Constellations of The Postdigital*. Amsterdam: Institute of Network Cultures.

Cornell, P. and Nilsson, J. A. (2017) 'Utopia and Built Environment', *Ennen ja nyt*. Available: www.ennenjanyt.net/2017/08/utopia-and-built-environment/ [accessed 9 July 2019].

Dante or Die (2019) 'About Us'. Available: https://danteordie.com/about-us [accessed 21 June 2019].

Dante or Die (2018a) *Chris Goode – User Not Found*. Available: www.youtube.com/watch?v=FZspLtiASw8 [accessed 9 September 2019].

Dante or Die (2018b) *User Not Found*. London: Oberon Books.

Debord, G. (1995) *The Society of Spectacle*. New York: Zone Books.

Deleuze, G. (2005) *Cinema 1: The Movement-Image*. London: Continuum.

Deleuze, G. and F. Guattari (1988) *A Thousand Plateaus: Capitalism and Schizophrenia*. London: Athlone.

Dias, M. (2012a) '*A Machine to See With* (and Reflect Upon): Interview with Blast Theory Artists Matt Adams and Nick Tandavanitj', *Liminalities: Journal of Performance Studies*, 8(1). Available: http://liminalities.net/8-1/blast-theory.html [accessed 1 September 2014].

Dias, M. (2012b) 'Experiencing *Ciudades Paralelas* – Cork Midsummer Festival, June 2012 (part 1 of 3)'. Available: https://marcosdias.word press.com/2012/07/31/experiencing-ciudades-paralelas-part-1/ [accessed 10 July 2019].

Dias, M. (2012c) 'Experiencing *Ciudades Paralelas* – Cork Midsummer Festival, June 2012 (part 2 of 3)'. Available: https://marcosdias.word press.com/2012/07/31/experiencing-ciudades-paralelas-part-2/ [accessed 10 July 2019].

Dias, M. (2012d) 'Experiencing *Ciudades Paralelas* – Cork Midsummer Festival, June 2012 (part 3 of 3)'. Available: https://marcosdias.word press.com/2012/07/31/experiencing-ciudades-paralelas-part-3/ [accessed 10 July 2019].

Dias, M. (2011) 'Transcript of Interview with Participants of *A Machine To See With*', unpublished.

Dias, M. P. and Adams, M. (2019) 'Participating in the City through Performative Urban Interfaces', *Leonardo Electronic Almanac*, 22(4). Available: www.leoalmanac.org/participating-in-the-city-through-perform ative-urban-interfaces-marcos-dias-matt-adams/ [accessed 16 May 2020].

Dias, M. and Adams, M. (2013) 'Reflecting on Participation: Changing the Status of the Spectator/Passers-by Through Artistic Strategies and New Technologies'. Draft paper (unpublished).

Dixon, S. (2007) *Digital Performance: A History of New Media in Theater, Dance, Performance Art, and Installation.* Cambridge, MA: MIT Press.

Dreysse, M. and Malzacher, F. (eds) (2008) *Experts of the Everyday: The Theatre of Rimini Protokoll.* Berlin: Alexander Verlag.

Easterling, K. (2016) *Extrastatecraft: The Power of Infrastructure Space.* London: Verso.

Eco, U. (1989) *The Open Work.* London: Hutchinson Radius.

Enciclopédia Itaú Cultural (2013) 'Neoconcretism'. Available: http://enciclopedia.itaucultural.org.br/termo3810/neoconcretism [accessed 29 September 2019].

Ernevi, A., Palm, S. and Redström, J. (2007) 'Erratic Appliances and Energy Awareness', *Knowledge, Technology & Policy*, 20, pp. 71–8.

Fischer-Lichte, E. (2008) *The Transformative Power of Performance: A New Aesthetics.* Oxon: Routledge.

Florida, R. (2004) *The Rise of the Creative Class: And How It's Transforming Work, Leisure, Community and Everyday Life.* New York: Basic Books.

Franklin, A. (2010) *City Life.* London: Sage Publications.

Frearson, A. (2013a) 'The Garment District by Bart Hess at Future Perfect', *Dezeen.* Available: www.dezeen.com/2013/09/12/the-garment-district-by-bart-hess-at-future-perfect/ [accessed 5 July 2019].

Frearson, A. (2013b) 'Chupan Chupai by Factory Fifteen at Future Perfect'. *Dezeen.* Available: www.dezeen.com/2013/09/23/chupan-chupai-by-factory-fifteen-at-future-perfect/ [accessed 5 July 2019].

Gabrys, J. (2016) *Program Earth: Environmental Sensing Technology and the Making of a Computational Plane.* Minnesota: University of Minnesota Press.

Giannachi, G. (2004) *Virtual Theatres: An Introduction.* London: Routledge.

Goffman, E. (1990) *The Presentation of Self in Everyday Life.* London: Penguin.

Goldberg, R. (1998) *Performance: Live Art Since 1960.* London: Thames and Hudson.

Goldberg, R. (1996) *Performance Art: from Futurism to the Present.* London: Thames and Hudson.

Graham, S. and Marvin, S. (2001) *Splintering Urbanism: Networked Infrastructures, Technological Mobilities and the Urban Condition.* London: Routledge.

Griffiths, A. (2015) 'Panoramic Animations Offer "Romantic Overview" of Dystopian Future Cities', *Dezeen.* Available: www.dezeen.com/2015/03/18/liam-young-tomorrows-thoughts-today-architecture-future-city-dystopia-cities-dystopian-animation/ [accessed 4 July 2019].

Guattari, F. (1995) *Chaosmosis: An Ethico-aesthetic Paradigm*. Bloomington: Indiana University Press.

Haas, B. (2017) 'Wiping Out Crime: Face-Scanners Placed in Public Toilet to Tackle Loo Roll Theft', *The Guardian*. Available: www.theguardian.com/world/2017/mar/20/face-scanners-public-toilet-tackle-loo-roll-theft-china-beijing [accessed 3 October 2019].

Hansson, K., Forlano, L., Choi, J. H.-J., et al. (2018) 'Provocation, Conflict, and Appropriation: The Role of the Designer in Making Publics', *Design Issues*, 34(4), pp. 3–7.

Hayles, N. K. (1999) *How We Became Posthuman: Virtual Bodies in Cybernetics, Literature, and Informatics*. Chicago: University of Chicago Press.

Illouz, E. (2008) *Saving the Modern Soul: Therapy, Emotions, and the Culture of Self-help*. Berkeley: University of California Press.

Interactive Institute (2020) 'STATIC! Increasing Energy Awareness'. Available: http://dru.tii.se/static/research.htm [accessed 2 June 2020].

Kaprow, A. (1993) *Essays on the Blurring of Art and Life*. Berkeley: University of California Press.

Kitchin, R. and M. Dodge (2011) *Code/Space: Software and Everyday Life*. Cambridge, MA: The MIT Press.

Kobie, N. (2019) 'The Complicated Truth About China's Social Credit System', *Wired*. Available: www.wired.co.uk/article/china-social-credit-system-explained [accessed 15 July 2019].

Koleva, B., Tylor, I., Benford, S., et al. (2001) 'Orchestrating a Mixed Reality Performance', *Proceedings of the SIGCHI Conference on Human Factors in Computing Systems (SIGCHI'01)*. Seattle, Washington, United States, March, pp. 38–45. Available: https://dl.acm.org/doi/abs/10.1145/365024.365033 [accessed 1 June 2020].

Kostka, G. (2019) 'China's Social Credit Systems and Public Opinion: Explaining High Levels of Approval', *New Media and Society*, 21(7), pp. 1565–93.

Kuo, L. (2019) 'China Bans 23m from Buying Travel Tickets as Part of "Social Credit" System', *The Guardian*. Available: www.theguardian.com/world/2019/mar/01/china-bans-23m-discredited-citizens-from-buying-travel-tickets-social-credit-system [accessed 15 July 2019].

Lash, S. (2010) *Intensive Culture: Social Theory, Religion and Contemporary Capitalism*. London: Sage.

Latour, B. (2005) *Reassembling the Social: An Introduction to Actor-Network-Theory*. New York: Oxford University Press.

Latour, B. (2004) 'Whose Cosmos, Which Cosmopolitics? Comments on the Peace Terms of Ulrich Beck', *Project Muse*. Available: www.bruno-latour.fr/sites/default/files/92-BECK_GB.pdf [accessed 9 June 2019].

Latour, B. (2000) *Pandora's Box: Essays on the Reality of Science Studies.* Cambridge, MA: Harvard University Press.

Latour, B. (1997) 'On Actor-Network Theory: A Few Clarifications', *Nettime.* Available: www.nettime.org/Lists-Archives/nettime-l-9801/ msg00019.html [accessed 1 June 2020].

Latour, B. and Woolgar, S. (1986) *Laboratory Life: The Construction of Scientific Facts.* Princeton: Princeton University Press.

Law, J. (2003) 'Machinic Pleasures and Interpellations', Centre for Science Studies, Lancaster University. Available: www.lancaster.ac.uk/fass/res ources/sociology-online-papers/papers/law-machinic-pleasures-and-inter pellations.pdf [accessed 3 May 2020].

Le Corbusier (1987) *The City of To-morrow and Its Planning.* New York: Dover.

Leonard, J. (2015) 'Cyberpunk: The Documentary (60p)'. Available: www. youtube.com/watch?v=UdvxPlhTjDU [accessed 1 June 2020].

Lighthouse (2011) 'BLAST THEORY – A Machine To See With'. Available: www.lighthouse.org.uk/programme/blast-theory-a-machine-to-see-with [accessed 23 April 2013].

Lighthouse Arts (2011) 'Matt Adams – Improving Reality'. Available: www.youtube.com/watch?v=skyn5KKBsUI&list=UUCZHVgTT_EpA9-pBaP1aotg&index=29 [accessed 1 June 2020].

Manovich, L. (2001) *The Language of New Media.* Cambridge, MA: MIT Press.

Maturana, H. and Varela, E. (1980) *Autopoiesis and Cognition: The Realization of Living.* Dordrecht: D. Reidel Publishing Company.

Marcus, G. E. (1998) *Ethnography Through Thick And Thin.* Princeton: Princeton University Press.

Marcuse, H. (2001) *Towards a Critical Theory of Society.* London: Routledge.

Massumi, B. (2003) 'Urban Appointment'. Available: www.brianmassumi. com/textes/Urban_Appointment.pdf [accessed 21 October 2011].

McDonough, T. (ed.) (2002) *Debord and the Situationist International.* Cambridge, MA: The MIT Press.

McQuire, S. (2016) *Geomedia: Networked Cities and the Future of Public Space.* Cambridge: Polity Press.

McQuire, S. (2008) *The Media City: Media, Architecture and Urban Space.* London: Sage.

Miles, S. and Miles, M. (2004) *Consuming Cities.* Houndmills: Palgrave Macmillan.

Mitchell, W. J. (2003) *Me++: The Cyborg Self and the Networked City.* Cambridge, MA: The MIT Press.

More, T. ([1516] 2016) *Utopia.* London: Verso.

Mosco, V. (2004) *The Digital Sublime: Myth, Power and Cyberspace.* Cambridge, MA: The MIT Press.

Mumford, L. (1934) *Technics and Civilization*. New York: Harcourt, Brace and Company.

Mumford, L. (2014) 'Tool Users vs. Homo Sapiens and the Megamachine', in Scharff, R. C. and Dusek, V. (eds) *Philosophy of Technology: The Technological Condition: an Anthology*. Chichester: Wiley-Blackwell, pp. 381–8.

Murphy, S. (2014) 'Dante or Die's I Do offers an unusual slant on weddings', *Metro News*. Available: https://metro.co.uk/2014/02/27/dante-or-dies-i-do-offers-an-unusual-slant-on-weddings-4323303/ [accessed 24 June 2019].

Nye, D. E. (1994) *American Technological Sublime*. Cambridge, MA: The MIT Press.

Osthoff, S. (1997) 'Lygia Clark and Hélio Oiticica: A Legacy of Interactivity and Participation for a Telematic Future', *Leonardo*, 30(4), pp. 279–89.

Papastergiadis, N. (2012) *Cosmopolitanism and Culture*. Cambridge: Polity Press.

PARN (2013) 'What Is PARN?'. Available: http://physicalnarration.org/content/what-parn-0 [accessed 24 April 2013].

Persuasive Games (2020) 'Fatworld: A Game About the Politics of Nutrition'. Available: http://persuasivegames.com/game/fatworld [accessed 5 May 2020].

Rancière, J. (2009a) *The Emancipated Spectator*. London: Verso.

Rancière, J. (2009b) *Aesthetics and its Discontents*. Cambridge: Polity.

Raunig, G. (2010) *A Thousand Machines: A Concise Philosophy of the Machine as Social Movement*. Los Angeles: Semiotext(e).

Raunig, G. (2007) *Art and Revolution: Transversal Activism in the Long Twentieth Century*. Cambridge, MA: The MIT Press.

Rimini Protokoll (2019) 'Rimini Protokoll'. Available: www.rimini-protokoll.de/website/en/about [accessed 9 July 2019].

Roberts, G. (2011) *The Man With the Movie Camera*. London: I.B. Tauris.

Rodenbeck, J. F. (2011) *Radical Prototypes: Allan Kaprow and the Invention of Happenings*. Cambridge, MA: The MIT Press.

Ruffino, P. (2018) *Future Gaming: Creative Interventions in Video Game Culture*. London: Goldsmiths Press.

Russon, M. (2015) 'Google DeepDream Robot: 10 Weirdest Images Produced by AI "Inceptionism" and Users Online', *International Business Times*. Available: www.ibtimes.co.uk/google-deepdream-robot-10-weirdest-images-produced-by-ai-inceptionism-users-online-1509518 [accessed 1 May 2019].

Sadler, S. (1999) *The Situationist City*. Cambridge, MA: The MIT Press.

Sassen, S. (2006) *Territory, Authority, Rights: From Medieval to Global Assemblages*. Princeton: Princeton University Press.

Schechner, R. (2006) *Performance Studies: An Introduction*. New York: Routledge.

Schiller, D. (2000) *Digital Capitalism: Networking the Global Market System*. Cambridge, MA: The MIT Press.

SCI-Arc (2019) 'Liam Young'. Available: www.sciarc.edu/people/faculty/liam-young [accessed 4 July 2019].

Science Gallery (2019a) *About*. Available: https://dublin.sciencegallery.com/#about [accessed 7 June 2019].

Science Gallery (2019b) *Lightwave*. Available: https://dublin.sciencegallery.com/files/u1/SG_LW09.pdf [accessed 7 June 2019].

Sell, M. (2008) *Avant-garde Performance and the Limits of Criticism: Approaching the Living Theatre, Happenings/Fluxus, and the Black Arts Movement*. Ann Arbor: University of Michigan Press.

Simmel, G. ([1903] 1950) 'The Metropolis and Mental Life', in Wolff, K. H. (ed.) *The Sociology of Georg Simmel*. Glencoe: The Free Press, pp. 409–24.

Stengers, I. (2005) 'The Cosmopolitical Proposal', in Latour, B. and Weibel, P. (eds) *Making Things Public: Atmospheres of Democracy*. Cambridge, MA: The MIT Press, pp. 994–1003.

Stevenson, D. (2003) *Cities and Urban Cultures*. Maidenhead: Open University Press.

Stewart, Gregg (2018) 'Interview: Daphna Attias and Terry O'Donovan on User Not Found', *Theatre Weekly*. Available: https://theatreweekly.com/interview-daphna-attias-and-terry-odonovan-on-user-not-found/ [accessed 2 October 2019].

Steyerl, H. (2017) *Duty Free Art: Art in the Age of Interplanetary War*. London: Verso.

Thrift, N. (2004) 'Remembering the Technological Unconscious by Foregrounding Knowledges of Position', *Environment & Planning D: Society & Space*, 22(1), pp. 175–90.

Turner, V. (1988) *The Anthropology of Performance*. New York: PAJ Publications.

Tuters, M. and Varnelis, K. (2006) 'Beyond Locative Media: Giving Shape to the Internet of Things', *Leonardo*, 39(4), pp. 357–63.

Twigg, C. (2015) 'What Happens to My Late Husband's Digital Life Now He's Gone?', *The Guardian*. Available: www.theguardian.com/lifeandstyle/2015/jul/04/what-happens-to-my-late-husbands-digital-life-now-hes-gone [accessed 25 June 2019].

United Nations (2018) 'World Urbanization Prospects: The 2018 Revision'. Available: https://population.un.org/wup/Publications/Files/WUP2018-KeyFacts.pdf [accessed 10 July 2019].

Voce, A. and N. V. Mead (2019) 'Watch New Cities Rise from the Desert, Jungle and Sea', *The Guardian*. Available: www.theguardian.com/cities/

ng-interactive/2019/jul/09/cities-from-scratch-100-and-counting-new-cities-rise-from-the-desert-jungle-and-sea [accessed 10 July 2019].

Wainwright, O. (2019) '"The Next Era of Human Progress": What Lies Behind the Global New Cities Epidemic?', *The Guardian*. Available: www.theguardian.com/cities/2019/jul/08/the-next-era-of-human-progress-what-lies-behind-the-global-new-cities-epidemic [accessed 8 July 2019].

Weiser, M. (1991) 'The Computer for the Twenty-first Century', *Scientific American*, September. Available: www.lri.fr/~mbl/Stanford/CS477/papers/Weiser-SciAm.pdf [accessed 24 September 2019].

Willis, H. (2017) 'Sense and the City: Liam Young's Speculative Cinema', *Mediapolis: A Journal of Cities and Culture*, 2(2). Available: www.mediapolisjournal.com/2017/06/sense-city-liam-youngs-speculative-cinema/ [accessed 27 June 2019].

Young, L. (2017) *I Spy with my Machine Eye*, E-flux Architecture. Available: www.e-flux.com/architecture/superhumanity/68672/i-spy-with-my-machine-eye/ [accessed 3 June 2020].

Young, L. (2014) *New City: Keeping Up Appearances*. Available: https://vimeo.com/channels/newcity [accessed 1 June 2020].

Young, L. (ed.) (2013) *Brave New Now*. Lisbon: Lisbon Architecture Triennale.

ZERO1 (2009) 'Locative Cinema Comes to Life with Commission from Sundance Film Festival, The Banff Centre, and Silicon Valley's ZERO1'. www.zero1.org/about/press/locative-cinema-comes-life-commission-sundance-film-festival-banff-centre-and-silicon-0 [accessed 20 October 2020].

ZERO1 San Jose Biennial (2010) *A Machine to See With*. Available: http://01sj.org/2010/artworks/machine-to-see-with/ [accessed 22 April 2013].

Index

Note: Artistic and literary works can be found under authors' names. Page numbers in italic refer to illustrations.

EU authorised representative for GPSR:
Easy Access System Europe, Mustamäe tee 50,
10621 Tallinn, Estonia
gpsr.requests@easproject.com